100 IDEAS THAT CHANGED GRAPHIC DESIGN

Steven Heller and Véronique Vienne

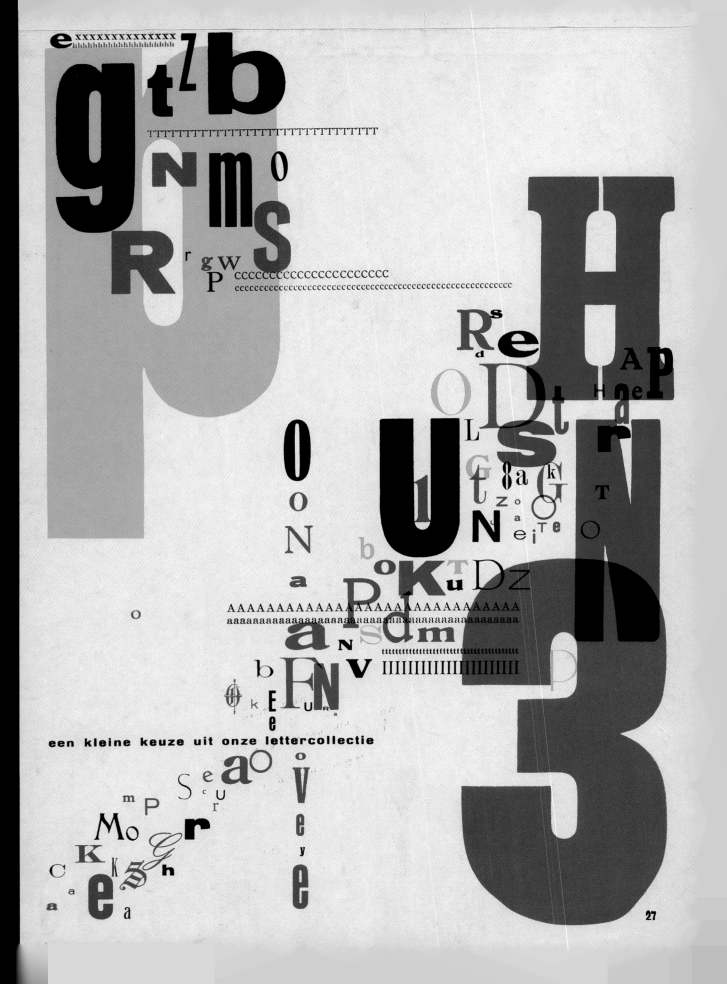

een kleine keuze uit onze lettercollectie

100 IDEAS THAT CHANGED GRAPHIC DESIGN

Steven Heller and Véronique Vienne

Laurence King Publishing

Introduction

Physicists cite the Big Bang theory to explain the origin of the universe. Likewise, we believe there are at least 100 big bangs in the history of graphic art that help explain why examples of graphic design look and feel the way they do. We call this the big idea theory.

So what's the big idea? Let's begin with the big idea for this book. Our aim is to determine, define, discuss, and illustrate the big ideas that created the critical mass that produced the art and craft of contemporary graphic design. Some of these big ideas derive from past centuries; others are situated squarely in the early to mid-twentieth; and still others were conceived during the late twentieth and early twenty-first centuries. We have attempted to position these ideas in chronological order, for some of them, like body painting, started centuries ago. Nonetheless, some of the moments of creation are fuzzy, so the chronology is approximate.

Now, what are big ideas? They are the notions, conceptions, inventions, and inspirations—formal, pragmatic, and conceptual—that have been employed by graphic designers to enhance all genres of visual communication. These ideas have become, through synthesis and continual application, the ambient language(s) of design. They constitute the technological, philosophical, formal, and aesthetic constructs of graphic design.

One of the key criteria for a big idea is what we call "legs." If an idea can be shown to have influenced the practice and theory of graphic design over time, then an argument can be made for its importance. Moreover, if the artifacts that embody the idea are numerous or recurrent, then arguably the idea is also significant.

This volume is not an anthology of "isms" (that has been done many times before), since we consider them as umbrellas for various big (and small) ideas. Under the "great" historical isms, there can be numerous big ideas, such as asymmetric or discordant typography or vibrating color, which are characteristic traits in one or more particular movements or schools. Rather than skim the surface using the shorthand of isms, this book unpacks those art historical categories and pulls out the individual big ideas within them.

A big idea can be situated in one time or span different time periods. It might go out of currency and be revived later. This book attempts to locate approximately when a big idea was invented (if possible) but examines its respective applications in whatever form it is best expressed. Where we can, we show a contemporary example that reveals how, for instance, an idea that became passé was subsequently rediscovered.

Are these 100 the only big ideas? We may have left some out or ignored others. The caveat at the beginning of this introduction that there are "at least" 100 ideas implies that others exist. In fact, narrowing the field down to these ideas was not easy. When we began to list and annotate the ideas, separate the wheat from the chaff, and avoid those that might seem like ideas but are actually tropes or conceits—as in stylistic manifestations rather than substantive design foundations—we determined that more "aha" moments exist than these. Yet 100 is a nice round number. And we hope that folded into these ideas are, perhaps, smaller ideas that also have resonance.

Style, as noted above, is a trope or conceit (words we like a lot) that may emerge as a by-product of an idea. The psychedelic graphic style is a combination of various ideas addressed here. And before that, Art Moderne or Art Deco was the overall manifestation of different graphic ideas.

How many graphic designers does it take to come up with a big idea? Breakthrough ideas might be credited to a single individual, but they are often ready for prime time, and waiting for someone to bring them forward. Still, the mystery remains: which came first, the big idea or the big change? How many Rodchenkos did it take to define the visual revolution of the Constructivist movement? Was Alexey Brodovitch a genius, or simply the product of his time? And how come no one remembers who designed the ubiquitous paper recycling symbol, while everybody knows that Paul Rand came up with the ill-fated Enron logo? You may never be credited for your contribution to graphic design, but the world might be a better place if you can help formulate a big idea.

Some of our big ideas started as small inventions (as mere technical improvements) or even as gimmicks, but have carved for themselves a comfortable niche over time. They've become familiar graphic artifacts. Then there are big ideas that turned out not so big after all. Manifestos come to mind: many of them were exercises in self-aggrandizement, but they were rites of passage, and as such they were important.

Are all the big ideas "good" ideas? Alas, no. We listed quite a few big ideas that didn't improve the way we communicate graphically, but had a tremendous influence on the graphic design profession and the visual culture all the same. Pastiches? Forced obsolescence? Graffiti? You'll be the judge. We were not shy about expressing our opinion when we thought that an idea was not as brilliant as it could have been. Sometimes we even challenged the official version regarding the value of certain design practices or the outcome of an invention. In other words, we acted as critics as much as historians. Our goal is to encourage readers to do the same. Graphic design needs more critics.

Are some big ideas bigger than others? While some ideas may not be "good" ideas, they are nonetheless big in their impact. Some comparatively small ideas may have import on the field and the culture as a whole. Split fountain printing, for instance, is not an earth-altering idea, but it helped define an aesthetic that defined the visual codes of the 1960s generation. Similarly, Kodalithing does not compare with inventing the wheel, but it contributed to the design language and how designers worked within limited budgets to get their messages into the world. As George Orwell might say, some big ideas are more equal than others.

What new big ideas will the future bring? As graphic design continues in the twenty-first century, and given the advances in technology and integration of different media (including motion and sound for numerous digital devices), big ideas are still essential. We hope this book is not the capstone (or tombstone) of the art and craft of graphic design. In terms of visual communication, many of the ideas in this book are still significant. Some could use a little tweaking or an overhaul. Yet others will doubtless give way to new ideas that will further define what we are and what we do.

Where ink meets paper: communicating words, pictures, and ideas

IDEA №1
THE BOOK

Ever since Gutenberg introduced movable type in the fifteenth century, the book has been a laboratory for writers, artists, designers, and typographers. And despite the advent of digital media, print is not dead. John Plunkett, creative director of *Wired* magazine, predicted that ordinary information would gravitate to electronic media, but that "extraordinary content is going to stay in the print domain."

While a great text will evoke mental pictures, a great design will give the reader added levels of perception. Even the most rudimentary design components—the texture of the paper, a fine cut of type, the style of the running head—are more than aesthetic niceties. The designer's role has always been to aid the reader by complementing the narrative. In the 1908 edition of Nietzsche's *Ecce Homo*, architect and designer Henry van de Velde replaced antiquated composition with Art Nouveau ornamentation. While a majority of commercial book publishers were content to produce pages of uninterrupted text, enlightened publishers aimed for the total integration of type and image.

By the early twentieth century, design became an integral part of the content as well. The Italian Futurist Filippo Marinetti's 1914 sound poem *Zang Tumb Tuuum* turned book composition on its head by introducing on the same page multiple typefaces in varying weights and sizes; the type was further arranged so that it conjured the roar of the machinery and engines described in the text. In 1923 the Russian artist and designer El Lissitzky collaborated with the poet Vladimir Mayakovsky on a collection of the latter's poems, *For the Voice*, designed to be read aloud at public gatherings: Lissitzky transformed text type into pictograms, giving the reader additional cues to follow for both inflection and meaning. And Fortunato Depero's *Depero Futurista* (bound with two metal bolts) energized typography so that reading the text was like experiencing the movement of a high-speed vehicle. These books were not neutral containers, but stages upon which words and images performed.

Innovation in book design is not defined solely by radical departures. Frederic Goudy's 1918 *The Alphabet* is based on central axis composition (when type is centered on the printing plane or surface) born of seventeenth- and eighteenth-century Italian and French book traditions, but not bound by them. This book was composed using Goudy's own typefaces and ornaments (influenced by the past) in an effort to achieve balance and harmony.

In the late twentieth century an experimental revival took place. Volumes such as *S,M,L,XL* by Bruce Mau and Rem Koolhaas, and Jonathan Barnbrook's 1997 *Damien Hirst* (a veritable catalog of pop-ups, pull-outs, slipheets, and die-cuts), not only tested the limits of the book but redefined the book-as-object. The book designer's increasing role as both form-giver and content-provider, brought on by new technologies, continues to make the printed book ever more fertile ground for creativity. ∎

S,M,L,XL (1998), a brick of a book designed by Bruce Mau, created a publishing trend in large scale, primarily in visual art, design, and architecture monographic tomes.

Depero Futurista *(1927), also known as "the bolted book" for the two industrial-strength screws binding it, was a self-promotional collection of words and advertising images by this Italian Futurist.*

"The type conjured the roar of machinery and engines."

Ecce Homo *(1908), title page spread of Nietzsche's masterpiece, designed by Henry van de Velde, rendered in a contemporary Jugendstil decorative style.*

Making the body the page

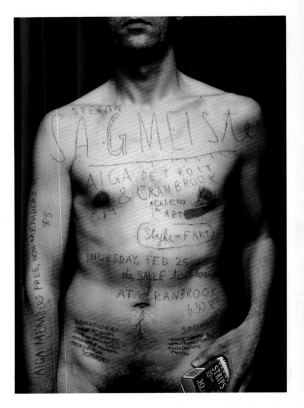

IDEA № 2

BODY TYPE

At least one graphic design genre dates back to Neolithic times. The tattoo, whether as decoration or symbolic icon, has stood the test of time—even if the actual injected images tend to fade and degrade as skin ages and wrinkles. Tattoos are more popular in some cultures and subcultures than others—sometimes even sacred—while other cultures strictly prohibit them.

The notion of tattooing and its cousin, body painting, has been frequently applied as a method of conveying typographic or illustrative messages in advertising art and design since the 1960s. Painting tattoo-like messages on the body can involve visual puns, such as Robert Brownjohn's poster for the 1963 "Obsession and Fantasy" exhibition at the Robert Fraser Gallery in London. A tattoo is not meant to be a commercial advertisement, but in this case it is one, and rather brazenly so. The pun part is that the nipples of the model, across whose naked flesh the

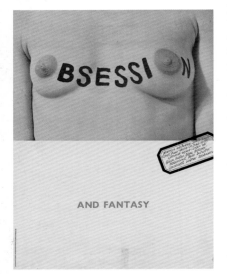

word "obsession" is painted, are the "O"s of the word. This idea riffs on the cliché of the sailor with his chest tattooed with an image such as a ship, a girl, or a flag. Brownjohn's iteration is not as elegant as most tattoos, but the message is clear, and the image is memorable.

Perhaps the most typographical body-markings are the ranchers' brands burned into the flanks of animals as marks of ownership. Some look like modern-day logos. Perhaps brands were what Stefan Sagmeister had in mind when he took a razor-blade to his body, literally cutting words into his flesh, in a kind of temporary designer-self-mutilation for a poster advertising an AIGA (American Institute of Graphic Arts) lecture of 1999. Forget about the pain-free body painting of the Brownjohn poster (and countless other examples)—cutting himself was a commentary on the absurdity of indelibly inking the body with tattoos. And yet it served its purpose. It was not only a startling way to communicate a message, but also an unforgettable lettering composition.

Placing words on the human body is an everyday occurrence. Drawing, printing, or tattooing letters, alphabets, and words is a staple of the design toolbox, used on magazine covers, book jackets, CD covers, and in advertisements to convey headlines or quotations

or simply catch the eye. The Russian designer Peter Bankov's 2003 cover for Russian advertising trade magazine *KaK*, in which words cover the female body, follows the Brownjohn model of the naked female form, but without the nipple pun.

Whether indelibly inscribed or temporarily tattooed on skin, body type's long tradition of use gives it continued resonance. ∎

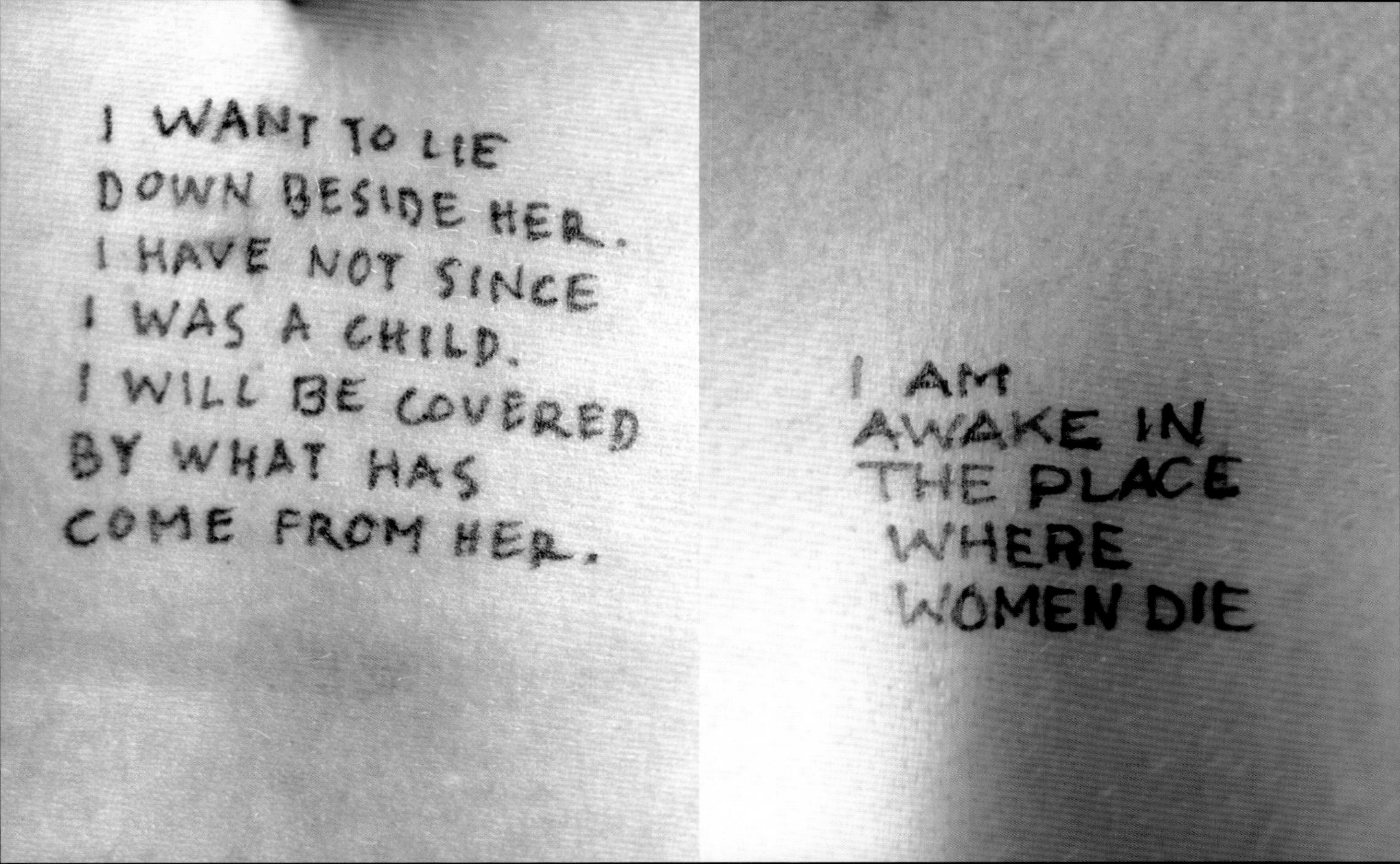

I WANT TO LIE
DOWN BESIDE HER.
I HAVE NOT SINCE
I WAS A CHILD.
I WILL BE COVERED
BY WHAT HAS
COME FROM HER.

I AM
AWAKE IN
THE PLACE
WHERE
WOMEN DIE

Lustmord *(1993), created by Jenny Holzer using ink on skin, shows the body both as canvas and message.*

Instant gratification

BELOW: Ich&Kar tree decals (2005), featuring arms and hands branching out, are an example of a new type of wall motif. Today, more and more graphic artists and illustrators are creating witty rub-on designs for residential use.

OPPOSITE: Letraset Instant Lettering (1970s) was a popular system of decals that allowed anyone to create professional-looking headlines and signs in a number of typefaces, sizes, and alphabets, including Hebrew and Arabic, shown here.

IDEA Nº 3
RUB-ON DESIGNS

Presented at first as an alternative to hand lettering, dry-transfer letterforms stood, for a brief moment, at the intersection of crafts and technology. Easy to use, the method nonetheless required some dexterity. Words had to be set carefully, one letter at a time, and rubbed down in perfect alignment. When done correctly, it could replace traditional typesetting. Anyone could feel the rush of composing elegant headlines within minutes.

For a graphic designer in the 1970s, holding a brand-new polyester sheet of 24 point Helvetica Medium Condensed, its neat rows of caps and lower cases ready to be applied on a clean surface, was pure ecstasy.

Letraset, a UK company specializing in art supplies, was the main provider of these handy alphabets, which were ubiquitous in design studios worldwide because they could be used to create high-quality camera-ready artwork. Even though setting headlines with these decals required a sure hand and a keen understanding of typographical rules (once the letters were down you could not move them), the result could be stunning: depending on how much pressure you had applied, the words or sentences could look letterpressed or silkscreened.

The idea of transferring motifs from one surface to another used to be called "decalcomania." It was popular in the nineteenth century for pressing decorative patterns on to everything from plates to guitars. The Surrealists used the same word to describe a way of applying uneven pressure on a thin layer of gouache to give it a mysterious-looking texture. In the 1950s, ready-to-transfer cartoon characters were popular with children. But kids had trouble mastering the delicate process, involving sliding the wet images off their transparent backing on to a page, resulting in crumpled figures so bizarre they inspired the term "cockamamie," a deformation of "decalcomania."

Decals today are peel-off designs, their sticky backing formulated to bond permanently with anything from automotive parts, model airplanes, football helmets, and surfboards to cell phones, computer cases, furniture, and walls. Letraset is no longer known for its innovative transfer letters—the company went back to its craft roots, selling such products as self-sticking adhesive film and metallic ink markers. Cockamamie is not dead, though. Wallpaper manufacturers are now proposing lines of mural-size rubdowns that reproduce eccentric or quirky patterns designed by artists whose sensibility is steeped in comic-book culture. Domestic, a French company, publishes wall stickers by avant-garde European graphic designers such as Antoine+Manuel, Marti Guixé, Geneviève Glaucker, and Ich&Kar. ∎

ICH&KAR
2005

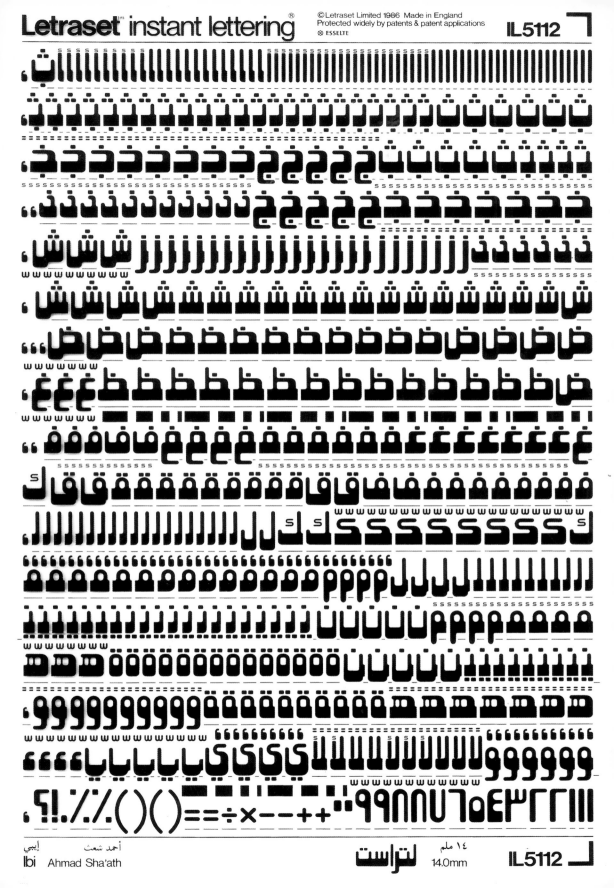

Mickey Mouse (2008) received a makeover for his 80th birthday. His radiant smile looks even more dazzling thanks to the addition of rays radiating from his head, a technique used on Chinese propaganda posters for Chairman Mao.

Radiating lines confer special status

IDEA № 4
RAYS

One of the most ancient iconographic symbols, rays were the attribute of gods and heroes, the hallmark of their supernatural power. Radiating from the head of Apollo, Buddha, or Christ, rays were the graphic interpretation of a rare optical phenomenon known as an aura, which occurs when moisture in the air is diffracted by sunlight around an object, creating a dazzling circular rainbow.

The first widespread nonreligious use of rays was on the flag of imperial Japan, "the Land of the Rising Sun." It featured 16 red beams emanating from a red disk. After World War II, with Japan defeated, the flag lost its rays to become the red circle it is today. Communist China promptly appropriated them for its own propaganda, displaying them as a full aureole surrounding Mao Zedong or as a sweeping fan of searchlights on the horizon, seemingly announcing the dawn of a new age. The rays, often red on a white, yellow, or blue background,

have since inspired designers who see in them a powerful graphic motif, similar to that of the red stripes of the American flag, but with the added reference to the now-nostalgic "red, bright, and shining" iconography of the Mao cult.

Rays showed up in the work of the American designer Seymour Chwast, who liked their Art Deco flavor but knew how to harness their graphic impact, as seen in his 1968 *End Bad Breath* antiwar poster. Rays were also ubiquitous in the posters of Japanese designer Tadanori Yokoo who, influenced by Chwast, Milton Glaser, and Push Pin graphic artists, was weaving culturally charged imagery in his compositions, often layering red rays with other traditional Japanese motifs. Rays were recently mobilized to give Mickey Mouse a radiating halo not unlike that emanating from the portraits of Chairman Mao. With his bright yellow aura, the face of the beloved rodent is now a sacred icon. Rays are today a staple of Shepard Fairey's artful graffiti, deliberate reinterpretations of Maoist posters, co-opted to serve a politically disruptive agenda.

Meanwhile, rays have found their way into the commercial realm as graphic gimmick. Surrounding an object, they highlight its importance. Flaring up around a price, they signal a

BELOW: Having Reached a Climax at the Age of 29, I Was Dead (1965) was the title of an exhibition by Japanese graphic designer Tadanori Yokoo announcing a retrospective of his work. Among the many visual references in his art are radiating rays, similar to the rays on the flag of imperial Japan.

ABOVE: "Smarter Planet" campaign (launched 2009), developed by Ogilvy & Mather New York for IBM, heralds the repositioning of IBM as an energy- and environment-conscious company. Circular emblems, symbolizing various industries or issues, all sport a diadem of rays, evidence of their special status.

bargain or a promotion. As short bursts of energy, they give an aura of modernity and excitement to a logo, a name, or an emblem. They also do wonders on detergent packaging to express the idea of "squeaky-clean."

The latest "Smarter Planet" IBM campaign, by Ogilvy & Mather's creative director Michael Paterson, features the Earth with "think rays" popping out on the top, as if it has just had a bright idea. As the campaign has developed, more ads with glowing spheres have been created. From brains to gears, the round emblems all wear a tiara of short beams, not unlike the Statue of Liberty. ■

Historical elements signal a period aesthetic

IDEA Nº 5
PASTICHE

ABOVE: The Works of Geoffrey Chaucer (1896), printed by William Morris at the Kelmscott Press, is the artist's best-known work. The Chaucer type was designed specifically for this book. The woodcut illustrations by Edward Burne-Jones (1833–1898) epitomize what the Pre-Raphaelites saw as the high moral tone of medieval illustration.

OPPOSITE: Chez Panisse Second Birthday Celebration (1973), a poster designed by David Lance Goines in an homage to the Jugendstil style of the Vienna Workshops and Vienna Secession movement.

BELOW: Old Advertising Cuts From A–Z (1989), published and designed by Charles Spencer Anderson for the French Paper Company, borrowed 1920s and 1930s advertising clichés, making nostalgic imagery into contemporary visual language.

Throughout the history of modern graphic design, designers have reprised elements from the past, as pastiche, either to signal a particular period aesthetic or to make a philosophical point. William Morris adopted medieval gothic for his Kelmscott Press editions as emblematic of the Arts and Crafts Movement's rejection of industrial standardization. Pastiche openly imitates the previous works of other artists, often with satirical intent and as a hodgepodge of incongruous parts.

David Lance Goines' 1973 poster celebrating the second birthday of San Francisco restaurant Chez Panisse may not have the same political underpinning as Morris's Arts and Crafts aesthetics, but Goines does reference Charles Rennie Mackintosh and Ludwig Hohlwein as primary influences, with emphasis on the latter. Like Morris, however, Goines has made the pastiche, in this case of

Art Nouveau, his own graphic signature for much of his work.

Why would a brand want to employ pastiche? Borrowing existing mannerisms provides familiar codes with limited risk. They are further designed to tap into some ersatz **nostalgia** for sensibilities popular, often, long before the target audience was even born, suggesting a primal effect that the power of pastiche can evoke. Brands need to appear new yet familiar, and pastiche design reconciles this paradox by giving new brands instant heritage and old brands a chance to flag their origins and authenticity. Liquor and beer companies value the vintage look: Fernando Creative's design for Meztizo beer hybridizes a Mayan look with a heavy metal typography, while their package for Chocolate Beer builds on a nineteenth-century aesthetic of wood type and Victorian cartouches.

American designer Charles Spencer Anderson, who has created a body of work using vintage icons and cultural kitsch, perhaps surprisingly finds graphic time-travel cynical and manipulative. He says the need of marketers to inveigle their products into the consumer's consciousness accounts for the increase of pastiche in mass-market packaging. While Anderson "quotes" (or

samples) historical artifacts as raw material, the fact remains that historical pastiche is useful for telegraphing specific codes that are used to manipulate perception and trigger consumer response. Some examples of styles and their intended implications include: Victorian = historic; Russian Constructivism = revolutionary; Bauhaus = progressive; Art Deco = elegant; Streamline = speed; American Socialist Realism = optimistic; Psychedelic = drugs; 1950s Atomic and 1970s Disco = goofy; and 1980s = hipster.

Arguably contemporary design technology has no look and no form to inspire a visual movement. This leads to the perpetual question that designers from all disciplines constantly deal with: what should it look like? It is in a stylistic vacuum that pastiche tends to be frequently used and abused. ■

CHEZ PANISSE
SECOND BIRTHDAY
CELEBRATION
TUESDAY AUGUST 28
SIX PM TO MIDNIGHT
CASSOULET
½ LITRE OF WINE
& SALAD :: $5.25
ALSO UN FILM DE
MARCEL PAGNOL

A printer's cliché becomes a visual trope

IDEA № 6
POINTING FINGERS

Whatever its intended message, a pointing finger is a declarative statement and a behavioral cue. Originally employed in graphics as a printer's cut (premade illustration), its primary purpose was to indicate direction— "This way," "Turn here," "Detour." Pointing fingers were also commonly used in nineteenth-century printing, on posters, bills, and advertisements, to be emphatic. When a finger pointed directly at a word or sentence it was a benign command to read whatever was being pointed out.

SOME COUNTRIES THINK THAT CIVILIAN DEATHS CAUSED BY A WEAPON'S FAULTS AND INACCURACIES ARE ACCEPTABLE. CLUSTER MUNITIONS. IT'S TIME TO POINT THE FINGER.
WWW.STOPCLUSTERBOMBS.ORG

ABOVE: Point the Finger *(c. 2011), poster designed for "Beat the Drum to Ban Cluster Bombs." The accusatory finger indicates those nations who have not signed the Convention on Cluster Munitions.*

BELOW: Are You Doing All You Can? *(1942) is a World War II poster of Uncle Sam created and published by the General Cable Corporation—one of many pointing fingers designed to boost morale on the home front.*

OPPOSITE: Auch Du bist liberal *(You too are a liberal) (1959), poster designed by Karl Gerstner, influenced by the famous pointing fingers from World War I used in posters by England, France, Russia, Germany, and the United States.*

The pointing finger acquired more gravitas when in 1914, at the outset of World War I, the British designer Alfred Leere created the famous recruitment poster featuring a picture of the secretary of state for war, Lord Kitchener, pointing directly out of the poster at the viewer, above the words "wants you." This was the first of many wartime (and postwar) recruitment posters to use the pointing finger in a similar way. It was later copied in the United States (James Montgomery Flagg, 1917), Italy (Achille Luciano Mauzan, 1917), Germany (Julius Ussy Engelhard, 1919), and Russia (Dimitri Moor, 1920). These were demonstrative, patriotic calls to arms rendered by both sides in both world wars, each side realizing the innate power of the trope.

Yet the militarist application was preceded by a less aggressive promotional point-of-purchase display for a soft drink. In 1911 Moxie, a popular American beverage, produced a sign showing a stern soda-fountain attendant in a white coat pointing directly at the customer over a label exhorting the viewer to "Drink Moxie." In line with the subsequent iterations, this was about winning a war: in this case against Coca-Cola.

The pointing finger has been used frequently and ubiquitously ever since. In some cultures it is considered offensive or rude to point, yet used decoratively or conceptually, as it is in much graphic design, the pointing finger nonetheless retains its benign character. And in the digital age, this pointing digit has taken on new relevance as the cursor on all computers. What the 1960s television show *Laugh-In* referred to as "the fickle finger of fate" is now the stalwart directional in the virtual world. ■

auch Du bist liberal

Designers grappling with mortality

IDEA № 7
VANITAS

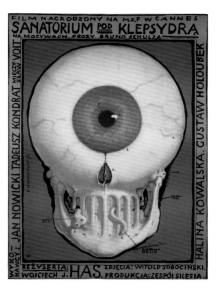

Macabre images involving skulls have been popular since antiquity; in ancient Rome the expression *memento mori*, meaning "remember you must die," was coined to remind the rich and famous of their mortality. Few icons are as recognizable as skulls, and every period of history has found a use for them, as religious emblems, as antiwar symbols, as danger signs, or as expressions of spiritual angst. Only the Moderns, those incurable utopians, seemed immune to their charm.

BELOW: Ossário (2006), a quarter-mile-long fresco by street artist Alexandre Orion. He turned a tunnel in São Paulo into a hellish vision by cleaning the walls with a wet rag to trace a garland of skulls.

ABOVE: The Hourglass Sanatorium (1973), a film poster by Polish artist Franciszek Starowieyski, turns a giant eyeball into a cranium, while the lower jaw suggests the bars of the cells in which inmates are left to die.

OPPOSITE: Apartheid/Racisme (1986), a poster by French collective Grapus, denounces racism by representing Africa as a skull in which eye sockets and nasal cavities are maps within maps, an image that evokes the partitioning between blacks and whites.

An artistic genre known as "vanitas" flourished in Europe during periods of prosperity, with illustrations of beautiful women peering at the face of death in the mirror as a recurring theme (Allan Gilbert's 1892 *All Is Vanity* is a prime example). During the first part of the twentieth century, when wars tore the world apart, skull imagery was mainly used to denounce violence: John Heartfield's gruesome 1928 photocollage *The Face of Fascism*, a decaying portrait of Mussolini, was devoid of sentimentality. In 1935, Magritte painted a rare vanitas, a nude woman with a skull as a head.

Decades later Polish poster artist Franciszek Starowieyski, the master of phantasmagoric dreams, rediscovered the skull for his generation. In 1973, from the other side of the Iron Curtain, he promoted the Polish cult film *The Hourglass Sanatorium* with a nightmarish vision: a bony jaw, its clenched teeth the bars of a festering prison, on top of which sat a cranium that was a huge menacing eyeball. Skulls were Starowieyski's specialty: he used them to depict female forms, lunar landscapes, or bristling weapons. After him, graphic designers competed to turn skulls into subjects of visual meditation. In 1986, the Grapus collective in France designed one of the most effective images against South African apartheid by turning a jagged map of Africa into the black silhouette of a skull whose lower jaw had been viciously ripped off.

Theater posters for *Hamlet* have long been a favorite venue for designers to muse on death. In 2004, Daniel Kunzi for Atelier BLVDR produced a masterly scribble for the Théâtre St. Gervais in Geneva. In 2006, Polish designer Piotr Miodozeniec created a striking cut-paper version of the scene in which the Danish prince stares at a skull as if it were his own image. But the prize for the most dramatic vanitas to date goes to the Brazilian graffiti artist Alexandre Orion for his macabre mural in "reverse graffiti" inside a tunnel in São Paulo. While cars were racing by, he drew a long garland of skulls by removing the soot from the wall with a wet rag. The fresco was about a quarter of a mile long before a cleaning unit hosed the wall down, erasing it all—a gesture as eloquent as the *tempus fugit* motto itself. ∎

The clenched fist is a symbol of power, authority, or anger

IDEA № 8

CLENCHED FISTS

The left have long claimed the clenched-fist salute as their exclusive property—a symbol of solidarity and defiance. During Germany's liberal Weimar Republic in the 1920s, for example, the raised fist was used by the Communists and the straight-arm salute by the Nazis. But images from World War I show that the iron fist was first a symbol of military power.

The term "iron fist" refers to the unbridled strength of a leader, perhaps coined to characterize the nineteenth-century Prussian statesman Otto von Bismarck, dubbed the "Iron Chancellor" for his famous speech about attaining power "not by speeches and votes of the majority," but through "iron and blood."

Since all political parties require symbols to propagate their ideologies, whoever repeatedly uses a given symbol will usually end up claiming "ownership." In the war of body-part language in the early twentieth century, the Nazis and

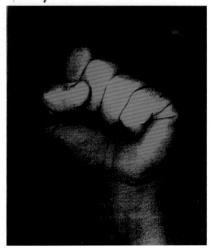

Fascists borrowed from the Roman emperors, whose imperial greetings included raised arms and fists on chests. The Communists took their clenched-fist gesture from the 1871 Paris Communards, the earliest Socialist revolutionaries.

"The fist was always part of something—holding a tool or other symbol, part of an arm or human figure, or shown in action," states cultural historian Lincoln Cushing. "But graphic artists from the New Left changed that in 1968, with an entirely new treatment." The new image was stark and simple, and, given its political echoes of German socialists and, indeed, Spanish Civil War Republicans, it was the perfect icon of militant rebellion. Its first New Left iteration was a poster by San Francisco Bay Area graphic artist Frank Cieciorka for "Stop the Draft" week in 1968, protesting the arrest of the anti-Vietnam War "Oakland Seven." The image was adapted from a poster he had done previously for "Stop the Draft" in 1967, which used a large, blocky figure wielding a fist.

The fist was raised high at all major rallies on posters and flyers for student, antiwar, women's, and other political activities throughout the world. In the United States the fist was adopted by Students for a Democratic Society in 1968 and by Harvard student strikers a year later in a poster created by Harvey Hacker, a design student. The Atelier

ABOVE: Clown (1906), an anti-Czarist Russian satiric periodical with cover illustrated by Vasilii Beringer, shows the clenched fist not as a symbol of leftist revolution but as representative of the masses.

BELOW: Citizen Designer (2003), with cover designed by James Victore created on a copy machine, suggests the radical spirit of citizen activism in art and design.

OPPOSITE: Strike (1969), silkscreen print by Harvey Hacker at the Strike Poster Workshop, Graduate School of Design, Harvard University. Arguably the first time the clenched fist was used in the 1960s, it enumerated the eight demands of dissent.

Populaire, the poster workshop set up by the students in the Paris 1968 uprising, issued fist images during strikes by students and workers protesting the policies of the president, Charles de Gaulle. And the fist is still employed as a symbol of dissent, if sometimes commercially co-opted—as was the case with the promotion for controversial American shock-jock Howard Stern when he moved from commercial to satellite radio. ∎

STRIKE FOR THE EIGHT
DEMANDS STRIKE BE
CAUSE YOU HATE COPS
STRIKE BECAUSE YOUR
ROOMMATE WAS CLUBBED
STRIKE TO STOP EXPANSION
STRIKE TO SEIZE CONTROL
OF YOUR LIFE STRIKE TO
BECOME MORE HUMAN STR
IKE TO RETURN PAINE HALL
SCHOLARSHIPS STRIKE BE
CAUSE THERE'S NO POETRY
IN YOUR LECTURES
STRIKE BECAUSE CLASSES
ARE A BORE STRIKE FOR
POWER STRIKE TO SMASH THE
CORPORATION STRIKE TO MAKE
YOURSELF FREE STRIKE TO
ABOLISH ROTC STRIKE BECAUSE
THEY ARE TRYING TO SQUEEZE
THE LIFE OUT OF YOU STRIKE

Make a statement that can't be missed

IDEA № 9
MONUMENTAL IMAGES

Monumentality has long been a tool for perpetuating myth and building heroes. Take the Colossus of Rhodes (292–280 BCE). This statue of the Greek god Helios, intentionally or not, is a model for the gargantuan advertising display; it celebrates Rhodes's victory over the ruler of Cyprus in 305 BCE. Similarly, the Statue of Liberty, designed by Frédéric Bartholdi, might be considered a giant advertisement "mascot" for the idea of freedom and the American way of life.

Architects working for bishops or kings have always understood the virtues of larger-than-life scale. These rulers themselves may have been human-sized in reality, but in images they could tower high above the multitudes. The gigantic figures that Benito Mussolini commissioned in 1935 for his Fascist city, EUR (Esposizione Universale Roma), exemplified the marriage of power and graphic monumentalism. A billboard with his own sculpted, oversized visage in Rome, with the word *sì* (yes) repeated as a background pattern, reflected the advertisements for commercial wares hawked on grandiose displays in every town and city in the world.

The enormous eye that menacingly overlooked the busy intersection of Fifth Avenue and 42nd Street in New York was not the portentous Big Brother of Orwell's *1984*; however, it was a decidedly

resolute display of corporate confidence. The eye in question stared from a billboard with the headline "Watch the Fords Go By," and was designed by A.M. Cassandre for the Ford Motor Company in 1937. And watch it did: doubtless many Fords—the largest-selling marque in the United States at that time—passed that corner every day. Cassandre's image was possibly the most monumental close crop of a human feature ever printed and was a paradigmatic example of a growing trend in graphic monumentality.

Cassandre's eye, with the V8 logo emblazoned on the pupil, was one of the many large-scale advertising "**spectaculars**" (the term applied to the mammoth Times Square electric-light billboards) commonly used to sell consumer goods, starting in the late nineteenth century. Today, scrims cover

A.M.CASSANDRE

V8

WATCH THE FORDS GO BY

entire buildings in the middle of cities, on which are emblazoned immense icons that through picture, color, and type can transmit messages on the street more effectively and imposingly than any common poster print.

The world indeed cowers and bows before monumental imagery, no matter what the message or image. Big reaps its own reward. The simple fact that something is incredibly larger than it should be triggers a sense of awe. To make the boldest statement possible, increasing the size of the most common-place objects or physical features, and adding the right words, phrase, or slogan, does wonders. ■

OPPOSITE: Si Si Si *(Yes Yes Yes) (1934). The designer of this enormous three-dimensional billboard hanging across from the Palazzo Braschi in Rome is unknown. It is likely Benito Mussolini gave permission for its design.*

ABOVE: Watch the Fords Go By (1937), a surreal image designed by A.M. Cassandre for Ford Motors. A multisheet billboard, it looked down upon the vehicular and foot traffic on 42nd Street and Fifth Avenue in New York City.*

Expressive female figures say "look at me"

IDEA № 10
FEMALE ARCHETYPES

The French painter and lithographer Jules Chéret invented one of the first commercial female archetypes at the end of the nineteenth century. She was a free-spirited Parisian girl, with a plunging neckline and a dizzying hourglass figure. Her twirling silhouette was posted on every wall of the French capital to advertise nightclubs, theatrical productions, horse races, and cabaret shows, but also liquors, perfumes, and cosmetics.

The image of *joie de vivre*, the Chérettes, as the figures were called, were typical of the *fin de siècle* frivolity that preceded the birth of Modernism. Portrayed with expressive hand gestures and a relaxed upper body, the young girls displayed the kind of self-confidence that would soon become associated with the liberation of women. A lively smile illuminated their faces as they looked over their shoulders at their admirers.

Though they looked sexy, their erotic appeal was carefully veiled in order not to interfere with the commercial message. By the end of the 1930s, Coca-Cola perfected the genre, presenting cheerful color illustrations of seductive housewives. Alluring but never risqué, these happy homemakers were not as provocative as the popular bombshells by Alberto Vargas whose likenesses were also used to adorn military aircraft during World War II and the Korean War. By the mid-1940s, the demure Coca-Cola females were replaced by more flirtatious beach beauties sipping from the iconic bottle.

The term "pinup" was coined in 1941 to describe the way young men liked to display glamorous images of scantily dressed girls. However, one of the most popular pinups of that period was not a classic beauty. "Rosie the Riveter," depicted in a painting by Norman Rockwell, was featured on the cover of the *Saturday Evening Post* on May 29, 1943. An allegorical figure who stood for the 11 million American women working in factories during World War II, she was shown eating her sandwich during her lunch break. Portrayed as a sturdy maiden in work clothes, she sat in a graceful pose that was just as compelling as that of a sex kitten. She too looked over her shoulder at the world at her feet, her can-do attitude evidence of the power of her femininity.

ABOVE: Rei Ayanami (1995), a fictional character created by Hedeaki Anno and drawn by Yoshiyuki Sadamoto for the Japanese television series Evangelion, was adapted as a Manga female figure with a fetching silhouette but an enigmatic personality.

BELOW: BEople #4 (2002), art directed by Base Design in Brussels, was a short-lived fashion magazine that featured models in nontraditional poses in an attempt to invent a new form of seduction.

OPPOSITE: Folies-Bergère, La Loïe Fuller (1892), a poster promoting a cabaret act in Paris, was one of many such images by the celebrated French affichiste Jules Chéret, who liked to represent women as twirling figures.

As photography replaced illustration, watercolor pinups morphed into carefully retouched portraits of movie stars, with Marilyn Monroe, Sophia Loren, and Brigitte Bardot making headlines in the 1950s. Playboy Playmates and Bond girls were not far behind. Today, actresses and TV personalities all over the world sell products with as much abandon as the Chérettes a century ago. But new female archetypes are being introduced: some provocative, like the Manga character Rei Ayanami, others deceptively demure, like the partially disrobed masked model gracing a 2002 cover of *BEople*, a magazine about a certain Belgium. ∎

Cut out of color, white forms become focal points

IDEA № 11

COLOR BLOCKS

French artists experienced a mini-renaissance at the end of the nineteenth century when they discovered traditional Japanese woodblock prints, or *ukiyo-e*—"pictures of the floating world." The Impressionist movement, and later Art Nouveau, owed a great deal to what was then perceived as an entirely novel art form.

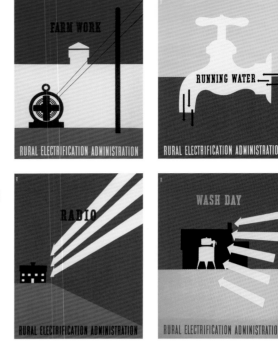

ABOVE: *Rural Electrification Administration posters (1934) demonstrate the versatility of Lester Beall, who combined the geometric impact of Russian Constructivist compositions with the graphic simplicity of Japanese* ukiyo-e *prints.*

BELOW: La Goulue *(1891) shows how Toulouse-Lautrec used large, flat fields of color in a dynamic fashion, often turning the white area into the most dramatic shape, as here with the white knickers of the can-can dancer.*

OPPOSITE: Boccaccio *(2007), theater poster by Swiss designer Stephan Bundi. The flatness of the white form is emphasized by the horn-shaped fingers that poke fun at the cuckolded hero.*

Poster artists, and Toulouse-Lautrec in particular, adopted the bold style of the primitive *ukiyo-e* printing technique, which had been popular in Japan from the seventeenth century onward. Lautrec's illustrations, with their flat color-fields, assertive black silhouettes, and loose brushstrokes, became instant icons. His lithograph of the celebrated Moulin Rouge dancer La Goulue lifting her white petticoats to reveal her frilly knickers is one of the most renowned examples of this phenomenon.

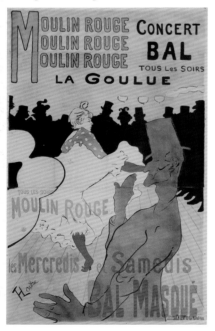

Color-blocking, as a style, acquired a life of its own, as poster artists worldwide kept inventing new ways of interpreting the trend of "Japonisme." In the United States in the 1930s, Lester Beall used flat color-fields as if they were stencils, a visual effect that had been mastered by Japanese printers but largely overlooked by their Western admirers. Beall's posters for the Rural Electrification Administration use geometric patches of blue, red, or yellow to trap, or "block," white silhouettes that pop up as dynamic graphic motifs against flat colors. The interaction between positive and negative space, so crucial in typography, had never before been applied to illustrations with so much vivacity.

Today, a number of graphic designers are still fascinated by the versatility of this blocking process, in which blank space becomes the focus of a composition. In 2004, Apple promoted its new iPod with a series of posters in electric colors featuring black silhouettes of hip-hop dancers. What made the posters memorable was the fact that the small earphones, thin cables, and diminutive iPod were white, and seemed to pop against their acid-green, dazzling-yellow, hot-pink, or bright-purple backdrops.

In 2007, Swiss art director Stephan Bundi updated, yet again, the *ukiyo-e* technique. His two-color poster for the operetta *Boccaccio*, for the Theater Biel Solothurn, is a consummate illustration of how powerful such an approach can be. Against a solid orange background, the striking white cutout of a man's head stands out, its flatness emphasized by the realistic photograph of two fingers that look like his horns. Poking fun at cuckolded husbands, the *Boccaccio* poster is also a graphic "V" sign—a victory sign for minimalist graphic expression. ∎

BOCCACCIO

OPERETTE VON FRANZ VON SUPPÉ
BIENNE DES LE 21|12|2007
BIEL AB 21|12|2007
SOLOTHURN AB 27|12|2007

THEATRETHEATER
BIEL SOLOTHURN BIENNE SOLEURE

Graphic veneers illuminate content

IDEA № 12
ORNAMENTATION

Is it fundamentally wrong to use decoration? Although architect Adolf Loos asserted with high-minded certainty that ornament was a sin in his 1908 essay "Ornament and Crime," decoration is neither inherently good nor bad. Although it is all too frequently applied to conceal faulty merchandise and flawed concepts, it can nonetheless enhance a product when used with integrity, to illuminate rather than obscure content.

A decorator taps into aesthetic allure to evoke a certain kind of pleasure. Critics argued that Art Nouveau (and later Art Deco and Postmodern) decoration on buildings and furniture and in graphic design rarely added to a product's functionality or durability, and locked the respective objects in their own time, thereby rendering everything eventually obsolete. However, decoration can also play an integral role in the total design scheme. Good decoration is that which frames a product or message. The euro paper currency, for example, is more appealing than the staid American dollar. The dollar bill lacks the dynamism of the euro, which has vibrant graphic elements in a variety of bright and pastel colors; it looks both official and human at the same time.

Decoration is a combination of forms (color, line, pattern, letter, picture) that does not convey a literal message, but serves to stimulate the senses. Paisley, herringbone, or tartan patterns are decorative yet can elicit a visceral response. Ziggurat or sunburst designs on the façade of a building or the cover of a brochure spark a responsive chord even when type is absent.

The worst decorative excesses are not the obsessively baroque borders and patterns such as the vines and tendrils that strangulated the typical Art Nouveau poster or page, but those that stem from the careless application of anachronistic details without function. A splendidly ornamented package, such as many of today's boutique tea, soap, and food wrappers, will have a quantifiable impact on consumers.

With the computer making complex decorative compositions easier, the 2000s have seen a revival of both old and newer decorative tendencies. A cult of the squiggly—modern-day Art Nouveau—has crept into the design of everything from type to packaging. Some is stunning in craft and artistry. Canadian letterer Marian Bantjes has emerged as the contemporary master. But some is excessive—an overabundance of twigs and tendrils that have not yet been pruned. ∎

BELOW: Kusmi Tea (2008) package. This Russian-style tea brand was started in 1867 by Pavel Michailovitch Kousmichoff, in St Petersburg, Russia.

ABOVE: Ver Sacrum (1902), poster designed by Koloman Moser for the XIII Vienna Secession exhibition, exhibits the decorative tendencies that rejected realism and the academic art of the time.

OPPOSITE: National Poetry Month (2010), poster designed by Marian Bantjes, features kaleidoscopic figures turning beneath a star-filled sky, inspired by the poetry of Wallace Stevens with lettered lines from "Final Soliloquy of the Interior Paramour."

Memorable logos recalling Victorian decorative style

IDEA № 13
DECORATIVE LOGOTYPES

"If in the business of communications, image is king," wrote Paul Rand in *Design, Form, and Chaos* (1993), "the essence of this image, the logo, is the jewel in its crown." Although Rand also said that a logo "cannot survive unless it is designed with the utmost simplicity and restraint" (*Paul Rand: A Designer's Art*, 1985), corporate marks come in many shapes, colors, and configurations, not all of them so restrained as to be void of decorative tendencies.

Some logos are indeed as ornate as jewelry. Quite a few of the world's most famous, and lasting, early commercial logos, including the GE (General Electric) monogram designed by A.L. Rich and trademarked in 1899, were imbued with restrained Art Nouveau ornamentation.

Stylized and abstracted ornamental motifs have been significant components of the designer's toolbox from the nineteenth century to the present. Despite warnings by reductivists, like Rand, who adhere to economy and for whom, as Adolf Loos pronounced in 1908, ornament is a crime, decorative approaches have more often than not proved effective within the bounds of taste and intelligence. Like the GE logo, Coca-Cola's swirl of Spencerian script (a formal penmanship style) designed by Frank Mason Robinson was conceived in 1885, when Victorian decorative tendencies dominated commercial art and popular culture. Although it has been fine-tuned over the past century, the logo continues to possess the decorative attributes of that time. Similarly, the original Ford Motor Company logo was a complicated seal with neo-Baroque filigree, which was changed in 1912 to an oval with a Spencerian "Ford." This more decorative approach has been retained despite attempts to change it.

The advent of the proto-Modern **object poster** in 1906 put a temporary halt to the era of Victorian decorative practices, and replaced them with stark, simplified logos and trademarks (although not everywhere). It was a move away from ornament but not a total end to it. Although the Modern design movements vociferously encouraged elementary composition—bold linear and geometric forms—there have been many who saw decorative mannerisms as a means of identification. The more unique attributes a logo has, the longer it will stick in the mind's eye.

The letter "A" from Seymour Chwast's 1968 typeface Artone has that quality, borrowing its curvilinear grace from Art Nouveau (the "A" is derived from a type style named "Smoke" because of its ethereal nature). Used on its own as an "A" it is further decontextualized, so that it can be read as both letter and abstract symbol.

Today the freedom to draw on historical precedents for inspiration or direct pastiche, without being condemned as (too) passé, has caused a resurgence in decorative logotypes and marks, such as Mucca's Sant Ambroeus logo, which suggests classic French and Italian patisseries. ∎

TOP: *Sant Ambroeus (2008) logo, designed by Mucca for a bake shop and restaurant, suggests Parisian patisserie papers.*

ABOVE: *Artone Studio India Ink logo (1964), designed by Seymour Chwast, is an Art Nouveau letterform created with the drip of ink in the positive and negative parts of the A.*

OPPOSITE: *GE (General Electric) (1900) logo, designed by A.L. Rich, evolved from an 1892 monogram in the Victorian script style. This iteration continues to use the Art Nouveau decorative flourishes.*

Irresistible trade characters

IDEA № 14

NAIVE MASCOTS

During the late nineteenth century, words were preferred to pictures in advertising. However, as the reproduction of images became cheaper, businesses that had relied solely on brand names and clever slogans sought new visual icons. Older pictorial trade characters evolved into contemporary mnemonic logos. To gain the public's trust, industry turned to signs and symbols—some abstract, but many with human characteristics.

One of the most successful mascots ever was designed for Michelin, the French tire company founded in 1888. Its trademark figure, Bibendum (dubbed "Bib the Michelin Man," among other nicknames), was created by French artist "O'Galop" (a pseudonym of Marius Rossillon), and introduced at the Lyons Exhibition of 1894, where the Michelin brothers displayed their wares. André Michelin commissioned this friendly, bulbous figure after his brother,

Édouard, observed that a stack of tires looked similar to a human form.

In 1923, Aleksander Rodchenko created an unusual advertisement for baby pacifiers. Designed in the Constructivist manner, it featured a wide-eyed, puppetlike infant with no fewer than nine rubber teats stuck between his lips. There was nothing cute about the child, yet the overall effect was endearing because neither Rodchenko nor his client felt compelled to present a rosy picture: the red and green baby looked like a hollering brat.

In France in the 1950s, a group of illustrators brought about what many consider to be the golden age of poster design with their carefree and naive drawing style. Cassandre's Dubonnet Man (see p.122) and Raymond Savignac's Monsavon cow are probably the most famous, but there were many more who worked in the same genre: Jean Carlu, who drew goofy-looking clowns for the Perrier "Pschitt" campaign; Hervé Morgan, who developed the simple-hearted Banania man; and Francis Bernard, known for his candid, working-class, broom-wielding housewives. Bernard Villemot, whose bright color palette and minimalist brushstrokes were almost Matisse-like, could turn an orange peel into the face of a silly man—

OPPOSITE: *Michelin Man (1898), a.k.a. Bibendum, designed by Marius Rossillon and one of the world's oldest trademarks, was conceived to look like a pile of white tires. The stout mascot eventually acquired the reputation of a cigar-smoking ladies' man.*

ABOVE: *Orangina Man (1955), created by Bernard Villemot, was a caricature of the frivolous yet endearing Frenchman, a Maurice Chevalier lookalike, complete with straw boater and silly grin. In subsequent ads, Villemot turned the iconographic orange zest into a parasol, a bikini, and a hula hoop.*

BELOW: *Pacifiers (1923), by Aleksander Rodchenko and Varvara Stepanova, claims that "Better pacifiers there have never been nor ever will be." The image suggests that Russian babies were as vocal as their revolutionary parents.*

and make the ad look smart—as he did for Orangina.

Marketers, eager for brands to appear sophisticated, almost managed to put an end to this delightful trend. From time to time, though, some graphic designers are able to get away with a ludicrous concept that is both absurd and marvelous, as was the case in a 1983 poster by Woody Pirtle for Knoll furniture. It featured a childlike drawing of an office chair upholstered in the guise of a chili pepper. "Hot Seat" was the tagline. In advertising, simple and brilliant are not mutually exclusive terms. ∎

Original design hits the marketplace

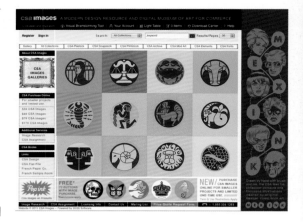

ABOVE: CSA Images (2008) is the website of Charles Spencer Anderson's archive, which sells old, new, and customized spot and stock art: just one of the latest Internet business models.

IDEA № 15
ENTREPRENEURSHIP

Design authorship—arguably synonymous with entrepreneurship—has been practiced since the late nineteenth century, when William Morris's Arts and Crafts workshops in London hand-produced objects, from typefaces to books to furniture, destined for sale in a marketplace. The movement extended to Aurora, New York, where Elbert Hubbard and his Roycrofters sold a wide range of products through catalogs and stores. The tradition evolved in Austria and Germany with the Wiener Werkstätte, Deutsche Werkbund, and Bauhaus, and in the nascent Soviet Union with the Productivists.

In the United States, Contempora, a design collective founded in 1928 that included the contributions of poster and type designer Lucian Bernhard, graphic artist Rockwell Kent, and furniture designer Paul T. Frankl among others, produced textiles, home accessories, and *objets d'art* sold in stores and galleries. Although the word "author" was not expressly used, these design authors and entrepreneurs dreamed up concepts that largely fulfilled their own creative and profit-driven needs.

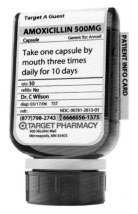

Designers like to make things—yet design is rarely an end in itself, but rather a vessel into which ideas are poured. The concept behind the design author is similar to that of the film auteur, where the top creative roles are in the hands of a single individual, although this need not imply that the individual visionary does it entirely alone.

The designer and ephemera enthusiast Charles Spencer Anderson created the CSA Archive in 1995, based entirely on his passion for vintage graphics. But simply acquiring the graphics is neither an idea nor a product. The entrepreneurial concept was to transform and manipulate them into distinct works of art that could be sold or licensed to designers in need of unique imagery. The business has grown to include a wealth of paper products and books based on the materials in or inspired by the archive.

However, authorship is not always entrepreneurship along the CSA Archive model. Often it involves developing (indeed inventing) new ideas to fill the needs of a market, culture, or society. The design author pinpoints an opening and then creates the concepts to fill the specific requirement—and sells them if lucky.

In 2005 a design student in New York, Deborah Adler, realized that a new prescription drug labeling system and redesigned bottle could save lives. Her prototype, which began as a thesis, turned into a real product when it was taken up by the giant retailer Target as part of a radical revision of its drug packaging. A self-generated, authorial work became a widely used alternative to the status quo.

The design author takes a leap away from the safety of the traditional designer role into that precarious territory where the public decides what works and what does not. ■

BELOW: Target ClearRx (2005), by Deborah Adler, began as a thesis project for her School of Visual Arts MFA. The "clear" typographic concept was purchased by Target stores and used as their signature pharmacy product.

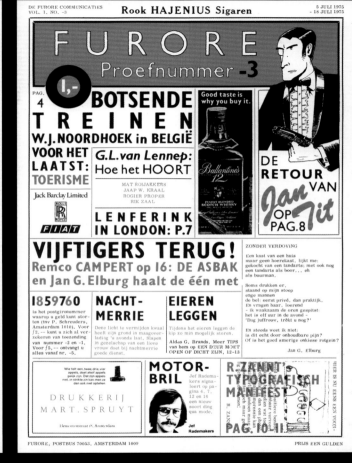

A Catalog of Roycroft Books
*(1905?), designed at the Roycroft
workshop in East Aurora, New York.
Influenced by William Morris's Arts
and Crafts Movement, Elbert Hubbard
established a crafts colony that sold
books, textiles, and other products.*

Furore *(July 1975) is the magazine of
Piet Schreuders, Amsterdam designer
and writer, whose entrepreneurship
centers on "pop culture archeology."
He is publisher of* De Poezenkrant
(about cats) and Furore *(about, he
says, "everything else").*

Novelty letterforms underscore words' meaning

IDEA № 16
METAPHORIC LETTERING

The word "novelty" when applied to typefaces now implies letters that are ephemeral or silly. However, when novelty typefaces were at their commercial apex during the mid- to late nineteenth century and again throughout the late twentieth, "novelty" was a term of distinction, meaning that an alphabet was something other than classic, and frequently metaphoric.

Metaphoric letters were imbued with symbolism and served as vessel and as idea. Often **visual puns**, they were used to enliven the printed word and add dimension to a page.

"Rustic" (later copied and renamed "Log Cabin") was designed in the 1840s by the London foundry owner Vincent Figgins, who had also begun cutting Tuscan letterforms (ornamented type with fishtail serifs) around 1815. Rustic had cut logs forming the letters (even the round ones), came only in capitals, and was used in periodicals, bills, and posters to inject a *trompe l'oeil* illusion, but also to imply naturalism (decades prior to Art Nouveau). In its various subsequent incarnations it was used to advertise in an obvious way rustic products and ideas, such as campsites, hunting cabins, and related items.

This genre of illustrative lettering, which in the twentieth century was commonly used to underscore visually specific businesses and services—including icicle-shaped letters for ice machines or air-conditioning, and chopstick or bamboo letters for Chinese food—was used by commercial job printers when customized illustration was too costly or unavailable. While such faces might be considered typographic stereotypes today—and perhaps even racially derogatory—they were meant as "typography *parlant*" (akin to architecture *parlant*, a structure that serves a basic function yet also conveys a secondary, semiotic meaning, as in a hot-dog stand shaped like a hot dog). The face called Fire, with flames emerging from the letters, has been part of novelty catalogs for years; as has Banana, with its letters in the shape of the fruit—this had more limited usefulness, but is still ripe for exploitation in some typographic realms.

At their peak, two or three novelties were released for every serious text or headline face. Many faces and one-offs were used on bills for carnivals and fairs, where a large array of *parlant* can be found. The rationale behind creating such a face is its hoped-for commercial viability, or, alternatively, its use as a means of solving a particular conceptual problem.

An avid lettering metaphorist, Austrian-born designer Stefan Sagmeister transforms everyday natural and industrial objects into letters to convey messages in which the metaphors trigger deeper understanding of the message—and they look intriguing too, which is the primary function. ∎

CHRISTMAS COMES BUT ONCE A YEAR
2454-3n
Hollyberry O*M Vol.2 p.706

CONFUCIUS SAY TAKES 2 TO MAKE QUARR
5229n
Governale Bamboo O*M Vol.2 p.707

CONIFEROUS—OR DO NOT FORGET TH
2026-2c
Rustic No.222 T*M Vol.2 p.707

Novelty lettering specimens (c. 1890s). Hollyberry, Bamboo, and Rustic (also known as Log Cabin) are among many nature-inspired lettering styles.

Death to Traitors *(c. 1860) was
printed on envelopes and letters as
vividly illustrative propaganda at the
time of the American Civil War. The
letters formed by soldiers, flags,
and—the most ominous—gallows,
spell the traitor's fate.*

Trying to Look Good Limits
My Life *(2004), part of Stefan
Sagmeister's typographic project "20
Things I Have Learned in My Life So
Far." Words are formed from natural
and industrial materials and*

Emphatic and elegant

SWASHES ON CAPS

Adding a flourish to an uppercase letterform is not unlike pinning a silk flower to the lapel of a gray flannel suit. It could look needlessly gaudy. Yet this is exactly what type designers have done since the end of the nineteenth century. They have fitted the capital letters of classical typefaces such as Caslon, Bodoni, Baskerville, and Bookman with special alternative characters adorned with curvy tails, tears, and strokes.

In doing so, they are harking back to medieval illuminated manuscripts. Swashed capital letters, so the reasoning went, would be useful to mark the beginning of a sentence or a paragraph, emphasize the first letter of a name, or highlight the title of a book. Like scribes before him, Gutenberg treated capitals as special characters, with each movable initial letter available in a fancy version, complete with filigrees, curlicues, and coiling ornaments. In the eighteenth century, swashes were also added to some lowercase letterforms to confer a distinctive calligraphic edge to announcements and calling cards. As long as they were used sparingly—and never in words set entirely in capital letters—these elegant squiggles gave the printed page a stylish swagger.

Pioneer of the Arts and Crafts Movement William Morris made extensive use of swashed capitals, combining them with generous borders, large margins, and woodcut-style illustrations. His black and white compositions recreated the rich feel and variegated texture of the most elaborate Gothic manuscript.

No sooner were the rules established than someone had to break them. In 1901, the French architect Hector Guimard created an alphabet of capital letters with ornamental offshoots whose top-heavy slabs and droopy swashes actually increased the legibility of words. First used for the graphic identity of the Castel Béranger, a Paris apartment building Guimard himself had designed, the face was eventually perfected and standardized, and used to label his famous entrances to the Paris Metro stations.

Trying to put a spin on capital letters is an irresistible challenge for some graphic designers. In San Francisco in the 1960s, **psychedelic** poster artists reinterpreted Guimard's alphabet, turning blocky capital letters into delirious letterforms. More recently, a new generation of type designers are going back to Gothic sources and, inspired by the work of Claude Garamond, are setting text in capital letters with a generous mix of ligatures and swashes. One of the most brilliant examples of this revivalist trend is Phil Baines's cover in 2004 for a book of meditations by Marcus Aurelius, part of the Penguin Books "Great Ideas" series, and Marian Bantjes's cover of *I Wonder*, a small gilded volume as precious as a medieval breviary (see p.61). ■

BELOW: Marcus Aurelius's Meditations (2004) was a breakthrough book cover by Phil Baines for the Penguin Books "Great Ideas" series. Its design, judiciously mixing swashes and ligatures, spearheaded a medieval-inspired typographic revival.

ABOVE: Métropolitain (1901), a distinctive typeface with top-heavy calligraphic strokes, was designed by the young architect Hector Guimard for the signage of the Art Nouveau entrances of the new Parisian Metro system.

OPPOSITE: Bookman Swash (1858), originally designed by Alexander Phemister, has gone through many different alterations and revivals since it was first introduced, but it has always had its coterie of fans who love its cursive flair and high legibility.

MARCUS AU
RELIUS·MED
ITATIONS·A
LITTLE FLES
H, A LITTLE
BREATH, AN
D A REASON
TO RULE ALL
—THAT IS M
YSELF·PENG
UIN BOOKS
GREAT IDEAS

AₐAₐABBᵦBCₒCₒDₐD

EEₐFFₐGGₐHHₐIIJJₐ

JKKₐKₐLLₐMMₐMNNₐNO

OPₐPPₐQQₐRRRRₐSSₐTTₐ

UUₐUVVₐVVₐWWWₐW

Wₐ₄XXₐXYYYₐZZZₐÆŒ

ØThₐ&&&ₐ(&(',:.;'")?!*⸱a

bßcddₐdeefffₐfighhₐijk

klmmₐmnnₐnooₐoppq

qₐrrₐrsttₐtuuvvₐwwₐxy

yₐzæₐæœₐœₐœₐøßß\$1234

567890123456789

O¢\$/¢£%° ⁂ «»@

Words become visual artifacts

IDEA Nº 18
TEXTS AS IMAGES

The relationship between words and images is one fraught with creative tension. Text people command the moral high ground as custodians of the printed word, while visual types counterattack by claiming that a picture is worth a thousand words. Their feuding is now legendary. In the publishing world, it is the responsibility of art directors to arbitrate their quarrels, but the conflict that pits words against images is as old, and as vexing, as the war between men and women.

At the beginning of the twentieth century, Italian Futurist Filippo Marinetti led a charge against printed matter, using words as ammunition to turn the page into a visual battlefield. The layout of his 1912 *Irredentismo* composition is an example of how to transform typography into a weapon against bourgeois values. Collaged over a map of Italy, fragments of newspaper headlines became rockets. Low-flying brushstrokes provided what looked like air support. For Marinetti, art was supposed to be radical strife whose objective was "the destruction of syntax."

Paradoxically, the best way to overthrow authority may be to become an author. Marinetti, who penned the Futurist **manifesto** in 1909 (see p.56), started what soon became a tradition among antiestablishment artists. Today, countless avant-garde painters, designers, illustrators, photographers, conceptual artists, and even performers use text as a form of visual protest. Bob Dylan was a pioneer of this genre when,

ABOVE: Parole in Libertà *(1912) by F.T. Marinetti uses phrases ("in freedom") to paint metaphorical pictures that are visually noisy.*

BELOW: Suckcess *(1965) is a cult image from Bob Dylan's "Subterranean Homesick Blues" video, in which the pop singer deliberately misspelled the word "success" to emphasize his distrust of the cultural and political establishment.*

OPPOSITE: Chaumont Festival *(2010), a poster by Dutch designer Karel Martens for a French international graphic design festival, treats the title of the event as a pretext for a typographical tour de force. Hard to decipher at first glance, the words become memorable once you have figured out what they mean.*

in 1965, he shot the music video of his "Subterranean Homesick Blues" single. In this amateur black-and-white film, he is seen casually tossing aside a series of cue cards inscribed with misspelled words from his lyrics. The frame that shows him holding the "Suckcess" card is an underground favorite.

Among contemporary graphic designers, texts as images are now commonplace. Recently, Dutch typographer Karel Martens indulged in some optical play when he was asked to create a poster for Chaumont 2010, a French graphic design festival. Easy to decipher from a distance, the sideways composition falls apart as you get closer, until all that is left is a kaleidoscopic experience. As the colors of the letters blend into a **pixelated** rainbow, the pleasure of the viewer increases. Pure white light seems to emanate from the words. ∎

21e
Festival
international
de
l'affiche
et du
graphisme
de
Chaumont

29
mai
–
20
juin

21st
International
poster
and
graphic
design
festival
of
Chaumont

may
29
–
june
20

Ville de Chaumont,
avec le soutien
du Conseil Général
de la Haute-Marne,
du Conseil Régional
Champagne-Ardenne et
de la Direction Régionale
des Affaires Culturelles/
Ministère de la Culture et
de la Communication.

Affiche: Karel Martens/ Impression: Lézard Graphique

let my people

GO

DAN REISINGER

A design essential: conveying multiple messages

IDEA № 19
VISUAL PUNS

A visual pun is an image with two or more meanings which, once combined, yield a single yet layered message. Graphic design could not exist without visual puns. Transforming or tweaking the meaning of images in ironic and comic ways, so that double meanings are possible, is the conceptual mainstay of a "visual idea." Forcing the viewer to decipher visual codes triggers both recognition and surprise.

OPPOSITE: Let My People Go *(1969), by Dan Reisinger, appealed to the Soviet government to allow Jews to leave the USSR. The biblical saying juxtaposed with the hammer and sickle makes the message clear.*

ABOVE: Gun Crime *(2010), illustrated by Noma Bar, is a commentary on the tragic toll of gun-related violence in the UK. The trigger serves as the mechanism and outcome of gun attacks.*

BELOW: Families *(1980), designed by Herb Lubalin as the logo for a Reader's Digest magazine. How lucky he was to have three letters that suggested a family; how astute he was to see them.*

Dan Reisinger's 1969 *Let My People Go*, referring to the Soviet Jews who were not able to emigrate to Israel, is a memorable visual pun, for it spells out the message while provoking a secondary level of understanding—and emotion. Using the hammer and sickle as a "G" indicates that the Soviets are the antagonists; using Moses's demand of the Egyptian Pharaoh adds drama to the missive. So the pun enters the consciousness through many openings. Similarly, in one of Reisinger's series of posters for Israeli airline El Al (1968–72), to evoke the destination Zurich the "A" is replaced by a snowy mountain peak, leaving no doubt what is on the airline's route.

These examples are evidence that not all puns are humorous in a slapstick way. In *Visual Puns in Design* (1982) author Eli Kince notes that puns have a "humorous effect" and an "analytical effect." The former is a mental jolt or

moment of recognition that creates a comedic "spark," which releases tension in the form of a smile or a laugh. The latter provokes comparison between one idea and another.

Then there are puns that use pictures, letters, and words, like Reisinger's. There are also more complex puns where letters and words are fused together, like Herb Lubalin's *Families*, where the letters "ili" are transformed into ciphers for mother, father, and son; likewise, in *Mother & Child* the ampersand fits inside the letter "o" of mother, suggesting a foetus in a womb. These puns appear easier than they are. Transforming "ili" into a family required keen perception. And making the ampersand fit so perfectly in the "womb" demanded typographic skill. For Lubalin, each of these elements were keys to the doors of perception, where for another designer "ili" or "o" might just have been letters.

Purely pictorial puns may seem easier than typographical ones, but are not necessarily so. Milton Glaser's 2004 Olympic poster *Column with Rings* may trigger a moment of recognition, but conjuring the pun takes a keen wit. Here Glaser pulls the rings of the Olympic logo apart into a ring toss. The Greek column (representing the Greek games) becomes the stick on which the rings are tossed. Finally there are suggestive puns, made by combining two or more unrelated or disparate references, sometimes as a substitution for a more literal reference, conveying two or more meanings. ∎

graphis diagrams

THE GRAPHIC VISUALIZATION OF ABSTRACT DATA

DIE GRAPHISCHE VISUALISIERUNG ABSTRAKTER GEGEBENHEITEN

LA VISUALISATION GRAPHIQUE DE DONNÉES ABSTRAITES

Graphis Diagrams *issue 165 (1974),
a square book edited by Walter
Herdeg, was a striking departure
from the magazine's rectangular
format. Just as unusual was its subject
matter, the visualization of abstract
data. Square formats often signal a
distinctive intention.*

A symbol of modernity—for over a century

IDEA Nº 20
THE SQUARE FORMAT

Art Nouveau was not all curves and floral motifs. In England, Scotland, Austria, and Germany, protagonists of this movement were just as interested in angularity as in serpentine lines, and they used squares as the central motif of many of their experiments. In these countries, publications with a square format were considered avant-garde, showcasing the work of such artists as Gustav Klimt, Joseph Hoffmann, and Koloman Moser. Compact, solid, flawless, the square was considered a pure form and was heralded as the ultimate antibourgeois motif.

BELOW: Ver Sacrum (1899) was the official organ of the Vienna Secession, an art movement characterized by square motifs and geometric designs. At the same time, the stylish square publication was ushering in the Jugendstil style and its Art Nouveau decorative patterns.

ABOVE: "Design&Designer" series (2001—11), a collection of square volumes by French publisher Pyramyd. Each book presents the work of a graphic designer, typographer, photographer, or product designer whose unique vision shapes the contemporary scene.

In 1898 the art magazine *Ver Sacrum* (Sacred Truth) chose the square format to publish the work of Austrian Art Nouveau artists. Short-lived but influential, it made even the most ornamented designs look spare and economical. For designers at the beginning of the twentieth century, the square format turned out to be the providential shape, one that seemed to accommodate within its neat perimeter the most extravagant layouts.

After World War I, the magazine *Wendingen* in the Netherlands took full advantage of the versatility of the square format, and from 1918 to 1932 turned out some of the most exciting cover designs to date. A monthly publication for architects and interior decorators, it displayed the work of sculptors, ceramicists, painters, and graphic artists. Its art director, architect Hendrik Wijdeveld, had picked the name of the magazine ("rotation") as a veiled reference to the revolutionary spirit of Modernism, yet at the same time he unwittingly described the very thing that makes a square format such a powerful shape: you can turn it every which way and it always looks good. This contrast between the stability of the square and its dynamic qualities was best exemplified by a 1921 cover designed by El Lissitzky. A collage of abstract forms that were assembled to give an impression of depth, it was a witty graphic exercise that pitted the **supreme geometry** of Mondrian against that of Malevich.

Since then, numerous art books have adopted the square format, the unusual shape of their cover often signaling the artistic nature of their content. Among the most iconic are Herbert Bayer's *Bauhaus* catalog, 1923; Walter Herdeg's *Graphis Diagrams*, 1974; Milton Glaser's *Graphic Design*, 1973; Takenobu Igarashi's *Alphabets*, 1987; and later editions of Herbert Spencer's 1969 *Pioneers of Modern Typography*.

Unlike square books, square magazines have been few and far between, and have retained an aura of uniqueness. In the late 1920s, *Das Neue Frankfurt* imposed a horizontal grid on a square format, always a winning design solution. In the 1970s there was *Avant-Garde*, designed by Herb Lubalin. "Almost" square magazines have also been launched from time to time, from the first editions of *Dada*, in 1917, to the groundbreaking issues of *Raygun*, designed by David Carson in the early 1990s. Today, square formats are still popular with publishers for books on design or architecture—the square remaining a symbol of uncompromising modernity. ∎

The human figure is reduced to graphic elements

IDEA № 21
PRIMITIVE FIGURATION

Primitive figuration—the simplification of body, head, arm, leg, and facial features—is the reduction of realistic forms into raw, abstract, interpretive shapes. It stems from primitive African art, which in 1905 was introduced to the West largely through German Expressionist graphics. Deformation of the figure was employed to heighten the intensity of personal expression, yet the method eventually became the cornerstone of Modern logo and trademark design after World War I.

ABOVE: Bonjour Voisin! *(1994), designed by Michel Quarez in a raw brushstroke, emphasizing the oversized red hand as a symbol of welcome—"hello neighbor!"*

BELOW: The cover woodcut for Die Aktion *(1918) by Hans Richter is emblematic of the political wing of German Expressionism, which critiqued society through distorted imagery.*

OPPOSITE: Anatomy of a Murder *(1958), by Saul Bass, was influenced by the outline drawn by police to indicate the position of a murder victim. Bass added a German Expressionist nuance to give it a more artful look.*

Initially practiced by a group of rebellious painters and printmakers, the Expressionist aesthetic vigorously repudiated the academic constraints that were strangling mainstream German art. Primitive woodcuts symbolically served as the protest medium but also suggested something more introspective—it was the opposite of the overly rendered, representational Romanticism that had swept over German art during the late nineteenth century. In the hands of such artists as Emil Nolde, whose periodical cover for the 1919 *Der Anbruch* (A New Beginning) uses a limited number of aggressively gouged marks to create an emotionally searing portrait, primitivism spoke viscerally and immediately rather than soothingly or contemplatively. This stark simplicity was the blueprint for graphic revolution.

Expressionism filtered through the avant garde and into the popular culture amid various artistic genres, painting, sculpture, and prints, as well as scene design on stage and screen. The latter influenced the New York-born, Los Angeles-based designer Saul Bass, who designed the (unique in its day) film poster and opening title sequence for *The Man with the Golden Arm* (1955) (see p.156), a movie that plumbs the depths of heroin addiction, starring Frank Sinatra. What separated Bass's work from the conventional static movie-title cards was his kinetic, sequential imagery representing an addict's needle-stained arm.

The raw impact was a direct result of animating the primitive graphic elements. Bass did not have to show the act of shooting up or needle marks to make the point. Substituting a sharp-edged black abstracted form that suggested a tense, pained arm and hand did everything the live-action film accomplished yet in a fraction of the time. In 1959 he reprised this primitive figuration with the poster for *Anatomy of a Murder*, which kinetically constructs a body in the abstracted form of a police outline.

Although it can project mixed signals when used primarily for the stylistic aesthetic—as was the case with the controversial logo for the 2012 London Olympics by Wolff Olins—neoprimitivism is still used as a counterpoint to more sterile graphic approaches. ■

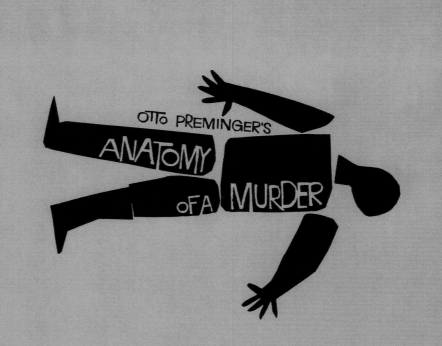

OTTO PREMINGER'S **ANATOMY OF A MURDER**

STARRING
JAMES STEWART
LEE REMICK
BEN GAZZARA
ARTHUR O'CONNELL
EVE ARDEN
KATHRYN GRANT

and JOSEPH N. WELCH as Judge Weaver

Influencing the thoughts and deeds of an entire population

IDEA № 22

PROPAGANDA

During the early twentieth century Edward Bernays's 1928 book *Propaganda* ensured that the word became synonymous with advertising and publicity. When Bernays was laying the groundwork for a new field called "public relations," advertising was a profession of copywriters and designers selling goods and services. In the 1930s the term "propaganda" took on more sinister meaning with the establishment of the Nazi Ministry of Propaganda and Enlightenment, making designers cogs in the propaganda machine's wheels.

ABOVE: Hope (2008), Shepard Fairey's independent expression of support for Barack Obama's presidential election campaign. It was propagated through an Internet campaign—one of the first in U.S. presidential politics.

OPPOSITE: Destroy This Mad Brute (1917), illustrated by H.R. Hopps, a World War I U.S. Army enlistment poster. An ape, wearing a German pickelhaube helmet and holding a ravaged woman, demonstrates enemy brutality.

BELOW: Der Stürmer (1941), edited by Julius Streicher, was a rabidly anti-Semitic weekly in Nazi Germany. Its slogan, "The Jews are our Misery," was writ large in every issue.

Propaganda was never entirely innocent, but it was certainly naive. The concept of propagating a message through textual and visual narratives, signs, and symbols—the backbone of branding today—was always designed to be manipulative, but not venal. And yet today propaganda is synonymous with spreading the big lie, whether a commercial one or a political one. One of the

biggest lies in recent times was the Nazi branding of the Jews as less than human. The film poster for *The Eternal Jew* exaggerates clichéd "Jewish" physical traits to portray a frightening specter.

Fearsome messages are not only the product of extremist and fringe groups; much is government sanctioned and professionally produced. To produce mass hostility toward one group or another, the object of abhorrence must be stripped of its human characteristics. "The war of icons, or the eroding of the collective countenance of one's rivals," noted Marshall McLuhan in *Understanding Media* (1964), "has long been under way. Ink and photo are supplanting soldiery and tanks. The pen daily becomes mightier than the sword."

Politics is often a war of dueling propagandas. Whatever breaches the individual's defenses and touches the right mental buttons wins the prize. During the 2008 U.S. presidential election, Shepard Fairey's *Hope* poster for Barack Obama managed to circumvent the innate resistance to propaganda and rouse the electorate. *Hope* is the graphic essence of that campaign.

These days commercial advertisements are not viewed as propaganda per se, but what else should manipulation of behavior be called? Ads push ideas through the idealization of products: convincing consumers that one brand is better than another is propaganda. However, commercial messages, in Bernays's meaning, may have positive implications in a capitalist society, where the market is driven by individual passions.

Propaganda can be a dangerous weapon, yet is not exclusively meant to induce fear. National virtues and patriotic fever must be promoted and stimulated. Visual depictions that instill pride, such as Fairey's poster, are every bit as necessary as those that trigger a negative reaction. Heroic, blemish-free effigies of leaders are de rigueur. This kind of propaganda is free from ambiguity, but not romanticism. ∎

The simpler the image, the more powerful the communicaton

THE OBJECT POSTER

The early twentieth-century advertising fashion known as "Sachplakat," or the object poster, originated in Germany and took the advertising and design world by storm. It was the jewel in the crown of a large stylistic movement called Plakatstil, or Poster Style.

With the advent of chromolithography during the late nineteenth century, a grand shift in advertising form and content altered the way design was practiced. The ability to reproduce color pictures gave birth to a popular art that not only persuaded but also entertained. Thanks to the new technology artists developed looser painting styles, and the resulting posters resembled grand canvases filled with fanciful figures and cool colors, all capped by artful letters. Then, as though in reaction to complexity, a more simplified style emerged, one that was easy for passers-by to read on jam-packed streets.

Sachplakat's inventor was an 18-year-old German cartoonist, Lucian Bernhard, who, in 1906, entered a poster competition sponsored by Berlin's Priester match company. As the story goes, Bernhard's first—rejected—sketch was typically Art Nouveau (called Jugendstil in Germany): a cigar in an ashtray on a checked tablecloth with dancing nymphets formed by the intertwining tobacco smoke. Next to the ashtray were two wooden matches. A friend mistakenly complimented Bernhard on the excellent cigar advertisement, which forced him to rethink the composition. Immediately he eliminated the tablecloth, ashtray, cigar, and smoke, until he was left with only two simple matches. Next, he enlarged the matchsticks, made them red with yellow tips, and placed them on a maroon field. At the top of the image area he hand-lettered the brand name "Priester" in bold block letters.

The object poster remained in vogue until 1914, when World War I brought commercialism to a halt. After the war, advertising techniques shifted again and a variety of new methods, including Art Deco styling, began to take hold. The Sachplakat lost its currency, but it was nonetheless influential. Eventually, it became just one of many tools in the advertising toolkit, along with more conceptual illustration, and later photography. ■

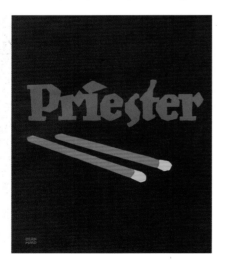

BELOW: Priester Matches *(1906), by Lucian Bernhard, is the first "Sachplakat" or object poster. With only two matches to illustrate the product along with the brand name, the poster bucked the trend for fanciful advertisements.*

ABOVE: Absolut Pears *(2007) is one of hundreds in a long-running series showing Absolut vodka bottles, starting in 1985 with a rendering by Andy Warhol. The bottles have been used in ironic contexts, but also as* objets d'art *on their own.*

OPPOSITE: Prevent Loose Heads Inspect Daily *(c. 1947), by Tom Eckersley, was created as a cautionary message for industry. Simply showing the object in question with unambiguous text was at once graphically startling and completely understandable.*

PREVENT LOOSE HEADS

INSPECT DAILY

ECKERSLEY

Issued by the Ministry of Labour and National Service and produced by the Royal Society for the Prevention of Accidents, Terminal House, 52 Grosvenor Gardens, London, S.W.1.

Printed by LOXLEY BROS. LTD.

MLD/168

Playful colors and shapes

IDEA № 24
PAPER CUTOUTS

Child's play and graphic design go naturally hand-in-hand. Cut-and-paste collages similar to those made in childhood are not inconsequential in the history of Modernist image-making. When Henri Matisse began to feel the effects of deteriorating health, he turned from paint to collage made from bright colored paper.

Matisse's 1947 *Icarus*, featuring a roughly cut black human figure floating against a sky of blue with cutout stars of yellow, influenced the approaches of Paul Rand, Saul Bass, Henryk Tomaszewski, Alan Fletcher, and Ivan Chermayeff, among many fine and applied artist acolytes. Each at one time or another employed similar techniques to effect an expressionistic graphic outcome. Although a time-honored method of early **do it yourself** art, **collage** was viewed in the early twentieth century as a Modern alternative to the even more traditional arts of painting and drawing.

The Fauvist Matisse had begun playing in his visual sandbox in 1943 when working on the limited edition book *Jazz* (published in 1947 by Tériade), an improvisational series of prints, which combined gouache-painted paper cutouts with handwritten text. "These images with their vivid, violet tones are grounded in crystallized memories of the circus, of popular tales or journeys," he concluded in the book, adding that he did them as "reactions to my chromatic and rhythmic improvisations, as pages that form a kind of 'ambient sound.'" Although they appeared ad hoc, they clearly were not.

Whether as abstracted forms used for handmade lettering on the cover of Alan Fletcher's *The American Art Book* (1999), or Henryk Tomaszewski's poster promoting sculptor Henry Moore (1959), or as back- and foreground texture in Alexander Liberman's layouts for *Self* magazine (1990), cut papers trigger a host of visceral responses in the receiver. Yet one common denominator is a sense of lightness and informality. Cut paper suggests youth—or at least play.

One of the most wittily ironic uses of this abstract manner—indeed one of the most informal—is Paul Rand's *H.L. Mencken, Prejudices: A Selection* (1958). Instead of settling for a frequently seen publicity photograph of the author for the cover, Rand cut it up in a childlike way into an abstract humanoid shape, with a demonstrative finger pointing in the air. The cut showed a distorted view of Mencken's head and shoulders yet did not accurately follow the contours. He then surrounded it with brightly colored (red and turquoise) boxes filled with the lettering. The intention was to make it rough and sloppy, as though an untutored hand had made it. The result, however, was a sophisticated emblem for Mencken as well as a playful book art object. ■

Wystawa rzeźb Henry Moore'a

Moore *(1959), poster by Henryk Tomaszewski, uses paper cutout letters to suggest Henry Moore's emblematic abstract sculpture. Atop the second "O" sits one of his distinctive stone works.*

Gaston CALMETTE
Directeur-Gérant

RÉDACTION — ADMINISTRATION
26, rue Drouot, Paris (9e Arr¹)

POUR LA PUBLICITÉ
S'ADRESSER, 26, RUE DROUOT
A L'HOTEL DU « FIGARO »
ET POUR LES ANNONCES ET RÉCLAMES
Chez MM. LAGRANGE, CERF & Cⁱᵉ
8, place de la Bourse

LE FIGARO

Le Numéro avec le Supplément == SEINE & SEINE-ET-OISE : 15 centimes == DÉPARTEMENTS : 20 centimes

H. DE VILLEMESSANT
Fondateur

RÉDACTION — ADMINISTRATION
26, rue Drouot, Paris (9e Arr¹)
TÉLÉPHONE, Trois lignes : 8⁰⁰ 102./2 — 102.47 — 102.48

ABONNEMENT
                          Trois mois Six mois Un an
Seine et Seine-et-Oise ..   15   30   60
Départements 18.75   37.50   75
Union postale 21.50   43   86
On s'abonne dans tous les Bureaux de Poste
de France et d'Algérie.

Samedi 20 Février 1909

« Loué par ceux-ci, blâmé par ceux-là, me moquant des sots, bravant les méchants, je me hâte de rire de tout... de peur d'être obligé d'en pleurer. » (BEAUMARCHAIS.)

Le Futurisme

M. Marinetti, le jeune poète italien et français, au talent remarquable et fougueux, que de retentissantes manifestations ont fait connaître dans tous les pays latins, vient d'une espèce d'enthousiasme discipliné, venu de fonder « l'Ecole ou « Futurisme » dont les théories dépassent en hardiesse toutes celles des écoles antérieures ou contemporaines. Le Figaro qui a déjà servi de tribune à plusieurs d'entre elles, et non des moindres, offre aujourd'hui à ses lecteurs le manifeste des « Futuristes ». Est-il besoin de dire que nous laissons au signataire toute la responsabilité de ses idées singulièrement audacieuses et d'une outrance souvent injuste par des choses éminemment respectables et, heureusement, partout respectées ? Mais il était intéressant de réserver à nos lecteurs la primeur de cette manifestation, quel que soit le jugement qu'on porte sur elle.

Nous avions veillé toute la nuit, mes amis et moi, sous des lampes de mosquée dont les coupoles de cuivre aussi ajourées que notre âme avaient pourtant des clartés électriques. Et tout en piétinant notre native paresse sur d'opulents tapis persans, nous avions discuté aux frontières extrêmes de la logique et griffé le papier de démentes écritures.

Un immense orgueil gonflait nos poitrines à nous sentir debout tous seuls, comme des phares ou comme des sentinelles avancées, face à l'armée des étoiles ennemies, qui campent dans leurs bivouacs célestes. Seuls avec les mécaniciens dans les infernales chaufferies des grands navires, seuls avec les noirs fantômes qui fourragent dans le ventre rouge des locomotives affolées, seuls avec les ivrognes battant des ailes contre les murs !

Et nous voilà brusquement distraits par le roulement des énormes tramways à double étage, qui passent sursautants, bariolés de lumières, tels les hameaux en fête que le Pô débordé ébranle tout à coup et déracine, pour les entraîner, sur les cascades et les remous d'un déluge, jusqu'à la mer.

Puis le silence s'aggrava. Comme nous écoutions la prière exténuée du vieux canal et crisser les os des palais moribonds sous leur barbe de verdure, soudain rugirent sous nos fenêtres les automobiles affamées.

— Allons, dis-je, mes amis ! Partons ! Enfin, la Mythologie et l'Idéal mystique sont surpassés. Nous allons assister à la naissance du Centaure et nous verrons bientôt voler les premiers anges ! — Il faudra ébranler les portes de la vie pour en essayer les gonds et les verrous ! Partons ! Voilà bien le premier soleil levant sur la terre !... Rien n'égale la splendeur de son épée rouge qui s'escrime pour la première fois dans nos ténèbres millénaires.

Nous nous approchâmes des trois machines renâclantes pour flatter leur poitrail. Je m'allongeai sur la mienne, comme un cadavre dans sa bière, mais je ressuscitai soudain sous le volant, lame de guillotine qui menaçait mon estomac.

La grande rafale de la folie nous arracha à nous-mêmes et nous poussa à travers les rues escarpées et profondes comme des torrents desséchés. Çà et là, des lampes maladroites, aux fenêtres, nous enseignaient à mépriser nos yeux mathématiques.

— Le flair, crisi-je, le flair suffit-aux fauves !...

Et nous chassions, comme d'une gangue hideuse et, entrons, comme de jeunes lions, la mort, dans sa large gueule pimentée d'orgueil, dans la bouche immense et torse du vent !... Donnons-nous à manger à l'Inconnu, non par désespoir, mais simplement pour enrichir les insondables réservoirs de l'Absurde!

Comme j'avais dit ces mots, je virai brusquement sur moi-même et j'avançai sous les caniches qui se mordent la queue, et voilà tout à coup que deux cyclistes me désapprouvèrent, titubant devant moi ainsi que deux raisonnements persuasifs et pourtant contradictoires. Leur stupide dilatoire discutait sur mon terrain... Quel ennui ! Pouah!... Je coupai court, net, et, de dégoût, je me flanquai dans un fossé...

Oh! maternel fossé, à moitié plein d'une eau vaseuse! Fossé d'usine! J'ai savouré à pleine bouche la boue fortifiante!

Le visage masqué de la bonne boue industrielle, pleine de scories métalliques, couvert de sueurs inutiles et de taches célestes, portant

nos bras foulés en écharpe, parmi la complainte des sages pêcheurs à la ligne et des naturalistes navrés, nous dictâmes nos premières volontés à tous les hommes vivants de la terre :

Manifeste du Futurisme

1. Nous voulons chanter l'amour du danger, l'habitude de l'énergie et de la témérité.

2. Les éléments essentiels de notre poésie seront le courage, l'audace et la révolte.

3. La littérature ayant jusqu'ici magnifié l'immobilité pensive, l'extase et le sommeil, nous voulons exalter le mouvement agressif, l'insomnie fiévreuse, le pas gymnastique, le saut périlleux, la gifle et le coup de poing.

4. Nous déclarons que la splendeur du monde s'est enrichie d'une beauté nouvelle : la beauté de la vitesse. Une automobile de course avec son coffre orné de gros tuyaux, tels des serpents à l'haleine explosive... une automobile rugissante, qui a l'air de courir sur de la mitraille, est plus belle que la Victoire de Samothrace.

5. Nous voulons chanter l'homme qui tient le volant, dont la tige idéale traverse la terre, lancée elle-même sur le circuit de son orbite.

6. Il faut que le poète se dépense avec chaleur, éclat et prodigalité, pour augmenter la ferveur enthousiaste des éléments primordiaux.

7. Il n'y a plus de beauté que dans la lutte. Pas de chef-d'œuvre sans un caractère agressif. La poésie doit être un assaut violent contre les forces inconnues, pour les sommer de se coucher devant l'homme.

8. Nous sommes sur le promontoire extrême des siècles !... A quoi bon regarder derrière nous, du moment qu'il nous faut défoncer les vantaux mystérieux de l'Impossible ? Le Temps et l'Espace sont morts hier. Nous vivons déjà dans l'absolu, puisque nous avons déjà créé l'éternelle vitesse omniprésente.

9. Nous voulons glorifier la guerre,— seule hygiène du monde, — le militarisme, le patriotisme, le geste destructeur des anarchistes, les belles Idées qui tuent, et le mépris de la femme.

10. Nous voulons démolir les musées, les bibliothèques, combattre le moralisme, le féminisme et toutes les lâchetés opportunistes et utilitaires.

11. Nous chanterons les grandes foules agitées par le travail, le plaisir ou la révolte : les ressacs multicolores et polyphoniques des révolutions dans les capitales modernes; la vibration nocturne des arsenaux et des chantiers sous leurs violentes lunes électriques; les gares gloutonnes avaleuses de serpents qui fument; les usines suspendues aux nuages par les ficelles de leurs fumées; les ponts aux bonds de gymnastes lancés sur la coutellerie diabolique des fleuves ensoleillés; les paquebots aventureux flairant l'horizon; les locomotives au grand poitrail dont les sabots piaffent sur les rails, tels d'énormes chevaux d'acier bridés de longs tuyaux, et le vol glissant des aéroplanes, dont l'hélice a des claquements de drapeaux et des applaudissements de foule enthousiaste.

C'est en Italie que nous lançons ce manifeste de violence culbutante et incendiaire, par lequel nous fondons aujourd'hui le Futurisme, parce que nous voulons délivrer l'Italie de sa gangrène de professeurs, d'archéologues, de cicérones et d'antiquaires.

L'Italie a été trop longtemps le marché des brocanteurs qui fournissaient au monde du mobilier de ses ancêtres, sans cesse renouvelé et soigneusement maintrié pour vendre le travail des tardis vénérables. Nous voulons débarrasser l'Italie des musées innombrables qui la couvrent d'innombrables cimetières.

Musées, cimetières!... Identiques vraiment dans leur sinistre coudoiement de corps qui ne se connaissent pas. Dortoirs publics où l'on dort à jamais côte à côte avec des êtres haïs ou inconnus. Férocité réciproque des peintres et des sculpteurs s'entre-tuant à coups de lignes et de couleurs dans le même musée.

Qu'on y fasse une visite chaque année comme on va voir ses morts une fois par an !... Nous pouvons bien l'admettre !... Qu'on dépose même des fleurs une fois par an aux pieds de la Joconde, nous le concevons !... Mais que l'on aille promener quotidiennement dans les musées nos tristesses, nos courages fragiles, notre inquiétude, nous ne l'admettons pas !...

Admirer un vieux tableau, c'est verser notre sensibilité dans une urne funéraire au lieu de la lancer en avant par jets violents de création et d'action. Voulez-vous donc gâcher ainsi vos meilleures forces dans une admiration inutile du passé, dont vous sortez forcément épuisés, amoindris, piétinés ?

En vérité, la fréquentation quotidienne des musées, des bibliothèques et des académies (ces cimetières d'efforts perdus, ces calvaires de rêves crucifiés, ces registres d'élans brisés!...) est pour les artistes ce qu'est la tutelle prolongée des parents pour des jeunes gens intelligents, ivres de leur talent et de leur volonté ambitieuse.

Pour des moribonds, des invalides et des prisonniers, passe encore. C'est peut-être un baume à leurs blessures, que l'admirable passé, du moment que l'avenir leur est interdit... Mais nous n'en voulons pas, nous, les jeunes, les forts et les vivants futuristes !

Viennent donc les bons incendiaires aux doigts carbonisés !... Les voici ! Les voici !... Et boutez donc le feu aux rayons des bibliothèques! Détournez le cours des canaux pour inonder les caveaux des musées!... Oh! qu'elles nagent à la dérive, les toiles glorieuses! A vous les pioches et les marteaux !... Sapez les fondements des villes vénérables !

Les plus âgés d'entre nous ont trente ans : nous avons donc au moins dix ans

pour accomplir notre tâche. Quand nous aurons quarante ans, que de plus jeunes et plus vaillants que nous veuillent bien nous jeter au panier comme des manuscrits inutiles... Ils viendront contre nous de très loin, de partout, en bondissant sur la cadence légère de leurs premiers poèmes, griffant l'air de leurs doigts crochus, et humant, aux portes des académies, la bonne odeur de nos esprits pourrissants déjà promis aux catacombes des bibliothèques.

Mais on ne nous trouvera pas. Ils nous trouveront enfin, par une nuit d'hiver, en pleine campagne, sous une triste hangar pianoté par la pluie monotone, accroupis près de nos aéroplanes trépidants, en train de chauffer nos mains sur le misérable petit feu que feront nos livres d'aujourd'hui flambant gaiement sous le vol étincelant de leurs images.

Ils s'ameuteront autour de nous, haletants d'angoisse et de dépit, et, tous, exaspérés par notre fier courage infatigable, s'élanceront pour nous tuer, avec d'autant plus de haine que leur cœur sera plein d'amour et d'admiration pour nous. Et la forte et la saine Injustice éclatera radieusement dans leurs yeux. Car l'art ne peut être que violence, cruauté et injustice.

Les plus âgés d'entre nous n'ont pas encore trente ans, et pourtant nous avons déjà gaspillé des trésors, des trésors de force, d'amour, de courage et d'âpre volonté, à la hâte, en délire, sans compter, à tour de bras, à perdre haleine.

Regardez-nous ! Nous ne sommes pas essoufflés... Notre cœur n'a pas la moindre fatigue ! Car il s'est nourri de feu, de haine et de vitesse !... Cela vous étonne ? C'est que vous ne vous souvenez même pas d'avoir vécu ! — Debout sur la cime du monde, nous lançons encore une fois le défi aux étoiles !

Vos objections ? Assez ! assez ! Je les connais ! C'est entendu ! Nous savons bien ce que notre belle et fausse intelligence nous affirme. — Nous ne sommes, dit-elle, que le résumé et le prolongement de nos aïeux. — Peut-être ! soit !... Qu'importe ?... Mais nous ne voulons pas entendre ! Gardez-vous de répéter ces mots infâmes ! Levez plutôt la tête !

Debout sur la cime du monde, nous lançons encore une fois le défi insolent aux étoiles !

F.-T. Marinetti

LA VIE DE PARIS

« Le Roi » à l'Elysée... Palace

Il y eut avant-hier soir dans tous les théâtres de Paris, à l'heure où généralement s'éteignent les derniers chandeliers et où les artistes complètement plâtrés se hâtent d'enfiler les sombres vêtements familiers les somptueux et éclatants oripeaux professionnels, un insolité et tout à fait surprenant brouhaha.

Les lampes électriques restèrent allumées dans les loges, et chacun échangea au contraire avec son voisin, de parts et d'autres du sombre et sérieux collègue de Cerdagne.

A l'heure où les autres suivent filent seulement leurs embryons de travaux les nombreuses quelques autos silencieuses ramenant vers les Passy ou les Auteuil, c'est que tous les artistes de Paris étaient conviés à venir fêter la joie représentation du Roi, le magnifique succès du théâtre des Variétés !

A cette heure, là, il fallait montrer patte blanche et carte longe personnelle à trois juges revêtus d'uniformes qui, gravement, pointalent les arrivants sur une feuille de contrôle. Quand on aurait franchi Minos, Eaque et Rhadamanthe, il fallait remettre sa carte à un cerbère, et alors seulement on était autorisé à recevoir la poignée de main de bienvenue d'un beau et élégant souriant, qui n'était autre que Fernand Samuel, directeur de l'heureux théâtre des Variétés et maire du palais sans soucis de triomphant roi de Cerdagne.

Le seuil franchi, il fallait montrer patte blanche et carte...

Un Monsieur de l'Orchestre.

Échos

La Température

Encore une très belle journée, hier, à Paris. Le ciel est de la plus grande douceur, et le soleil — réjouissant prélude du printemps — brille du plus vif éclat. Quant à la température, elle est sensiblement la même que celle de la veille, pendant la matinée. A sept heures du matin le thermomètre marquait 2° au-dessus de zéro; mais à midi il accusait 11° au-dessus, la pression barométrique, qui s'était un peu relevée, accusait, à midi, 759 millimètres.

Une aire anticyclonique couvre l'Europe centrale, et le maximum barométrique se trouve près de Vienne (770mm).

Des neiges et des pluies sont tombées dans le nord et l'est du continent. En France, la température s'est relevée partout, et sa mer est très houleuse sur les côtes de la Méditerranée.

La température se relèvera notablement sur nos régions du Sud.

Départements, le matin, au-dessus de zéro : 7 à Boulogne, 4 l'île d'Aix, 2 à Cherbourg, 2 à Biarritz et à Bordeaux, 3° à Nantes, 4° à Toulouse, 6° à Marseille, 8° à Perpignan et à Cette, 11° à Oran, 16° à Alger.

Au-dessous de zéro : 1° à Clermont et à Limoges, 2° à Nantes, au Mans et à Lyon, 3° à Dunkerque et à Charleville, 5° à Nancy et à Besançon, 7° à Belfort.

En France, le temps va rester beau et frais, sauf dans le Midi où des pluies sont probables. La température va s'abaisser un peu. (La température du 19 février 1908 était à Paris : 8° au-dessus de zéro le matin et 9° l'après-midi; pression : 758mm) grande faible.

Monte-Carlo. — Température : à dix heures du matin, 12°; à midi, 14°; temps doux; mer belle.

Nice. — Température : à midi, 15°; à trois heures, 14°.

Du New-York Herald :

A New-York : Temps pluvieux. Température, 10° ; minima, 4° : vent sud-est; faible. Baromètre, 764mm .

A Berlin : Temps beau. Température,

maxima, 8° ; minima, 0°. Vent sud-est; faible. Baromètre : 766mm.

A Berlin : Temps beau.

Les Courses

Aujourd'hui, à 2 heures, Courses à Vincennes. — Gagnants du Figaro :

Prix Michelet : Frivole; Pergame.
Prix de Mayenne : Fada ; Bourgogne.
Prix Léda : Fanem : Frégoli.
Prix Mambrino : Fresnay; Escapade.
Prix Marseille : Nazareth ; Electa; Relayeur.
Prix de Plaisance : Fred Leyburn ; Elisabeth.
Prix de La Varenne : Elysée; Etendard.

A Travers Paris

Le roi des Bulgares a chargé M. Stancioff, ministre de Bulgarie à Paris, de déposer en son nom une couronne sur le cercueil du marquis Costa de Beauregard et d'offrir ses condoléances à la famille du défunt.

M. Jean Richepin a fait jeudi son entrée sous la Coupole au son du tambour. C'est le rite. Lorsqu'un nouvel académicien vient s'asseoir au fauteuil vert, il est représenté devant la lourde porte verte, des militaires portent les armes et le tambour bat aux champs. Depuis Napoléon Ier, il y a toujours eu dans le vestibule du palais, aux jours de réception académique, un piquet d'honneur et un tambour.

Toujours, sauf une fois, et cette exception de la règle date de plus de trente ans. La scène se passe au moment où M. Etienne Lamy vint prendre séance. Ce jour-là il n'y avait ni piquet d'honneur, mais le tambour manquait. A sa place, il y avait un clairon.

La tradition voulait le tambour. On avait en hâte le mande et l'on courut pour le prier de se taire. M. Etienne Lamy fut reçu sans tambour ni trompette.

Le secrétaire de l'Institut fit au ministère de la guerre les démarches nécessaires pour retirer le retour d'un pareil incident. On lui promit que jamais plus on ne verrait de clairon sur le passage du récipiendaire. Mais, pour plus de certitude, le secrétaire perpétuel, chaque fois qu'il devait au ministre pour lui demander le piquet, prend soin d'ajouter : avec un tambour.

RUPTURE
FABLE

J'ai vu, jeudi soir, sur le quai
Noir de gens quittant la Coupole,
Une belle fille au gai visage
Digné d'un fronton d'Acropole,
Comme elle était un sage,
Je l'abordai, flaneur qui muse :
Santé, Andrée Sylvano, Spiriuco, Turanne,
Lore, elle dit : « C'est que j'étais la Muse,
La Muse de Jean Richepin ! »
Or, il me quitta, il me lâche, il m'explique :
« Oh ! je ne me plains pas d'ailleurs,
Car il n'a couverte de douze,
Et dans les trames les meilleurs !
Mais, avec l'habit vert et le chapal à claque,
Je sens, quitta à le regardant,
Qu'il ne peut plus me prendre !
Le voilà décormais porte
D'être sage comme une image,
Officiel et compassé !
Pour trancher au contraire
Chaque pensée et chaque mot,
Je parle trop vite et trop haut !
Je ne pourrai plus que le compromettre !
Puis, ces vingt-quatre hommes graves, à l'important géré prix ?
Donc il doit me mettre à la porte !
C'est que mon buste,
C'est pour cela que j'en déménage
Et de tai qui me transporte
Au clou palais, chez Ponchon ! »

Louis MARCOLLEAU.

M. Alphonse Lemerre, éditeur du Parnasse, vient de mourir, à Ville-d'Avray, où il était maire, maire de Ville-d'Avray, depuis de longues années.

Chaque année, en effet, depuis du Tapis-Vert, M. le maire faisait donner une tente foraine de ses artistes célèbres, représentations de plus belles représentations du monde. C'étaient Worms et Mme Barretta-Worms; Coquelin, Le prix placés tombant dans le tronc tricolore des œuvres municipales. On ignore si le successeur de M. Alphonse Lemerre à la mairie lui succédera aussi comme imprésario. Et que faire aujourd'hui pour les pauvres ?

Réponse collective.

Pour répondre aux nombreuses demandes de renseignements que nous adressées, Henri Petit, le grand tailleur-couturier, annonce que l'inauguration de ses nouveaux salons du boulevard Malesherbes aura lieu dans une huitaine de jours. Ses clients ne pourront faire leur attendre, car il a bien promis des révélations et des créations sensationnelles au point de vue du genre, et des incomparables établi.pour cette circonstance.

Faire venir le public est bien, le retenir est mieux encore; tel est le cas de la Revue des Folies-Bergère qui va cha-que soir... Il est vrai que cette merveilleuse revue est interprétée par une troupe unique, comme Campton, Marthe, Lavallière, Clara Faurens, Claudius, Pougaud, Maurel, Morton et Mario Marvilhe, tels sont les incomparables interprètes du « clou de la saison ».

Le commandant Pini quittera Paris aujourd'hui. Il se rend à Londres, où il compte passer quelque temps.

A Londres : Temps beau. Température,

Guyon, président de la société « le Sabre », qui donnait, en son honneur, un élégant dîner d'escrimeurs.

La plus goûtée, la plus appréciée de nos grandes marques françaises par la haute société russe est la plus aristocratique de nos marques, la Lorraine-Dietrich.

Une admirable six-cylindres Lorraine-Dietrich, destinée au prince Orioff, ce dilettante de l'automobile, vient précisément d'arriver à Monte-Carlo.

Elle l'a gagné de haute lutte, conduite par Rougier, on maître du volant, qui, avec elle, a brûlé les étapes. Ne nous pas en combien peu de temps, pour ne point effaroucher les célérophobes.

Le chasseur-statisticien :

Il ne s'agit pas d'un adepte de saint Hubert, mais du chasseur du théâtre Michel. En effet, ce jeune factotum s'étant amusé à relever chaque jour, pendant les cent premières représentations du Poulailler et du Feu la Mère de Madame, les deux observations pièces du théâtre Michel, le nombre d'autos et de voitures de maître dont il a ouvert les portières, nous donne à cet effet un chiffre fantastique de 6,302 automobiles, 1,985 voitures attelées et double et 3,832 voitures attelées d'un cheval.

Il n'a pas daigné occuper les taxi-autos ni les fiacres.

Les réceptions académiques ont toujours été de très brillantes manifestations d'élégance auxquelles l'augustie Coupole prête un peu de son imposante solennité. Celle de M. Jean Richepin n'a point failli à une tradition qui nous donne que toute autre risque de périclité. Aussi fut-elle pour la « Parfum de la Dame en noir » la plus importante de la saison pour supérieure élégance, comme une consécration dernière de cette « captivante et adorablement désespérée d'être » que fit einsna l'héroïne de Gaston Leroux, avant qu'elle fut adoptée par toutes les Parisiennes.

Nouvelles à la Main

Les crédits de la marine.
— On assure que M. Caillaux et M. Picard ne s'entendent guère. Il y a choc.
— Il y a même abordage.

Les agents des P. T. T. malmènent fort M. Simyan.
— Mais M. Simyan a du caractère. Il va prendre une rude revanche.
— Mais non, non !
— Mais non, car le public !

— Comment finiront ces manifestations de nos postiers ?
— On les fourrera quelques-uns à la boîte.

Le Masque de Fer.

Le complot Caillaux

M. Caillaux fomente un petit complot (tout petit) avec ses collègues du ministère, et en particulier contre le président du Conseil auquel il voudrait bien succéder.

Le pétard éclaterait au lendemain du vote de l'impôt sur le revenu et par conséquent à la veille de la discussion des crédits de la marine.

On sait que M. Alfred Picard va demander au Parlement les 225 millions qu'il estime indispensables pour la mise en état de notre flotte actuelle, c'est-à-dire de la flotte qui est sur mer ou dans les chantiers. D'autres sommes seront par la suite votées pour l'augmentation de nos escadres, si nous ne voulons pas tomber à bref délai au cinquième rang des puissances navales.

Mais on ce moment il n'est question que des dépenses immédiatement nécessaires pour l'entretien, l'achèvement, les réparations, les bassins de radoub, le matériel d'armement, les munitions, etc., que notre défense nationale exige de puis longtemps et qu'il est urgent de voter.

C'est sur cette question de défense nationale (la chose est à peine croyable) que M. Caillaux a décidé d'engager la lutte contre le cabinet Clemenceau.

D'après le ministre des finances, il n'y a aucune nécessité pour lui de voter ces 225 millions, et il s'en rapporte à l'évaluation de ses dépenses. Il faut, selon lui, connaître d'abord les réformes que M. Alfred Picard prépare dans le personnel des arsenaux, dans le mode de nos constructions navales, etc. Ces réformes, qui demandent encore plusieurs mois d'études et que M. Picard veut faire connaître avant tout, tendant à supprimer définitivement l'état, si affreux que sa collègue de la marine exagère à plaisir le péril de la flotte et le vide de nos arsenaux.

— Et puis, ajoute-t-il, je ne veux pas être le trésorier de la faillite de la République, ce que la faillite sont les dépenses de la guerre et de la marine. »

Plutôt que d'accepter le devis de M. Picard, M. Caillaux donnera donc sa démission, au lendemain du jour où aura été voté au Palais-Bourbon l'impôt sur le revenu, qu'il considère comme la grande pensée de sa vie, et dont il s'attribue le mérite à l'exclusion de ses deux ministres qui l'ont réellement défendu, à savoir MM. les rapporteurs.

On assure aussi que le terrain de M. Caillaux et l'adhésion de deux autres de ses col-

Artists taking a subversive stand

IDEA № 25
MANIFESTOS

Provocative pronouncements by groups of artists tend to share one characteristic: they favor stark black-and-white typography, on the assumption that colorful statements could be construed as frivolous. In fact, many of them look like ordinary pamphlets, as if their authors had gone out of their way not to let the form of their proclamations detract from the content of their subversive messages.

OPPOSITE: Manifeste du Futurisme (1909), written by Filippo Tommaso Marinetti, published in French in Le Figaro, an elitist newspaper which did not support Marinetti's revolutionary ideas. Its publication launched Futurism, an Italian art movement, on the international scene.

ABOVE: First Things First (1964), published by British designer Ken Garland, who intended to radicalize the design practice that was fast becoming a subset of advertising. In 2000 an updated version was printed in cutting-edge magazines including Adbusters, Emigré, Items, and Eye.

BELOW: Altermodern (2009) is an example of a museum introducing a new art movement as a "manifesto." The Tate Gallery poster, designed by M/M (Paris), addressed "the death of postmodernism and the rise of a new modernity, reconfigured to an age of globalization."

One of the first such art manifestos, a diatribe by Filippo Marinetti, looked like a regular newspaper article, and was printed in French in *Le Figaro* in 1909. The medium the Italian Futurist chose for his "mission statement" was reminiscent of Emile Zola's famous open letter *J'accuse*, published in *L'Aurore* 11 years earlier in defense of Alfred Dreyfus, an army captain falsely accused of being a spy. At first glance one could not guess that Marinetti's mild-looking manifesto would launch one of the most seminal art movements of the twentieth century. Futurism would soon be known as a celebration of speed, violence, war, and machine art.

The Futurist manifesto predicted the kind of seditious attitude that was to spread across Europe in the coming decades. Many more art manifestos would follow, with different purposes and rhetorics, but all adopting the format pioneered by Marinetti—that of an official announcement. The 1918 Dutch De Stijl manifesto listed nine bullet points, the 1930 French Art Concret six. Later manifestos expressed their philosophy using the typographical vocabulary of newspapers, with bold headlines and well-marked paragraphs. One important detail was always the list of signatories. The fact that these texts were endorsed by a group of artists is one reason why their layouts were not more distinctive. To reach a consensus between supporters with big egos, whoever designed and penned these manifestos had to adopt as neutral a style as possible.

There were some exceptions to the neutral style, though none uses color. Among the more graphically arresting documents are the 1963 Fluxus manifesto, a mostly lowercase, hand-printed document incorporating **collages**; and the 1978 Crude Art manifesto, roughly

drafted on an old typewriter. A recent manifesto, *First Things First*, originally written and published in 1964 but updated in 2000, attempts to spell out the social responsibilities of graphic designers. Given the subject matter, you might expect a provocatively laid-out statement, but true to form, it is a low-key graphic artifact.

But things are changing. Today, one could argue that contemporary art itself is a formidable statement: artists who work on manifestos are creating antiestablishment pronouncements that must be deciphered carefully, each work an "open letter" to the public. In 2009, London's Tate Britain chose the manifesto approach to introduce the theme of its fourth Triennial, *Altermodern*. The poster, representing a world map, is a mesmerizing assemblage of letterforms, images, and words that defy the very idea of "visual communication." ∎

Offset *(1926), for* Buch und Werbekunst *(Book and Advertisements), was a technological and aesthetic journal edited by Bauhaus student and teacher Joost Schmidt. This cover by Schmidt suggests the theme of printing.*

DER OFFSET-VERLAG·G·M·B·H·LEIPZIG·

OFFSET
BUCH UND WERBEKUNST
HEFT 7
1926

ENTWURF: JOOST SCHMIDT. BAUHAUS IN DESSAU
AUHAUS-HEFT
CKEREI VON C DÜNNHAUPT.G·M·B·H·DESSAU

Propagating styles and methods of design

IDEA № 26
GRAPHIC DESIGN MAGAZINES

Graphic design evolved during the late nineteenth century from a sideline of the printing industry into a distinct field with its own practitioners. The crucial link in this evolutionary process was trade magazines. Initially they established professional standards for printing and typesetting, but as businesses demanded more aesthetically complex layouts and typography, trade magazine editors were forced to analyze and critique new advances in design.

BELOW: Campo Grafico (1933), cover designed by Enrico Kaneclin for Italy's Fascist-era graphic design magazine, combined commercial art with the visual philosophy of Italian Futurism.

ABOVE: Dot Dot Dot 7 (2004) is an unconventional design magazine that looks at the culture and history of graphics through a theoretical lens. Printed, for the most part, in black and white, it eschews eye candy.

The Berlin-based *Das Plakat* (The Poster), with its focus on conventional and avant-garde sensibilities, emerged as a more historically influential review than any other. Founded in 1910 by Hans Josef Sachs, it aimed to champion art poster collecting and increase scholarship among amateurs and professionals. By *Das Plakat*'s demise in 1921 commercial artists and typographers were influenced by Futurism, De Stijl, Constructivism, and Dada, and some of the keepers of tradition gradually began to apply these methods to their commercial work.

In 1925 *Typographische Mitteilungen*, the monthly organ of the German Printers' Association in Leipzig, shocked the professional nervous system by sanctioning the most radical approaches. Under the guest editorship of Jan Tschichold, *Typographische Mitteilungen* advocated graphic design and typography from the Bauhaus, De Stijl, and Constructivism as appropriate for use among the wider-spread profession. It was the first time that the German printing and graphics industry had been offered a full dose of the type and layout later known as the New Typography.

The role of these magazines was to record, observe, and report on the field, but some also excited the passions of designers and altered the popular perception and styles of design. This was certainly true of *Gebrauchsgraphik*, founded and edited by Dr H.K. Frenzel, starting in 1923. A bilingual (English and German) chronicle of "new" international graphic art styles and techniques, it was distinguished by the guiding editorial notion that advertising art was a force for good in the world.

After World War II the most significant graphic design clarion was *Graphis*. This Zurich-based, multilingual, international magazine, founded in 1946 by poster designer Walter Herdeg, was an outlet for iconoclastic designers and illustrators from around the world, especially Soviet Eastern European countries. But the most groundbreaking of all was *Portfolio* (1949–51). Edited for three issues by Frank Zachary and designed by Alexey Brodovitch, *Portfolio* defined a late-Modern sensibility that viewed the concept of good design as weaving throughout culture as a whole. *Portfolio* leveled the field between high and low art and in so doing changed the fundamental definition of a trade journal.

The banner of these internationally focused magazines is still waved by such journals as *Etapes* in France and *Eye* in Britain, both with long tenures and a critical edge. Younger design magazines are harder to publish in the present-day print environment, but those that survive, such as *Dot Dot Dot*, are not trade-oriented but rather culture-concerned, focusing on the design and visual culture. ∎

Floral patterns are rediscovered

IDEA № 27
BOTANICAL GEOMETRY

The idea that one can turn natural, organic forms into highly stylized patterns had always intrigued artists. However, at the turn of the twentieth century, floral patterns began to be thought too quaint. Around 1900, all over Europe, avant-garde graphic artists began to combine curvilinear floral motifs with rectilinear elements as a reaction against the pervasive sentimentality and fastidious elegance of Art Nouveau.

BELOW: "Scylla" wallpaper design (1902) is a geometrical floral pattern by Koloman Moser, a cofounder of the Wiener Werkstätte. Though curvilinear and graceful, the forms prefigure the more rigorous ornamentation that would become synonymous with Modernism.

ABOVE: The identity system for dance company Centre Chorégraphique National de Tours (2002) is a playful and overgrown design by French duo Antoine+Manuel. Loosely based on Helvetica, the central motif acts as a logo that changes and blossoms according to the seasons.

Charles Rennie Mackintosh in Scotland, Koloman Moser in Austria, and Peter Behrens in Germany were at the forefront of this aesthetic rebellion. In their work, serpentine lines were intersected by checkerboards, leafy designs were forced into grids, and rigid type treatments took precedence over fluid ornaments. To assess the difference between the two decorative approaches—before and after the turn of the century—one has only to compare the floral wallpaper patterns designed by Eugene Grasset in 1897 to those designed by Koloman Moser in 1902. In five short years, natural forms had almost been eradicated.

Floral ornaments remained on the endangered species list for a century. They were briefly rediscovered by the "flower children" of the late 1960s, when psychedelic plants were the rage. Blossoms, vines, and leaves were part of the visual vocabulary of poster artists such as Victor Moscoso, Peter Max, and Milton Glaser. It was a short-lived revival, though, and it would be another 40 years before graphic designers turned to nature again for inspiration.

Today, thanks to computer technology, designers can "grow" organic-looking decorative borders or letterforms. In Canada, graphic artist Marian Bantjes designs patterns as exotic as hothouse plants. In France, where Art Nouveau originated, a number of graphic designers are inventing ways to bring organic forms back into their work: Antoine+Manuel have a predilection for letterforms that branch out like overgrown bushes, while Jocelyn Cottencin likes to cross-breed typefaces and has recently introduced on the market BF15, an interactive alphabet that shoots roots in every direction. ∎

THE BIG DRINK THE STORY OF

REG. U.S. PAT. OFF.

Coca-Cola

E.J. KAHN JR

Text as representational imagery

IDEA № 28
CALLIGRAMS

The technical constraints of metal typographic makeup prior to the age of photocomposition, from the 1950s to the 1980s, did not allow for much tomfoolery. Most typesetting was composed in a straightforward, symmetrical, linear manner. In the nineteenth century, however, book designers—and even some authors—experimented with **texts as images**, using words, sentences, and paragraphs to metamorphically, and thus metaphorically, represent the ideas put forth in the text. Type was contorted into many different pictorial forms. This kind of linguistically meaningful image is called a calligram.

Every student of type and typography has heard the term "crystal goblet," as described in a 1955 essay titled "The Crystal Goblet, or Printing Should be Invisible" by type expert Beatrice Warde. The idea behind this analogy is that type, rather than content alone, is the vessel of meaning—a very transparent vessel at that. And ostensibly this is correct. Transforming words and sentences into illustration where the text is still readable often adds to the expressiveness of the message.

Few nineteenth-century examples were as wry or witty as Lewis Carroll's 1865 "The Mouse's Tale," a poem from *Alice's Adventures in Wonderland*. Carroll's tale is clearly readable even as the type swirls like a skier on the slopes down the page, the size of the letters becoming ever smaller until the end. The mouse's tale is revealed in the shape of a mouse's tail. But make no mistake: setting of this kind was not easy using traditional techniques. Patience and skill were the principal virtues.

With the advent of photocomposition, the ability to cut and paste and morph letters to fit specific shapes and contours made metamorphic typography easier—and considerably more common (indeed clichéd)—in advertisements, editorial features, and book covers.

Influenced by Guillaume Apollinaire's 1916 "It Rains," a poem (one of the *"calligrammes"* for which he was famous) in which words drizzle vertically down the page, in 1958 American designer Bradbury Thompson created "Rain Rain Rain" for the trade magazine *Westvaco Inspirations*, showing multiple images of the same woman (each printed in a process color) walking through a storm of falling sentences. But this poetic approach using body text is not the only kind of metaphoric type.

Headline type, either hand-lettered or photographically (and now digitally) distorted to fit the shape of the respective form, provides a metamorphic visual *double entendre*—a graphic pun. Because some are deliberately harder to read than others, it is imperative that the shape taken by the type underscores the message. ■

"Fury said to a mouse, That he met in the house, 'Let us both go to law: I will prose- cute you.— Come, I'll take no de- nial: We must have the trial; For really this morn- ing I've nothing to do.' Said the mouse to the cur, 'Such a trial, dear sir, With no jury or judge, would be wast- ing our breath.' 'I'll be judge, I'll be jury,' said cun- ning old Fury: 'I'll try the whole cause, and con- demn you to death'."

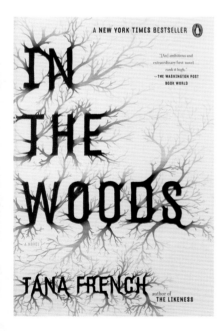

BELOW: In The Woods (2007), designed by Jennifer Wang, is not a classic calligram, but the lettering takes on the shape of the idea it is representing. In this case, words grow into a leafless, branchy tree.

ABOVE: "The Mouse's Tale" (1865) ends a poetic paragraph by Lewis Carroll in Alice's Adventures in Wonderland. Shaped like the mouse's tail, it is both a "constructive" typographic treatment and a visual pun.

Books (1925), designed by Aleksander
Rodchenko for the Leningrad branch
of the state publishing house Gosizdat.
One of the first times lettering was
used, like a comic-book speech bubble,
to simulate the voice.

Loud and clear

IDEA № 29
LOUD TYPOGRAPHY

"Making type speak" is a phrase used by contemporary designers who seek to release words from the conventional strictures of neutrality and transparency. Loud typography is perhaps as old as the earliest commercial poster—since the goal of a poster has always been to draw attention to itself by figuratively screaming a message as demonstratively as the size of the typefaces (and the paper on which they are printed) will allow.

Oil: A Lethal Addiction? *(2006), designed by Stephen Coates for the* New Statesman. *Often the larger the type, the louder the message; here the word "oil" speaks more profoundly than the other headlines.*

Aleksander Rodchenko's 1925 advertisement for the Lengiz publishing house titled "Books in all Branches of Knowledge," where the word "Books" boldly projects from the mouth of the shouting woman, is the most literal manifestation of loud typography. The triangular composition of the word in the shape of a megaphone, and the sound lines emanating from it, reinforce the symbolic aural experience. Frequently parodied during the late twentieth century (after Russian Constructivism was revived), the poster was a model for how voice had been typographically approximated.

Accents may change from culture to culture, volume may be modulated from project to project, yet type continues to speak at all levels. Culturally, the level of loudness is not dictated by any one movement. Italian Futurist Filippo Marinetti's onomatopoeic poems, known as *parole in libertà* ("words in freedom"—sound effects created by words), were loud as a means of cutting through the noise of the entrenched traditions in art and politics. But it was not necessary to be in the avant garde to raise the typographic timbre. The main headlines in sensationalist tabloid newspapers are called "screamers" for obvious reasons.

Screamers come from the need to make noise, but also produce eye-catching results. When President Kennedy was assassinated in 1963, many magazines used "soft" headlines that were solemn and refined. But even the more sophisticated newspapers around the world—not tabloid or sensational—used 72 point or larger type to sound the alarm that a tragedy had occurred. Of course, loud type needn't always signal disaster. When World War II was won by the Allies, happy messages such as "VJ Day" or "WAR OVER" were screamed across pages in any language and any typeface.

With so many reasons for loud type and dialects from which to choose, it is no wonder the contemporary din of typographic babble is getting louder. Paul Rand referred to the talking type of the early 1990s as "rap typography," literally suggesting the syncopation, rhythm, and rhyme found in rap music (not a far cry from *parole in libertà*). After Rodchenko's poster, loud type evolved into being more improvisational like jazz, more varied like rock, or more structured like a motet. Loud can be anything as long as it shouts off the page. ∎

The Modern alternative

IDEA № 30
ASYMMETRIC TYPOGRAPHY

Die Neue Gestaltung (The New Design) was born in 1925, when the German typographer Jan Tschichold guest-edited a special issue of a Leipzig printing trade journal and gave it the title "Elementary Typography." This unenticing term signified a curiously quiet revolution—a spare, economical, and functional approach, typified by asymmetrical composition and sans serif, often lowercase letters devoid of excess ornamentation—which would come to underscore the Modern aesthetic in graphic design.

This radical issue of an otherwise conventional printer's magazine became a manifesto of the burgeoning Neue Typografie (New Typography) through which Tschichold set forth a radical concept: "The purpose of the New Typography is functionality."

In calling on designers to reject unnecessary ornament and abandon the symmetrical structures that had for so long dominated printing and design, Tschichold wrote: "Asymmetry is the rhythmic expression of functional design." In 1928 he published *Die Neue Typografie*—the book—a handbook for the new approach, which showed by example how unadorned, rational, elementary composition was a pristine and readable alternative to books composed with black letter on a central axis.

Through posters done for the Phoebus-Palast movie theater in Munich and the Graphisches Kabinett art gallery, Tschichold truly practiced what he preached. As a member of the Group of Radical German Advertising Designers and founder (in 1928) of the Ring of New Advertising Artists, which included such Moderns as Kurt Schwitters, Piet Zwart, and Paul Schuitema, he helped introduce asymmetric design—and Modernism in general—to business throughout Europe.

Tschichold was eventually called (by Swiss designer Max Bill) a betrayer of the movement he codified for renouncing the New Typography after Hitler's rise to power. Once away from Germany (having moved to Basel, Switzerland, in 1933) he returned to classical tenets of design, believing that the rigid rules of the New Typography had a fascistic element.

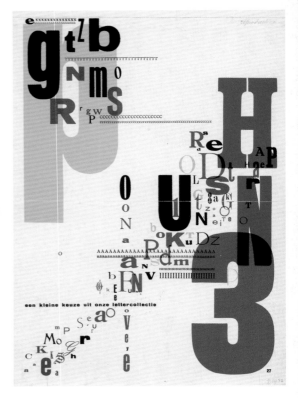

ABOVE: Drukkerij Trio *(1931), one of Piet Zwart's asymmetric typographic exercises for the Trio printing company in The Hague. The random overprinting of modern and vintage letterforms prefigures the deconstructive approaches of later decades.*

OPPOSITE: Die Frau Ohne Namen *(1927), a film poster designed by Jan Tschichold for the Phoebus-Palast, embodies all the geometrical characteristics of the New Typography of the 1920s.*

BELOW: Architectural Typography II *(1984), designed by Willi Kunz for an exhibit at Columbia University in New York, is rooted in twentieth-century European Modernism. This design shows what Kunz calls "theory based on practice/practice based on theory."*

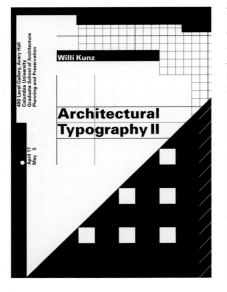

It may seem in restrospect that asymmetric composition was not such an earth-shattering feat. Yet in the history of design it was none other. Symmetry, balance, and order are classic virtues, which had become tired and turgid standards in typography, printing, and graphic design. Although these varieties continued to have resonance during the early twentieth century, the alternative of asymmetry both symbolized and propagated modern life. Piet Zwart's *Trio* was not simply an anarchic display of letters, but a statement about the chaos of the mechanical world. Asymmetric typography was more than a means of transparent communication, it was a statement, which ultimately became a method practiced by evangelical Modernists, such as Willi Kunz, and eventually turned into a style. ■

DIE FRAU OHNE NAMEN
ZWEITER TEIL

GEORG JACOBYS WELTREISEFILM

PHOEBUS-PALAST
ANFANGSZEITEN: 4, 6¹⁵ 8³⁰   SONNTAGS: 1⁴⁵ 4, 6¹⁵ 8³⁰

IN JEDER VORSTELLUNG AUFFÜHRUNG VON
HONEGGER: PACIFIC 231
DIESE ZEITGEMAESSE MUSIKSCHOEPFUNG WIRD VON EINER
EIGENS DAZU KOMPONIERTEN LICHT-DICHTUNG (FILM) BEGLEITET

ENTWURF: JAN TSCHICHOLD, PLANEGG B. MCH.   DRUCK: GEBR. OBPACHER AG. MÜNCHEN

A powerful partnership

IDEA № 31
RED WITH BLACK

With his 1919 poster *Beat the Whites with the Red Wedge*, the Russian avant-garde artist El Lissitzky capitalized on the stimulating power of red with black, unleashing in the process forces he could not control. Red with black, which he had carefully monitored in a perfectly balanced layout, turned out to be an aggressive duo. As a color combination, it has dominated the graphic design world ever since, prevailing against all odds as the most ubiquitous, all-purpose, universal color code.

Lissitzky's mentor, Suprematist painter Kasimir Malevich, had already experimented with pure red with black in numerous abstract compositions, but Lissitzky's version innovated by conferring on each color a symbolic meaning: red stood for the Revolutionary forces, while black was supposed to represent the darkness surrounding the White monarchists. He was also able to exemplify the tension between the two colors by giving them antagonistic geometric shapes.

After him, countless graphic artists emphasized the friction between red and black, pitting them against each other as if they were prize champions. Kurt Schwitters and Theo van Doesburg used them in a frantic Dada **collage**

(*Kleine Dada-Soirée*, 1922), then Aleksander Rodchenko trapped them into claustrophobic compositions (*Young Guard*, 1924). The Bauhaus artists were also fond of them, while Gustav Klutsis deployed them in his celebrated photocollages (*Great Works*, 1930).

At the service of Soviet **propaganda**, red and black had demonstrated their pugnacious nature and versatility. But sadly, during the 1930s and 1940s, they were used to brand totalitarian regimes, including official portraits of Lenin, Nazi flags, and fascist posters. Other color schemes would never have survived such a dark episode, but red and black managed to bounce back. They were rescued by a handful of American designers who were able to expunge their shameful past and recast them as the yin–yang of a new modernistic aesthetic.

At first, it took all the creativity and humor of Lester Beall, Paul Rand, and Alvin Lustig to soften the Constructivist image of red and black. In 1937 Beall, for *PM* magazine, deliberately mismatched a small ornate red "P" with a tall and skinny black "M." In 1940 Rand, for *Direction* magazine, cut freeform holes out of a solid red background. In 1944, Lustig, for the cover of *A Season in Hell*, created a playful red and black Mirò **pastiche**. By mid-century, the codes of the once-vilified color scheme had undergone a total transformation. Gone were the gimmicky angles and the heroic motifs. Designers such as Karl Gerstner, Armin Hofmann, Rudy VanderLans, and Wim Crouwel put a finishing touch on this makeover with graphically arresting designs that steered clear of color symbolism. ∎

Gigantic graphic art

IDEA Nº 32
SUPERGRAPHICS

The term "supergraphics" was coined in the late 1960s to describe a fad inspired by Op art. Huge arrows, numbers, words, or rainbows were painted on walls to transform bland interiors into exciting visual environments. Though the movement was short-lived, supergraphics never went away altogether. Today they turn up on building façades, on palisades in front of construction sites, on walls and ceilings in pop-up stores, in hallways and stairways in schools and dorms, and as part of interactive installations in theaters, malls, and museums.

During World War I, British and U.S. navy warships were painted with gigantic stripes and abstract patterns. Called Razzle Dazzle paintings, these motifs were carefully engineered to trick the rangefinders of the enemy naval artillery. Unlike traditional camouflage designs that blend in with the background, these supergraphics tried to stand out to confuse the viewer's perception of depth and sense of direction.

Large geometric forms tend to obliterate their background by creating a graphic diversion. It is a technique Paula Scher has used to transform a depressing

Victorian red-brick school building in New Jersey into an upbeat performing arts center. She painted the exterior walls white while emphasizing the heavy cornices with black. To emphasize further the horizontal lines, she covered the upper portion of the building with an intriguing typographical latticework of large black gothic letterforms, a dramatic scheme somewhat reminiscent of the décor created by Aleksander Rodchenko in 1925 in Moscow for the Mossel'prom department store.

French designer Pierre Bernard's exterior signage for the Pompidou Center, Paris, during the 1996 renovation of the museum was a typographic landmark. A gigantic five-story billboard served as a background for a long list of upcoming events. When a show closed, its reference would be crossed out, each individual letter obliterated with a line of a different color. As time went by the billboard became an increasingly colorful arrangement of vibrating strokes.

Temporary installations often become opportunities for supersized graphic expression. Architecture, a permanent art form, is less likely to attract bold graphic gestures. Yet in the last few years, some architects have realized that building surfaces do not have to be blank billboards. Herzog & de Meuron's iconographic program for the Eberswalde Library in Germany is a rich tapestry of vintage newspaper clippings etched directly on the glass façade. Other architects apply supergraphics on the outsides of buildings with LED installations, as Jean Nouvel did for the Torre Agbar in Barcelona (see p.111). At night, computer-controlled illuminations by Yann Kersalé turn the tower into a huge candy-colored lighthouse.

Razzle Dazzle was the inspiration for the décor staged by New York creative agency Formavision for a Reebok Flash pop-up store in 2008. The design of the space tricked the eye with huge distorted graphic patterns in hot pink and bright turquoise. Disconcerted visitors hesitated before entering: they felt as if they were about to step into a printed image rather than a real, three-dimensional environment. ∎

Eberswalde Library (2000), by architects Herzog & de Meuron in collaboration with photographer Thomas Ruff, is a modern interpretation of supergraphics. Using a serigraphic process, precast concrete and glass panels are printed with images on themes such as love, mortality, and politics.

In the early days of Modernism, black, not white, was the color of perfection

IDEA № 33
SUPREME GEOMETRY

For the Russian painter Kasimir Malevich, the black square was the perfect icon. It did not represent anything, yet it was the expression of an absolute reality in its purest form. The founder of a short-lived art movement called Suprematism, Malevich was an admirer of Cubist artists and sculptors like Sonia Delaunay and Alexander Archipenko.

A pioneer of abstract art, Malevich believed that it was possible to convey specific impressions through the interaction of squares, rectangles, circles, and triangles. In his 1915 *Black Rectangle with Blue Triangle*, the tension between the black and blue shapes is so intense that one can almost feel it, taste it, and hear it. Malevich contributed to graphic design by celebrating the supremacy of black over all other colors. As far as he was concerned, a black square was the most powerful form there was. Dutch architect and typographer Piet Zwart, whose surname means "black," agreed with Malevich: he used a stark letter "P" alongside an oversized black square as the logo for his letterhead. To this day, black is perceived as the color with the greatest graphic impact. Not only did Malevich influence the Constructivists, the De Stijl neoplasticists such as Zwart, and the Bauhaus minimalists, but also

his work never ceased to be a reference for countless designers eager to understand the principles of Modernism.

As recently as 1987, French graphic designer Etienne Robial created a Malevich-inspired logo for the television station M6 that is edgy yet at the same time as dynamic as a Suprematist painting. A red number 6 is placed dead-center on top of a massive black "M," their combined geometries expressing self-confidence and authority.

Proponents of pure forms have so far avoided **nostalgia**. The black square was never the subject of a revival because it never went out of style. For example, it is still a living ideal for B. Martin Pedersen, the present owner and publisher of *Graphis* magazine, who has been a stalwart supporter of the most stringent Modernism for decades. The cover of his 2010 *Graphis Poster Annual* is an ode to abstract space and perfect figures: on a black background, a neatly folded strip of colored paper forms the letter "P"—the initial of "poster" as well as an icon to symbolize "pure." ∎

ABOVE: Piet Zwart's monogram (c. 1930) is a minimalist interpretation of the word zwart ("black" in Dutch). The artist focused on the quintessential expression of his name: the letter "P" and a black square.

BELOW: The M6 logo (1987) is the work of Etienne Robial for a French television station. The logo, with its imperative black "M," is as powerful as a Malevich abstraction.

OPPOSITE: Graphis Poster Annual (2010), by Martin Pedersen, is one of a series that manages, year after year, to be both playful and strict. The stark black covers of these annuals are now an integral part of the Graphis brand.

Wit and ornament

IDEA № 34
FUNNY FACES

Goudy Stout is not a thick malt beverage but a quirky typeface designed in 1930 by one of America's most prolific type designers, Frederic W. Goudy. One step above comic-book lettering, it has one stand-out attribute: its uppercase "A" appears to be based on the comical gait of Charlie Chaplin's famed character the Little Tramp. "In a moment of typographic weakness," Goudy wrote, "I attempted to produce a 'black' letter that would interest those advertisers who like the bizarre in their print."

Although he might protest otherwise, the requisites of the advertising business were clear when he made this minor folly; attention in the growing marketplace was not going to be wrested by elegant or classic typefaces, but by eye-catching combinations of letterform and image. The stranger the letter, the more resilient it would be. Funny letters and typefaces were called to action in the competitive war to win consumer attention. In fact, many respected type designers added their own weird types to a fertile field of faces used for everything from leaflets to billboards. Many funny faces are inelegant but some, including A.M. Cassandre's Bifur of 1929, are handsome beyond their novelty quality.

In *Printing Types: An Introduction* (1971), Alexander Lawson wrote that the typographic fashion for funny faces began in the early 1800s, when English type founders produced "a variety of embellished types designed to emphasize their unique characteristics for the single purpose of attracting attention. Fat faces, Grotesques, and Egyptians—decorative types when compared to the Romans, which had undergone minor changes since the Italian fifteenth century—were not flamboyant enough for the new requirements of advertising display." Furious competition sprang up among type founders to outdo each other in the production of ornamented and fancy faces.

The fashion for funny faces comes and goes. In every era comic faces are revived to give an explicitly humorous edge to contemporary visual communications. Milton Glaser's comically titled Baby Teeth (1968), derived from a popular Italian Art Deco alphabet, may not really look like any recognizable teeth, but is a spirited and lighthearted design. Seymour Chwast's Weedy Beasties (2007), a more goofy font in which each character is endowed with eyes and a mouth, could add wit to any design.

The outpouring of funny faces has not diminished, even during more orthodox modern times. Their usefulness is dependent on the messages they are trying to convey. But when paired with the appropriate (or at times inappropriate) content they can communicate more effectively than neutral letters. ■

ABOVE: *Bifur, et al (c. 1946), specimen sheet for a selection of novelty typefaces produced by Deberny & Peignot, Paris. The funniest of the faces is Bifur, designed by A.M. Cassandre in 1929.*

OPPOSITE ABOVE: *Bestial Bold (1982), a typeface designed by Seymour Chwast for* The Mental Menagerie: A Five Year Retrospective. *The bulbous face is made comic by the addition of mouths and eyes.*

OPPOSITE BELOW: *Foonky Starred (2008–09), designed by Rian Hughes, is a starstruck open face from the Foonky family.*

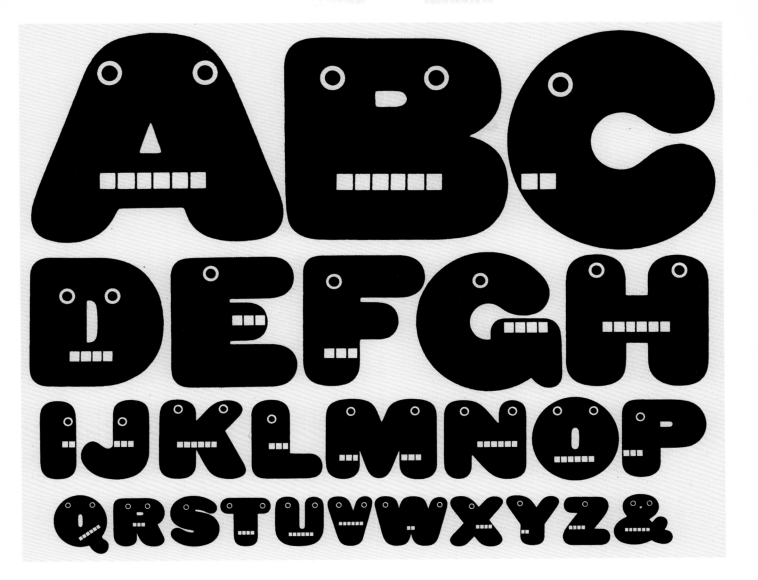

abcdefghijklmnopqrstuvwxyz
ABCDEFGHIJKLMNOPQRSTUVWXYZ
1234567890,.;:?!%&(([]))-£$@*

Flying off the page

IDEA № 35
EXPRESSION OF SPEED

With the invention of trains, planes, and automobiles came a reverence—if not a fetish—for speed among artists and designers. Industrialization during the mid-nineteenth century had introduced mass production, but subsequent engineering marvels enabled high velocities that were once only the subject of fiction, and which captured artists' imaginations.

Of the artists who were obsessed with speed, the Italian Futurists most avidly propagated the concept. However, an American expatriate in London, Edward McKnight Kauffer, made perhaps the most enduring graphic homage to speed. One of Europe's most prolific advertising and graphic designers of the 1920s–30s, Kauffer was influenced not only by the Futurists but also by the lesser-known Vorticists. His 1916 *Flight* combined abstraction and naturalism when used in a startling poster for

London's *Daily Herald* newspaper. Soaring birds represented hope, while the Cubist aesthetic suggested progress.

The Italian Futurist Fortunato Depero, a contemporary of Kauffer, took the speed fixation into even more accessible decorative realms. For him the graphic symbolism of speed was a means to raise the banner of Futurism and at the same time to appeal to the commercial masses with graphics that suggested new, improved, and up-to-date ideals.

After them, graphic artists used every trick at their disposal to visualize on paper—a static medium—the rush of a fast car or airplane. The arrow became the preferred symbol for speed, with two or more arrows able to suggest competition, acceleration, and revved-up momentum.

Max Huber's 1948 *Monza* poster, created for the legendary Italian motor-racing event, showed two arrows negotiating a parabolic turn in the pursuit of another speeding ahead of them. Huber understood that speed can best be experienced in the context of other interacting patterns. In the *Monza* poster, the headlines are leaning backward, as if sucked in by the force of the veering arrows.

In the 1970s, a new generation of graphic artists rediscovered speed, no longer as a way to celebrate progress but to mock its values. Graffiti artists had to work fast as they illegally spray-painted

subway trains in New York City. Owing to circumstances rather than deliberate intent, a wide range of styles evolved, all expressing genuine speed of execution.

Reminiscent of the work of Italian Futurists and Vorticists, contemporary graffiti writers such as PHASE 2, Shame 125, Daze, and JonOne often use dashing lines, intricate triangular motifs, or fat curving arrows when spelling their names. Written a century earlier, the words of Umberto Boccioni best describe the fascination these street graphic artists exert today: "The gesture which we would reproduce on canvas shall no longer be a fixed moment in universal dynamism. It shall simply be the dynamic sensation itself." ∎

Think small.

Our little car isn't so much of a novelty any more.

A couple of dozen college kids don't try to squeeze inside it.

The guy at the gas station doesn't ask where the gas goes.

Nobody even stares at our shape.

In fact, some people who drive our little flivver don't even think 32 miles to the gallon is going any great guns.

Or using five pints of oil instead of five quarts.

Or never needing anti-freeze.

Or racking up 40,000 miles on a set of tires.

That's because once you get used to some of our economies, you don't even think about them any more.

Except when you squeeze into a small parking spot. Or renew your small insurance. Or pay a small repair bill. Or trade in your old VW for a new one.

Think it over.

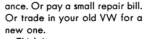

A logo speaks for a company

IDEA № 36
CORPORATE IDENTITY

At the beginning of the twentieth century businesses and industries branded or identified themselves in more or less ad hoc ways. The idea of developing a unified design scheme with standards and templates was unheard of until 1907, when the German architect and graphic designer Peter Behrens changed the face of business identity forever by creating the first corporate identity system.

When Behrens was retained as the design consultant for AEG (Allgemeine Elektricitäts-Gesellschaft), Germany's largest electrical company, **naive mascots** and trademarks were commonly registered, but the concept of an overall corporate identity did not exist. Behrens then developed a logo—reducing the unwieldy name to the initials AEG placed in a honeycomb configuration. Applied to all printed materials and signs, the logo became an aide-memoire that was recognizable as much outside as within the company. As a member of the German Werkbund, Behrens had dabbled with Jugendstil (German Art Nouveau) in posters and book illustrations, yet with the AEG identity he removed much of the stylish ornamentation.

Corporate identity developed its own rules, enforced by corporate identity standards manuals. These codified strict design requirements so that no room was left for deviation in terms of typefaces, colors, and marks. However, those identities that allowed for variation (not deviation) fared better in the long term. The best corporate identity designers maintained that within the parameters design could sprout wings.

One of the most savvy was the industrial designer Eliot Noyes. His involvement first with IBM and later with Westinghouse, and the hiring of Paul Rand to overhaul the identities of both corporations, formed a direct link to Behrens's model. Today it is unthinkable that a corporation would not start out with an integrated (if not evolving) graphic design system that helps define itself and create allure.

While Noyes focused on architecture and product design, Rand brought his graphic "play principle" to the fore. After defining the typographic and color palettes, and making certain the layout formats were tight, he went to work injecting graphic personality into advertisements, posters, packages, and other printed materials. This meant that one graphic concept did not fit all occasions. Each ad for Westinghouse or annual report for IBM was a different notion and look, like a new piece of art every time. As long as the anchor elements applied to them, anything else was possible.

The best designers understand that stagnation kills a corporate personality. Without variation an organization appears inflexible and, therefore, unable to adapt to new developments. Too much anarchy, however, and shareholders become wary of the corporation's stability. Corporate identity is a fine balancing act for a graphic designer. ■

OPPOSITE: **Think Small** *(1962), a Volkswagen® campaign created by Doyle Dane Bernbach and art directed by Robert Gage. Its simplicity contrasted with conventional exaggerated auto ads. The white page emphasized the undersized Beetle®, while the copy pointed to the virtues of owning a small car.*

TOP: AEG Allegemeine Elektricitäts-Gesellschaft (c. 1920). In 1907 the architect Peter Behrens became AEG's artistic adviser, responsible for the design of all products, advertising, and architecture—especially the logo.

ABOVE: Apple iPad package (2010). The original rainbow Apple logo (no longer used) was designed in 1977 by Rob Janoff. The Apple has changed from colored to black, aqua (2001–03), and glass (2003–present).

"The jacket made as much of a splash as the book."

Three Tales *(1945), designed by Alvin Lustig, differentiates this edition of Flaubert's work in a witty modern manner.*

Animal Farm *(2008), designed by Shepard Fairey as part of a series of George Orwell reprints, exudes a contemporary poster aesthetic.*

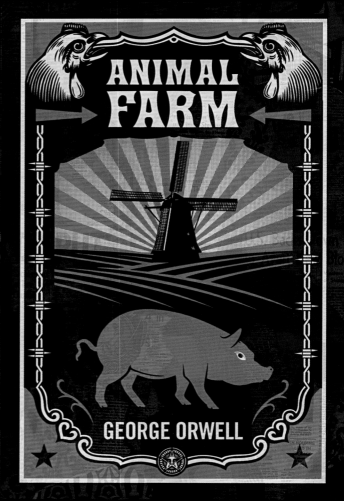

Telling a book by its cover

IDEA № 37
DUST JACKETS

In 1833, when the very first book jacket was used (by a British publisher, Longman & Co.), its purpose was to protect books from the damaging effects of dust and light. The heavy paper wrapped around and folded into the binding was meant to be discarded after purchase. Such were the humble beginnings of a form that would become a showcase for graphic design.

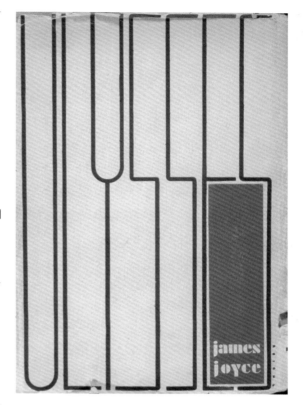

Ulysses *(1934), hand-lettered and designed by Ernst Reichl, was said to be influenced by the paintings of Piet Mondrian.*

For 50 years following that milestone event, the covering known as the dust jacket was primarily utilitarian—a plain paper wrapper usually with a window cut out to reveal the title and the author's name. For decoration, the binding (the spine and front and back covers) of the average trade book (a book marketed to the masses, as opposed to expensive fine editions) was stamped or embossed with a modest vignette. This was standard until the late 1880s and '90s, when the trade binding began to be decorated more often. The designs of Aubrey Beardsley in England and Will Bradley in the United States were reproduced on book bindings as a kind of miniature poster. Soon publishers allowed these designs to be printed on the paper jacket as well, for additional advertising appeal. By the turn of the century the dust jacket was the standard advertising tool, but was still considered a disposable wrapper. By the 1930s the jacket had become a new form of design art.

For purists from the old school of bookmaking, the dust jacket was ephemeral while the book itself was designed to endure. Yet for the German-born American designer Ernst Reichl the jacket and the interior were equal parts of a whole. His jacket for the first American edition of James Joyce's controversial *Ulysses*, which had been banned in the United States for 12 years before its eventual publication in 1934, broke many of the rules of jackets at that time. It was all type—and fairly large and curiously abstract type at that—with a limited color palette. The jacket made as much of a splash as the book.

Nonetheless, dust jackets were unquestionably the low end of graphic design practice during the 1920s and '30s, because they were tainted by the crass practice of advertising. In fact, most dust jackets were mini-posters or billboards, illustrated in accordance with the principles of mass marketing. The sole purpose of the jacket was to hook a reader, so the artists took many liberties with a book's content. The disparity between the author's intent and the artist's interpretation was rarely questioned. The jacket's allure was most important—and in some cases the jacket was the best part of the book. ∎

Seeing alphabets everywhere

IDEA № 38
FOUND TYPOGRAPHY

Ersatz letterforms and numerals can be discovered in almost anything in both the natural and the manmade environment. Truly "found" typography comprises those objects that were never intended to be letterforms yet through individual interpretation, skewed vision, and magical transformation, appear to be so, particularly when in the context of other ersatz letters forming an alphabet.

ABOVE: Alphabet with Tools *(1977), by Mervyn Kurlansky, takes everyday objects found in homes and workshops and transforms them into the letters of the Western alphabet.*

OPPOSITE: Hooks Alphabet *(2008), by Jeffrey Tribe, was created while Tribe was playing with picture hooks. Such visual discoveries are often overlooked, until the designer's eye becomes focused on the possibilities of the commonplace.*

The serendipity of shape and form found in everyday things that sometimes results in thematic groupings of letter-like objects can provide an "aha moment" of discovery for designers with keen eyes (and extraordinary patience). While some letters are joyously obvious, such as the A frame of a sharply pitched roof, the H of a football goalpost, or the O of a bagel, others are a little more contorted—the Y of a twin parking meter or the J of a drainpipe and gutter.

One of the earliest examples of this phenomenon was Abraham de Balmes's alphabet from his *Grammatica Hebraea* (1529), in which common objects, including a horseshoe, a knife, a sickle, and other tools and utensils took on the properties of individual letters. These were drawings; more recent found typographies are routinely photographed.

Mervyn Kurlansky's 1977 *Alphabet with Tools* is a case of how keen observation resulted in a satisfying typographical family made up of small office tools and machines. Starting with the A of a compass, moving through the K of a butterfly paperclip and the S of a French curve, to the Z of a combination knife and corkscrew, the sum of its parts is a total alphabet that is a conceptual *objet d'art*.

On a slightly more absurdist note, the lettering for the word "for" in Stefan Sagmeister's *Having Guts Always Works Out For Me* (2007) is made from sausages. Although the sausages were cut to form the letters, the raw material was indeed found. It took a perverse wit (and witty carnivore) to make hot dogs into an alphabet. And as vision and tenacity goes, Jeffrey Tribe's 2008 *Hooks Alphabet*, made of common picture-hanging hooks, required some clever maneuvering to make all 26 letters.

The purpose of these alphabets is less one of functionality than of curiosity. Designers see letters everywhere. The notion that letters can be constructed from such a broad range of objects continues to fascinate. These witty natural and industrial objects work their way into designs, to tickle the funnybone or toy with perception. ■

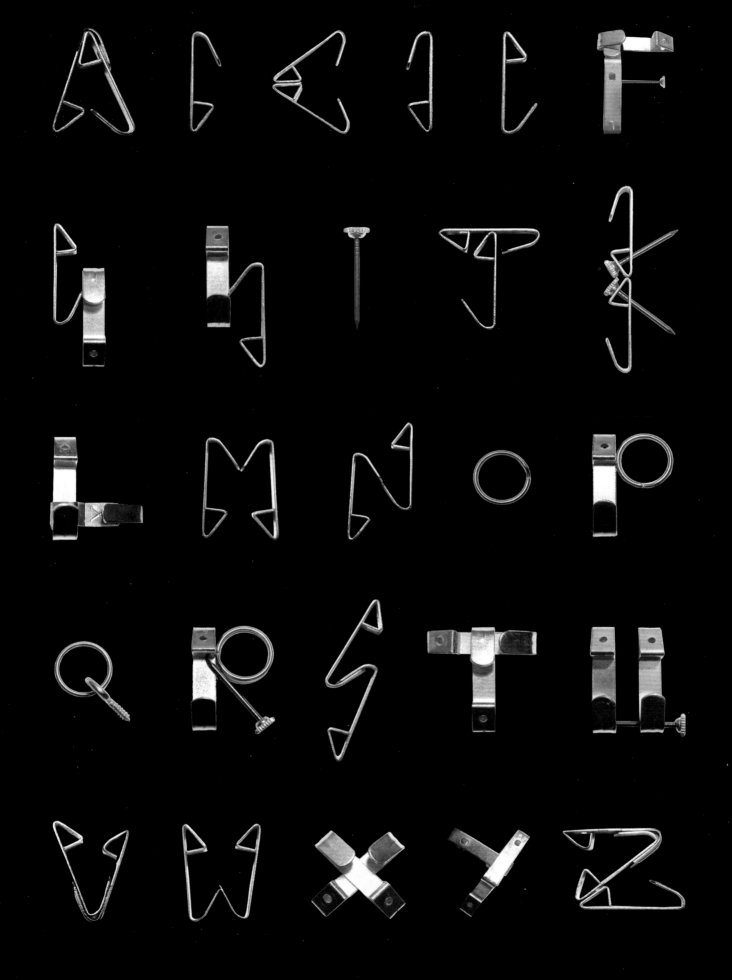

Careless composition grabs attention

IDEA № 39
RANSOM NOTES

The jumbled-type or ransom-note school of graphic design gained its name from the clichéd style—cutout letters intended to hide the identity of the sender. It has its roots in the late nineteenth century, when common job printers carelessly mixed disparate wood and metal type styles together on the same page, resulting in a cacophony of typographic noise.

ABOVE: God Save the Queen *(1977), the cover art for the 7" Sex Pistols single, was designed by Jamie Reid in a manner that became emblematic of punk design.*

OPPOSITE: Runaway Opposites *(1995), illustrations by Henrik Drescher, is a book of poems for children. The ransom letters and handwriting suggest immediacy.*

BELOW: Mecano *(1923), designed and edited by Theo van Doesburg, is rooted in the 1920s Dada aesthetic of ad hoc composition.*

Born as much of necessity (the printers did not always have complete fonts on hand) as of intent (to achieve visual exuberance), the approach became emblematic of the Victorian era. There was a commercial strategy too: since urban thoroughfares were increasingly cluttered with posters and advertisements, printers went through typographic contortions to attain eye-catching prominence. Raucousness was its own reward, particularly when the purpose was to capture and hold a viewer's attention.

What started as naive practice turned more calculated during the early twentieth century. The ransom method in the hands of Italian Futurists and German Dadaists was the total rejection of canonical legibility. Typographic poets, such as Berlin Dadaist Raoul Hausmann, aggressively dismantled accepted tenets through hysterical type that was not simply a metaphor for the new order but the archetype of a distinctly new visual language. Hausmann's "optophonetical poem" KP'ERIOUM (1918–19) was meant to be read out loud, the tonal directions established through the typographic size and weight. While there was logic to the anarchic composition, it nonetheless signaled rebellion.

Throughout the twentieth century, jumbled ransom-note lettering was designed to throw the eye off balance, and so too the equilibrium. In the early 1970s, punk emerged as the next generational aesthetic to exploit jumble. Jamie Reid's 1977 cover for the Sex Pistols' single "God Save the Queen" was deliberately untidy and amateurish. Taking Dada a step further, punk was so contemptuous of conventional beauty that it proffered a kind of "haute-ugly." To the astute observer, the primitive torn-and-tattered style, especially the ransom-note typography and anarchic collages on publications, record covers, and posters, suggested a usable, indeed a co-optable, style. What began as a means to address an exclusive audience became shorthand for youth culture.

Anyone with a pair of scissors and a glue pot could emulate this punk styling. And the most flagrant samplers were Condé Nast's fashion magazines in the early 1980s under creative director Alexander Liberman, who believed that elegant design was irrelevant. He spent millions making the magazines under his control, including *Vogue*, *Self*, and *Mademoiselle*, look jumbled. ∎

WHAT IS THE OPPOSITE OF
HAT?
IT ISN'T HARD TO ANSWER THAT.
IT'S SHOES.
FOR SHOES AND HAT TOGETHER
PROTECT OUR TWO EXTREMES FROM WEATHER.
BETWEEN THESE TWO EXTREMES THERE LIES
A MIDDLE
WHICH YOU WOULD BE WISE
TO CLOTHE AS WELL, OR YOU'LL BE CHILLY
AND RUN THE RISK OF LOOKING
Silly.

Yo! THAT WRITING LOOKS LIKE CHINESE FROM THIS ANGLE.

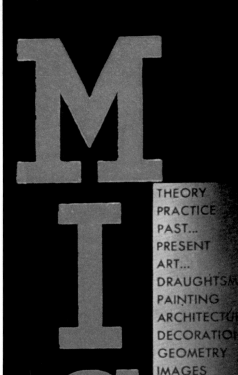

A. TOLMER

M I S E

THEORY
PRACTICE
PAST...
PRESENT
ART...
DRAUGHTSMA
PAINTING
ARCHITECTUR
DECORATION
GEOMETRY
IMAGES
THE BOOK
PUBLICITY
PRECEDENT
WRITING
PRINTING
TYPOGRAPHY
SLOGANS
PHOTOS
BLACK AND
FORM
ESPRIT
STYLE
SIMPLICITY
DARING
BALANCE
AVANT-GARD
MASS

EN

the theory and
practice of lay-out

PAGE

THE STUDIO LTD

Distilling theory from practice

IDEA № 40
DESIGN HANDBOOKS

During the 1920s and '30s certain eminent designers in Europe and the United States took delight in telling other designers how to design. During these nascent years of Modernism they were so convinced they had discovered the rightness of form that, to spread the word (and image), they issued detailed manuals setting out their ideas.

The two most influential books of their time, W.A. Dwiggins's *Layout in Advertising* and Jan Tschichold's *Die Neue Typographie* (The New Typography), both published in 1928, provided different formulas for transcending antiquated commercial art conventions. Dwiggins celebrated a new kind of naturalistic ornamentation, while Tschichold promoted Bauhaus- and Constructivist-inspired principles that reduced all design to basic geometric and asymmetric formats. Both attracted their share of followers, yet it is Tschichold's book that is today considered the key document of Modernist typography.

A few years later, another tome defined the new mainstream aesthetic

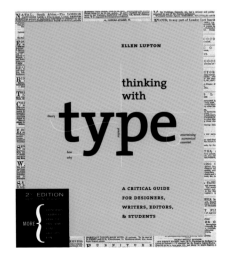

and became the design bible of its time. The French publisher Alfred Tolmer's *Mise en Page: The Theory and Practice of Lay-Out*, published in 1932 in separate English and French editions, codified the most widely practiced of the early twentieth-century design styles. Tolmer's goal was to provide formal guidelines while encouraging creative invention, and this lavishly printed primer, with its slipsheets, tip-ins, embossed and debossed pages, and foldouts, was an alluring guide.

Tolmer attempted to present solid intellectual arguments for why Modern design, both avant-garde and in its more mass-market incarnations, was the perfect form for the age. "The art of layout," he wrote, "is born at the moment when man feels the urge to arrange in an orderly fashion the expression of his thoughts." Tolmer asserted that "real freedom in typography seems to be confined at the present time to advertising lay-outs"; showed how Egyptian, Greek, and other classical forms evolved into Modernistic mannerisms in typography and illustration; and hailed the use of photomontage as the foremost progressive design conceit. With his handbook Tolmer fervently and single-handedly smoothed the edges off orthodox Modernism, making once-radical design concepts palatable for business.

Predictably, Tolmer's fashionable manual became unfashionable as the

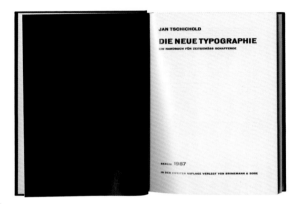

OPPOSITE: Mise en Page *(1932), written and designed by Alfred Tolmer, was a bible for Art Moderne (Art Deco) typography and image styling.*

BELOW: Thinking with Type *(2010), written and designed by Ellen Lupton, picks up where the modern and Modernist manuals left off—detailed instruction in contemporary typography.*

ABOVE: Die Neue Typographie *(first published 1928), written and designed by Jan Tschichold, was the foremost manual for minimalist and asymmetric design.*

age of austerity prompted by World War II hit the European continent. But manuals continued to be published, perhaps with slightly less panache. Designers and those who thought about design continued to push their different truths, which evolved into rules and standards or styles and mannerisms. Eventually, the manual became a template for certain kinds of practice. Each year one or more is published with the aim of becoming adopted by schools whose job it is to make design production easier, and if lucky a little more creative into the bargain. ∎

DIE GUTE REKLAME IST BILLIG.

Ein geringes Maß hochwertiger Reklame, die in jeder
Weise Qualität verrät, übersteigt an Wirkung eine vielfache
Menge ungeeigneter, ungeschickt organisierter Reklame.

Max_Burchartz.

MERZ

11

RED. MERZ, HANNOVER, WALDHAUSENSTR. 5 II.

TYPO

REKLAME

EINIGE THESEN ZUR GESTALTUNG DER REKLAME VON MAX BURCHARTZ:

Die Reklame ist die Handschrift des Unternehmers. Wie die Handschrift ihren Urheber, so verrät die Reklame Art, Kraft und Fähigkeit einer Unternehmung. Das Maß der Leistungsfähigkeit, Qualitätspflege, Solidität, Energie und Großzügigkeit eines Unternehmens spiegelt sich in Sachlichkeit, Klarheit, Form und Umfang seiner Reklame. Hochwertige Qualität der Ware ist erste Bedingung des Erfolges. Die zweite: Geeignete Absatzorganisation; deren unentbehrlicher Faktor ist gute Reklame. Die gute Reklame verwendet moderne Mittel. Wer reist heute in einer Kutsche? Gute Reklame bedient sich neuester zeitgemäßer Erfindungen als neuer Werkzeuge der Mitteilung. Wesentlich ist die Neuartigkeit der Formengebung. Abgeleierte banale Formen der Sprache und künstlerischen Gestaltung müssen vermieden werden. Zitiert aus Gestaltung der Reklame, Bochum, Bongardstrasse 15.

K. SCHWITTERS.
Signetentwurf für Adolf
Rothenberg

DIE GUTE REKLAME

ist sachlich, ist klar und knapp, verwendet moderne Mittel, hat Schlagkraft der Form, ist billig.

MAX BURCHARTZ.

Merzrelief von Kurt Schwitters siehe Seite 91

Magazines as laboratory for artistic experiment

IDEA № 41
AVANT-GARDE ZINES

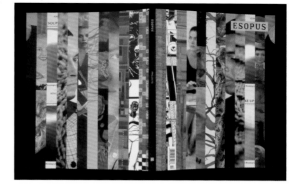

OPPOSITE: **Merz** 11 (1925), created and designed by Kurt Schwitters, was his personal design zine. This issue was devoted to his distinct advertising stylings.

ABOVE: Esopus 14 (2010), edited and designed by Tod Lippy, is an ad-free journal devoted to art and culture and unusual combinations thereof.

BELOW: OZ 41 (1972), the Crime & Conspiracy issue of this 1960s alternative magazine, led to the editor's trial for obscenity and blasphemy.

The early twentieth century was littered with journals and gazettes created by artists to serve as soapboxes for their quirky ideas. Futurist, Dadaist, and Surrealist art provocateurs wrote dissonant poetry, composed **asymmetric typography**, pasted expressive **collages**, and printed it all in crudely produced publications. Each movement, in its own way, proffered the Modernist notion that art was a total experience. These art and culture periodicals, or "zines," were weapons of cultural warfare, attacking convention.

Alternative culture periodicals informed and entertained, but they also provoked action and reaction. Type and image on paper triggered visceral responses. Avant-gardists flagrantly refused to appeal to mass taste. In Italy, Germany, Switzerland, and France avant-garde periodicals such as *Futurismo, Noi, Dada, Merz,* and *La Révolution Surréaliste* were designed to rally the faithful while offending the conventional.

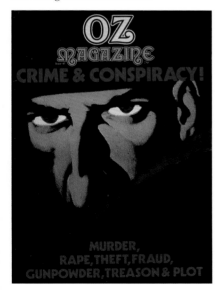

Radical ideas had to *appear* avant-garde to *be* avant-garde. Graphic design was the code of revolt. Words were the building blocks of meaning but typography, layout, and image did more than simply frame ideas: they telegraphed intent. The sensory impact on the reader effected through raw type composition marked the end of beauty as the accepted standard. The design of most Dada publications during the early 1920s, for example, both intentionally and intuitively disrupted professional design standards. Dadaists, such as Kurt Schwitters, appropriated graphic elements from mainstream printing sources and wedded them to Futurist and Cubist pictorial theories of disruption and fragmentation. Standard typefaces were not just mere letterforms composed in neatly regimented columns; they were used as textures applied to a *tabula rasa*.

Radical design ideas, however, eventually filtered into the mainstream. Jan Tschichold's *Die Neue Typographie* (see p.87) codified Modern design. Kurt Schwitters's personal zine, *Merz,* was at various times transformed from an experimental outlet for avant-gardisms into a sample book of progressive graphic design, where he exhibited ways of applying Tschichold's principles to commercial advertisements.

The lifespan of an avant-garde zine depended on how long it continued to offend or surprise or both. Once entrepreneurs saw the profitability in controlled offensiveness, radical ideas were invariably consumed by the very culture they once affronted. After the initial shock of Surrealism wore off it quickly became a favored advertising and marketing style, tapping into the public's fascination for dreamlike allure. Strands of Futurist DNA were present in many 1970s zines, which borrowed the punk aesthetic.

As digital media rise in prominence, today's print magazines must jump through hoops to be truly avant-garde. The twice-yearly arts magazine *Esopus* does not take advertising, which in itself is radical. But it also publishes art and artists who are on the fringes. If avant-garde pushes the boundaries, then print design—which could be considered retrograde—is now arguably avant-garde. That *Esopus* continues the tradition so boldly makes it a viable model for the new avant-garde zine. ∎

Cutting-edge appeal

IDEA Nº 42
COLLAGES

The idea that you can use scissors and glue instead of paint and brushes appealed to Dada artists, who relished the notion of destruction as a radical form of creation. Raoul Hausmann, considered the inventor of photocollages, believed that you can pick and choose images and words from the supply of existing material and recycle them to express an original thought. But collages were also conceived as a critique of a materialist culture that assaulted individuals with a profusion of images, messages, and slogans.

The graphic vocabulary of early collages (sometimes called montages) consisted of cutout photographs, either contoured or torn, combined with partial headlines from newspaper clippings. The central motif of Hausmann's most often reproduced collage, *ABCD*, is a close-up of his own face, with his mouth open in what looks like a shriek. What provoked Hausmann's reaction was probably the riot of facts and figures closing in on him to the point of almost smothering him. A virtuosic balancing act of letterforms, graphs, maps, textures, and sketches—including a banknote and a medical illustration—the lopsided composition is strangely gratifying.

Countless graphic artists have studied Hausmann's hectic medley of scraps and tried to learn from it, Russian Constructivists in particular. In the West, collage artists relied mostly on commercially produced visuals to construct provocative narratives. In the 1950s, British Pop art precursor Richard Hamilton pasted together figures and silhouettes plucked from various magazine advertisements, for a montage titled *Just what is it that makes today's homes so different, so appealing?* Meant to be a satire on the frenetic acquisitiveness encouraged by rampant consumerism, it represented the interior of a living room, with everything in perspective yet somehow uncomfortably flat and stiff. The main figure, a bodybuilder, serves as a metaphor for the buildup of goods and products that characterizes our culture, as well as the buildup of images typical of collages.

The collage that became the biggest commercial and critical success worldwide is probably the cover of the 1967 Beatles album *Sgt. Pepper's Lonely Hearts Club Band*, designed by Peter Blake and Jann Haworth. Constructed as a full-size set, it was a psychedelic assemblage of cutout cardboard figures of famous people in the middle of which the Fab Four stood, dressed in Day-Glo military-style uniforms. Wax figures of their younger selves, borrowed from Madame Tussauds, were also part of the setup.

In the 1980s, Dada-inspired collages mixing typography and photograms became popular with a generation of graphic designers partial to the work of Man Ray and László Moholy-Nagy. Rudy VanderLans was the author of visually exciting montages printed as posters to promote *Emigré* magazine. Though not slavishly copying the structure of *ABCD*, these collages were juggling exercises in which typographic elements drifted together to form a playful aggregation of visual flotsam. ∎

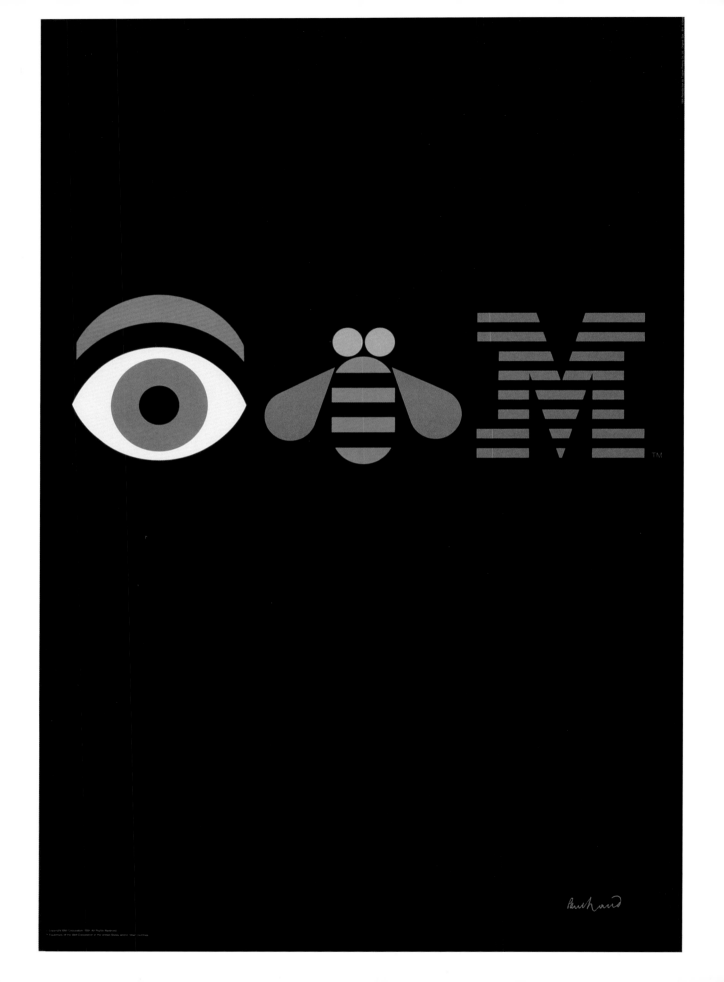

Visual pranks can incorporate concealed messages

IDEA № 43
RIDDLES AND REBUSES

Symbol, sign, cipher, rebus, icon, graphic pun, emblem... the difference between such terms can be more confusing than the messages they are trying to convey. Figures of graphic speech, each in their own way strives to bridge the gap between words and images. As such, they are invaluable assets in developing a sophisticated visual language. René Magritte's famous painting of a pipe is first and foremost an image of a pipe, but its caption, *Ceci n'est pas une pipe* (This is not a pipe), says this is not so.

OPPOSITE: Eye-Bee-M *(1981). The celebrated poster by Paul Rand for IBM breaks down the conventional logo into a rebus with the identifiable striped "M." It was originally rejected as being too playful.*

BELOW: Couleur *(1975), created by Swiss graphic designer Jean Widmer for an exhibition on colors at the Pompidou Center in Paris. The words are spelled in the wrong color, a Magritte-inspired technique.*

ABOVE: I Love NY *(1977), one of the most most familiar and copied rebuses today, is the work of Milton Glaser for the New York State Department of Commerce. If Glaser had signed a royalty agreement, he would be probably the richest graphic designer on earth.*

Why did Magritte feel compelled to remind viewers that a picture of a thing is not the thing itself? Or did he mean to use the outdated sense of the word "pipe," synonymous with "fib," as some linguists have argued? "This is not a fib"? Experts point out that the official title of the 1929 painting, *The Treachery of Images*, is further evidence that Magritte was a trickster. Carefully rendered, his pipe was not only an illustration of the deceptive nature of all representations,

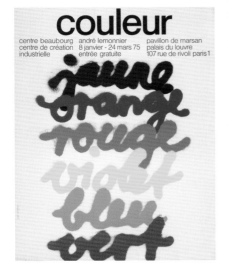

it was also meant to confuse viewers regarding the intention of its author.

In 1975, Jean Widmer paid homage to Magritte's semiotic exercises with his poster *Couleur*, announcing a design exhibition. It spelled out the names of six colors of the rainbow, but none of the words was written in its corresponding color. It made reference to another of Magritte's visual pranks, *La clef des songes* (The interpretation of dreams), in which everyday objects are incorrectly labeled—a bowler hat being identified as "snow," for example.

Unlike semiotic riddles, rebuses are fairly easy to translate into words. The word "rebus" comes from the Latin "by things" or "made by things." Sequentially combining pictures with letters and/or word fragments to form a word or phrase, rebuses have evolved to become a staple of modern conceptual graphic and typographic design.

The nature of most rebuses is to be accessible. Milton Glaser's I Love NY trademark vividly proves the old chestnut "a picture is worth a thousand words." Yet rebuses can be used to challenge perception. In many instances, clues that appear to be self-evident are in fact ambiguous.

Such is the case with Paul Rand's beloved *Eye-Bee-M* poster, which he designed in 1981, in the later part of his long-lasting relationship with IBM. A beautifully designed rebus, it is, like Magritte's pipe, a clever play on words. Yet, when you look closely at this witty interpretation of the famous striped logo (which Rand had designed in 1962, see p.164), you begin to wonder what was going on. Was Rand trying to say something? Was he insinuating that the business-machine giant was becoming too stodgy and that its image was due for an overhaul? As far as executives at IBM were concerned, the poster did contain a message—the wrong message—and, even though it was only meant to advertise an in-house event, they refused to approve its too-playful design. ∎

A new tool for propagandists

IDEA № 44
PHOTOMONTAGE

In 1917, the German satirist and designer John Heartfield developed a dynamic new visual technique that he used for political satire. The photomontage was the manipulation of two or more different photographs, combining negatives and positives, to form a convincing new image. It was a mechanical art for the mechanical age and changed forever how both political satire and nationalist propaganda were produced.

Heartfield's anti-Nazi graphic commentaries in the pro-Communist weekly periodical *AIZ* (Workers' Illustrated News) were considered the most inflammatory political dissent. Photographically situating real people, such as Hitler and his henchmen, in imagined yet plausible pictorial contexts opened them up to greater ridicule than could drawings and paintings. After World War I, Heartfield joined the newly formed German Communist Party (KPD) and produced many of its posters and periodicals, which is how photomontage came to be viewed as a left-wing medium.

The advent of photomontage intersected with the spread of photojournalism around the world and among right and left ideologies. The French illustrated weekly *Vu*, founded in 1928 and edited by the photographer Lucien Vogel, was one of the most innovative in terms of the picture essay. Vogel used the power of photography to document and critique current events. Graphic design was essential to the success of his magazine, so *Vu*'s logo was designed by French poster artist A.M. Cassandre, and Deberny & Peignot set the type. Irene Lidova, a Russian émigrée, was the first art director, and in 1933 her layout assistant was the Russian-born Alexander Liberman, who introduced plenty of photomontage to the magazine.

AIZ also influenced the six-language edition *USSR in Construction*, which was published monthly between 1930 and 1940. Founded by the writer Maxim Gorky, its declared editorial mission was to "reflect in photography the whole scope and variety of the construction work now going on in the USSR." Photomontage was used to juxtapose multiple realities into one ideal fantasy, and could serve the needs of whoever harnessed it.

Photomontage was not solely a political medium: it was perfectly adapted to commercial use, to add elements to a picture that were not actually there.

Although it is still used in some political or satirical contexts, contemporary photomontage (achieved with ease with Photoshop) is the tool of choice for a wealth of other tasks, from advertisements to CD covers.

Viktor Koen's precisionist photomontage is the quintessence of twenty-first-century surrealism. Borrowing from sci-fi and symbolist art traditions, his images are at once apocalyptic and utopian. ∎

7

Illustrierte
Geschichte der
Russischen
Revolution

OPPOSITE: Die Neue Linie *(1938),*
designed by Xanti Schawinsky,
combines the icons of Fascist Italy—
classic column, Duce, and the boot.

ABOVE: Illustrated History of
the Russian Revolution *(1927),*
designed with photomontage by
John Heartfield, juxtaposes news
photographs with symbols of
revolution.

Worth a thousand words

PICTOGRAMS

The International System of Typographic Picture Education (Isotype) was introduced in the 1930s by the Viennese political economist and museum director Otto Neurath and his wife, Marie Reidemeister. Isotype was originally designed as an alternative to text, a starkly graphic means of communicating information about locales, events, and objects on the one hand, and complex relationships in space and time on the other.

This set of pictographic characters was intended "to create narrative visual material, avoiding details which do not improve the narrative character," as Neurath wrote in one of his books propagating his unique idea to improve visual literacy. He believed that Isotype, formed of pictograms, icons, or symbols, could, as the world's first universal pictorial language, transcend national borders. Neurath's Vienna School was rooted in a simple graphic vocabulary of silhouetted symbolic representations of every possible image, from men and women to dogs and cats to trucks and planes. This storehouse of icons was a kit of parts that could be used to present any informational or statistical data. Neurath's illustrators, the German Gerd Arntz and the Viennese Augustin Tschinkel and Erwin Bernath, created a wealth of simplified characteristics that distinguished between, for example, laborers, office workers, soldiers, and police officers. The neutral silhouette was preferred because it avoided personal interpretation. It could also be viewed as a signpost rather than a critique.

Neurath was keen on objectivity and ordered the artists to make silhouettes from cut paper or simple pen-and-ink drawings. Yet Arntz injected warmth and humor through gestures in the way a figure held a newspaper or carried a lunchbox.

Neurath's work influenced the cartographic and information graphics of his day and well into the late twentieth century. He also used pictograms to stand for quantities—what he called "statistical accountability"—so they could convey numerical information at the same time as their primary meaning.

In addition to conveying quantifiable data, Isotype foreshadowed today's common pictorial sign symbols. Neurath's colleague Rudolf Modley's *Handbook of Pictorial Symbols* (1976) and industrial designer Henry Dreyfuss's *Symbol Sourcebook* (1972) are key references for their inclusive compilation of symbols. Otl Aicher's event symbols for the 1972 Munich Olympic Games take the basic icons in a more streamlined direction. And the American Institute of Graphic Arts' system of 50 symbol signs, designed by Roger Cook and Don Shanosky, a collaboration between the AIGA and the U.S. Department of Transportation, has become the standard for pictograms in airports and other transportation hubs and at large international events. ∎

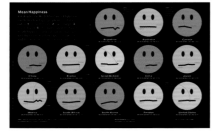

BELOW: Mean Happiness *(2008), designed by Scott Stowell and Ryan Thacker for* Good *magazine, to track the world database of happiness.*

ABOVE: *Munich Olympics pictograms (1972), designed by Otl Aicher, introduced the Isotype sensibility to the Olympic playground. These proved a huge influence on Games to follow.*

Pictographs Today and Tomorrow
*(1938) by Rudolf Modley is, along with
Otto Neurath's Isotypes, the prototype
of contemporary graphic sign-symbols.*

A portrait becomes a trademark

IDEA № 46
FLOATING HEADS

The first artist to depict a human head chopped off its body as a means of sending a graphically vivid message is anyone's guess. But beheading became a common trope in graphic arts early on. During the nineteenth century Aubrey Beardsley's image of Salome admiring the severed head of John the Baptist in *The Dancer's Reward* (1893) is stylishly striking and decidedly gory—but the head does not "float," it sits on a pedestal looking somewhat forlorn.

A less gruesome, and more frequently used, approach to disembodiment is found on an infamous black-and-white election poster from Adolf Hitler's failed 1932 attempt to be elected as chancellor of Germany (he gained power in 1933). Its designer is unknown (probably from the Nazi Party's Propaganda Atelier) but the photograph was by Heinrich Hoffmann, Hitler's personal photographer. Hitler's silhouetted face emerging from a black background with the sans serif capitals spelling out HITLER was an unusually modern design approach for political posters at the time, when most were starkly colored and boldly typographical. The floating head alluded to the idea of an omniscient presence, but might also be construed as a savior coming from the darkness (the Weimar Republic) into the light of a "new order." In retrospect the image was an ominous portent of the horrors to come.

The cover for the 1963 *With the Beatles* album (their second, issued in the United States the following year as *Meet the Beatles!*), seemed to follow a similar visual scheme. Photographed in natural light and wearing black turtleneck sweaters, the Beatles' heads look as though they are floating in space. While many photographic album covers for jazz recordings at the time were dramatically posed, this approach, focusing on the lads' mop-top hairstyles, suggested an iconic yet ghostly otherworldliness. Although highlighting four individuals, the album cover reinforced the unity of the Beatles as a group—more than the sum of its parts. It became a veritable logo until their next iconic photo session.

The floating head—both large and small and whatever the subject—is a reductive design element that by its very nature is potentially a trademark. As a graphic idea this arguably holds true for any object that is removed or severed from its context, but the come-hither features of the head (especially the eyes, nose, and mouth) are prime elements of a logo. ∎

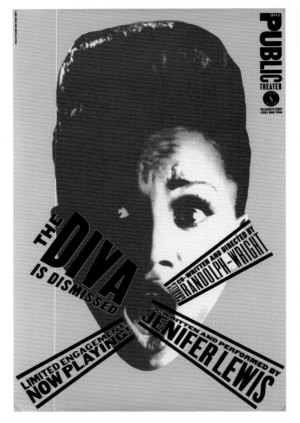

ABOVE: The Diva is Dismissed *(1994), wall poster designed by Paula Scher for the New York Public Theater. The floating head was influenced by nineteenth-century collage.*

BELOW: Hitler *(1932), election poster with photo by Heinrich Hoffmann, was a prototype for the "Big Brother" image. The floating head was omniscient.*

OPPOSITE: Für das Alter *(1949), poster designed by Carlo Vivarelli, was an early example of the "International" or "Swiss Style." The head against black focuses the eye on the elderly woman.*

Für das Alter

Freiwillige Spende

Entwurf: C. Vivarelli v/o Zürich   Foto: Werner Bischof Zürich   Druck: Art. Institut Orell Füssli AG, Zürich

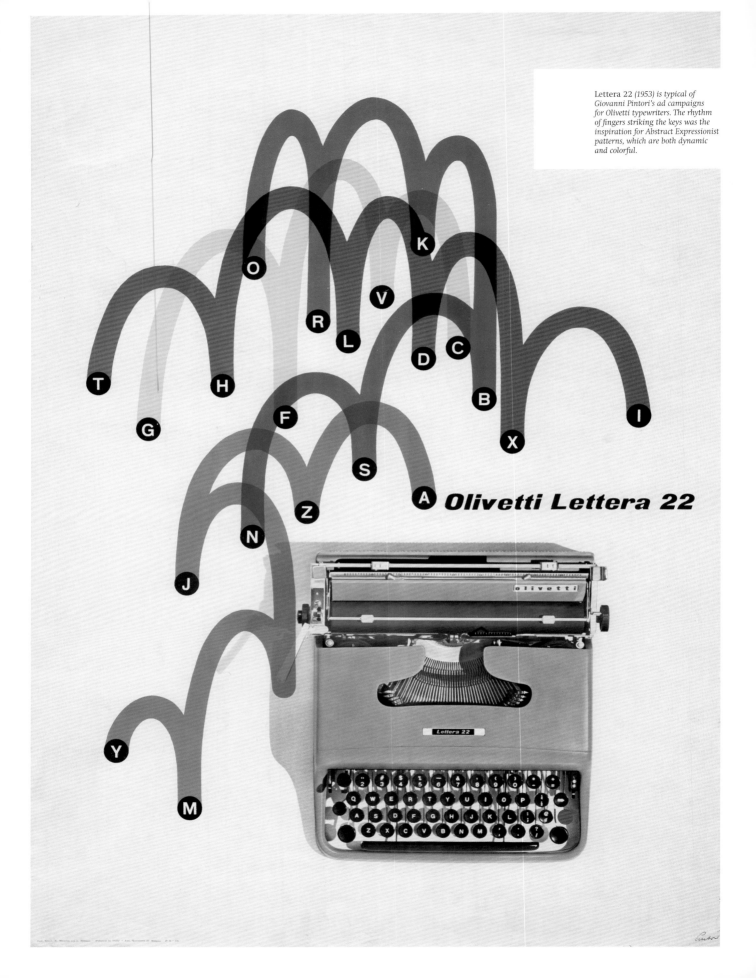

Olivetti Lettera 22

Translating emotions into graphic form

IDEA № 47
ABSTRACTION

Can abstraction communicate persuasively? Few graphic designers use abstract motifs to express an idea, promote an event, or tell a story, but when they do, the results are proof that you do not have to be visually explicit in order make yourself understood.

Joost Schmidt's famous poster for the 1923 Bauhaus exhibition in Weimar, done when he was still a student, is an abstract composition whose only figurative element was a hardly noticeable human profile. This profile, set in a disk, formed the Bauhaus official seal, as designed by Oskar Schlemmer the previous year. The poster, created to herald the new direction of the school—now dedicated to the celebration of machine art rather than crafts—could be interpreted as an allegory of man's new relationship with technology. Had the human profile not been part of it, though, the image might have been less anecdotal and more powerful. As it is, the message conveyed by this robotic-looking amalgam of shapes is ambiguous: are machines under our control, or do they control us?

It does not take much for an abstract pattern to become overtly illustrative. The mere suggestion of an eye, a star, a wheel, or a flower, for example, can be enough to turn blobs of colors or geometric forms into representational art. Most so-called "conceptual" imagery falls in this category. Designers such as Giovanni Pintori remain an exception. In the 1950s, for Olivetti, he created advertisements whose abstract patterns were meant to transcribe visually the "feel" of a particular typewriter rather than describe its features. The 1953 poster for the Lettera 22 typewriter is a good example, one of the few nonliteral designs applied to commerce. In the background, colorful clusters of graceful arcs evoke the rapid movements of deft fingers on the keys.

During the heyday of Abstract Expressionism, American painter Frank Stella was commissioned by the Lincoln Center cultural complex in New York City to design a poster for its 1967 summer festival. The abstract pattern of intertwined circles he created was a dynamic and playful composition. Rather than trying to say explicitly "dance" or "music" or "theatre" or "film," it translated pictorially the pleasure and excitement that performances elicit.

Music is often an inspiration for designers in creating abstract composi-

BELOW: Bauhaus Exhibition, Weimar (1923) by Joost Schmidt, influenced by Constructivism and De Stijl. Combining serif letterforms with industrial-looking motifs, the composition is striking but oddly off-balance.

ABOVE: Jazz in Willisau (1998), by Swiss graphic designer Niklaus Troxler, is one of more than a hundred such festival posters that make extensive use of abstraction to evoke the rhythms and tempo of jazz performances.

tions. The contemporary Swiss graphic designer Niklaus Troxler is a master of this genre. He translates his fascination for jazz into geometric silhouettes, scribbles, splashes, and chromatic exercises that make subtle reference to avant-garde movements of the twentieth century, from Dada to Abstract Expressionism and Op art. Director of the Willisau Jazz Festival in central Switzerland, which he founded in 1975, he is one of the rare individuals who has managed to combine two unrelated passions into a single expression. Looking at his posters, we realize that jazz and graphic design are both abstract languages that celebrate the dynamic qualities of space and time. ■

МОСКВА
1927

АРХИТЕКТУРА

АРХИТЕКТУРА

ВХУТЕМАС

Building on Constructivist foundations

IDEA № 48
TRIANGULATION

The idea of buttressing the visual components of a layout against each other to form a network of right angles and diagonals was initiated in Bolshevik Russia in the 1920s by designers whose creativity was sparked by the post-Revolutionary construction boom.

El Lissitzky was one of the most inspired proponents of this ideologically driven Russian movement, which came to be known as Constructivism. His famous red, black, and sepia poster, featuring the hand of an architect holding a compass, epitomized the basic principles of this early Modernist aesthetic. On this simple and bold layout, Lissitzky superimposed typographical and pictorial elements at 90- and 45-degree angles. He triangulated the heavy lines of type, the fingers of the hand, and the arms of the compass the same way an architect would have triangulated girders, timbers, and beams to strengthen a tall structure. The use of capital letters, sans serif type, and industrial-looking colors reinforced the impression of stability that this composition strove to achieve.

Perfected in Russia by Lissitzky and also Aleksander Rodchenko in the 1920s, triangulated layouts went on to capture the imagination of designers worldwide. Countless artists adopted and further developed the Constructivist style: first in the Netherlands, where Theo van Doesburg and Piet Zwart borrowed some of its tropes to spearhead the De Stijl movement; and later, in the 1930s, in Eastern Europe, where the likes of László Moholy-Nagy and Jan Tschichold combined diagonals and angles with Bauhaus typography to create their own distinctive signature look.

Forgotten for nearly 50 years, triangulated layouts had to wait until the late 1970s to make a comeback. Lissitzky-inspired designs became all the rage in the post-Modernist era as a new generation of graphic designers suddenly discovered this hitherto untapped source of inspiration. Roman Cieslewicz for the Pompidou Center in Paris, Rudy Vander-Lans for *Emigré* magazine, or Paula Scher for the Public Theater in New York (see p.98), are examples of talented designers who have used triangulation to evoke the avant-garde spirit of pioneering Modernists, and to emulate their upbeat, cutting-edge, dynamic outlook. ■

OPPOSITE: Architecture at Vkhutemas *(1927), one of El Lissitzky's most eloquent compositions. The book suggests that Constructivist rigidity should be tempered with a humanist sensibility.*

BELOW: Bauhaus Journal, *Number 2 (1928), designed by Herbert Bayer, who edited the journal. It is a remarkable example of the way Bauhaus teachers, among them Wassily Kandinsky, Josef Albers, and Moholy-Nagy, influenced each other.*

ABOVE: The Best of Jazz *(1979), a typographical masterpiece by Paula Scher, was done when she was discovering Aleksander Rodchenko and El Lissitsky. She recalls her work being acclaimed as "new wave" and "postmodern" when in fact it was a private homage to the pioneers of the Russian avant garde.*

PONTRESINA

Engadin

Tiefdruck Conzett & Huber, Zürich

Bigger is better

IDEA № 49
EXTREME CLOSE-UPS

Graphic designers tend to objectify photographs, cropping, distorting, retouching, slicing, or enlarging them in order to transform them into graphic artifacts. They are particularly fond of close-ups that decontextualize a picture and allow them to emphasize the difference between the foreground and the background of an image. Needless to say, photographers and graphic designers often fail to see eye to eye.

The Russian Aleksander Rodchenko was an exceptional artist. A prolific photographer as well as a graphic designer, he manipulated his own photographs, often magnifying and cropping parts of them for his **collages**. In his well-known poster for Dziga Vertov's 1924 documentary film *Kinoglaz* (Cine-Eye), the motif of a large eye took center stage. Rodchenko's influence is evident in the travel poster for the Swiss ski resort Pontresina by Swiss-born American photographer and designer Herbert Matter: the over-

scale face of a man dwarfs the image of a skier with snowy mountain peaks in the background. In Matter's *Engelberg* poster, an embroidered ski glove gets top billing, while everything behind it recedes in the background. Like successive flats in theatrical scenery, the larger the image in front, the deeper the stage seems to be.

Another Swiss graphic designer, Josef Müller-Brockmann, used photography sparingly, but when he did, everyone noticed. His road-safety poster featuring an extreme close-up of the wheels of a racing motorcycle is highly memorable—as it should be in order to act as an effective deterrent to speeding. The small figure of a child running to cross the street completes the impression of impending tragedy. Indeed, blown-up photographs are almost always alarming, one of the reasons they are fascinating. They show details we often do not see, and suggest an uncomfortable closeness. We cannot help staring at them while at the same time wanting to look away.

Contemporary designers are banking on this aspect of extreme close-ups, and even emphasizing it, by drawing on top of enlarged photographs to accentuate the in-your-face impression. The Parisian team Mathias Augustyniak and Michaël Amzalag, who work under the name

M/M (Paris), were among the first to exploit this technique successfully. Their 2001 posters for the fashion house Balenciaga showcase severely cropped portraits of top models, defaced with strangely beautiful hand-drawn doodles. In this collaboration with the fashion-photographer duo Inez van Lamsweerde and Vinoodh Matadin, the photographers did not mind their work being treated as a canvas. Today, augmenting the experience of looking is more important than preserving the integrity of a photograph. ∎

Body language can motivate, excite, or outrage

IDEA № 50
THE PROVOCATIVE GESTURE

Through the turbulent decades of the early twentieth century, graphic designers created iconic heroes in meaningful poses in the service of democracies and dictatorships alike. Extreme posturing has since developed into a sophisticated mode of expression. From **clenched fists** to thumbs up, for savvy visual communicators, the language of gestures is as expressive as that of letterforms.

ABOVE: Herkules-Bier (1925), a beer ad by Ludwig Hohlwein, evokes the robust qualities of the brawny beverage in a proud male figure flexing his muscles.

BELOW: We Can Do It! (1943), a propaganda poster commissioned by Westinghouse from commercial artist J. Howard Miller to encourage women to work in factories. In the 1970s the Women's Liberation Movement took the image as a symbol of female power.

OPPOSITE: Liberty and Justice (2004), by Mirko Ilic, was conceived as a cover for the Village Voice. It was inspired by an article about a ban on same-sex marriage being discussed in the U.S. Congress. The image is widely used in support of gay marriage.

Every period has its own imagery of gesture. The German poster artist Ludwig Hohlwein's so-called Munich style dominated German advertising from the 1920s to the 1940s. His depictions of lock-jawed, broad-shouldered human mannequins in heroic attitudes mythologized patriotic masculinity. America's famous monument to heroism, the Marine Corps War Memorial at Arlington, Virginia, was based on Joe Rosenthal's iconic photograph of a flag-raising during the Battle of Iwo Jima in February 1945. The United States Senate called for a national monument modeled on the picture, and the sculptor Felix de Weldon was commissioned for the work. The monumental bronze captures the drama, effort, and valor of the moment, its posed, frozen figures reflecting an authentic heroism.

During World War II the language of gesture was used extensively in propaganda posters. An interesting example is J. Howard Miller's poster featuring Geraldine Hoff, a seventeen-year-old metal presser in a Michigan factory (sometimes confused with Norman Rockwell's iconic Rosie the Riveter). Under the headline "We Can Do It!" Hoff was portrayed rolling up her sleeve to play her part in the war effort by taking the kind of manual job traditionally performed by men. Rediscovered in the 1970s the poster, with its gesture of female strength, was given a new lease on life by advocates of women's equality in the workplace.

Women in advertisements were often pictured striking provocative poses, but they seemed coy, even when they were shown in a sexually explicit attitude. In 1990, the ever-provocative singer Madonna was featured on the cover of *Interview* magazine grabbing her crotch, in a photograph by Herb Ritts. With this gesture she earned a place in the history of visual communication.

The stark black-and-white photograph became as much a graphic symbol of women's liberation as the painted image of Geraldine Hoff's raised elbow.

However, Ritts's cover seems quaint compared with Yugoslavian illustrator and graphic artist Mirko Ilic's airbrushed rendition of Alfred Eisenstaedt's famous 1945 photograph, taken on VJ Day, of an American sailor kissing a nurse. In Ilic's version, two women embrace: Justice and the Statue of Liberty. What shocked the editors of the *Village Voice* newspaper, who gave Ilic the assignment for their cover, was the fact that he had tinkered with a patriotic image *and* defiled, so to speak, two beloved American symbols. The illustration ended up inside. ∎

Hear the pictures, see the music

BELOW: The Child (1999), an animated music video by design collective H5 for Alex Gopher, a French DJ. Set in a typographical version of Manhattan, it features a wild car chase in which everything—people, cars, and buildings—is represented as words.

OPPOSITE: Präludium (1919), by Hans Richter, is a Dada-inspired hand-painted film that attempts to visualize the abstract shapes of rhythmic expression, and lets viewers experience the dynamic relationship between lines and curves.

IDEA Nº 51
MOTION GRAPHICS

A new discipline has emerged at the crossroads of film, video, animation, and **film title sequences**, and borrowing from all these genres. "Motion graphics" is neither art nor commerce, but a novel form of communication, one that combines moving effects and sounds. These singing and dancing visuals are to graphic design what the talkies were to silent films. Indeed, it is the addition of an audio component, more than that of movement, that propels graphic design into a temporal dimension.

The earliest experiments with what was then called "musography," or "eye-music," coincided with the commercialization of sound cinema in the mid-1920s. Artists began to turn their paintings, illustrations, and visual ideas into animated motifs that danced on the screen, often to the sound of jazz. German avant-garde artist Hans Richter and Swedish painter Viking Eggeling are considered the first abstract film-makers to translate musical principles into sequences of images. The real breakthrough for graphic artists came with Eggeling's *Symphonie Diagonale* (1924) and Richter's *Filmstudie* (1926), both released with an original soundtrack. Viewed today, these primitive, black-and-white art films feel surprisingly contemporary.

German Expressionist Oskar Fischinger is best known for his brief contribution to the *Fantasia* (1940) sequence set to the Toccata and Fugue in D Minor by J.S. Bach. Even though Disney's cartoon animators tampered with Fischinger's pulsating geometry, diluting his graphic verve with sentimental imagery, the film's slogan "Hear the picture! See the music!" was a perfect description of his art. His rich color palette and inexhaustible inventiveness influenced generations of graphic designers.

Motion graphics came into their own as a popular genre in the 1960s with Saul Bass. Heir to Richter, Eggeling, and Fischinger, he created for Hitchcock a series of semi-abstract film titles that appealed to a wide audience (see p.156). His Bauhaus-inspired graphic style was in perfect sync with the repetitive motifs of composer Bernard Herrmann's suspenseful scores. After him, a growing number of graphic designers ventured into filmmaking, exploring new techniques or perfecting old ones, including clay animation, frame-by-frame action, cinematography, cartooning, and digital animation.

Among the most original recent creations is *Combo* (2009), a giant animated graffiti photographed in stop-motion, the work of Italian mural artist Blu in collaboration with David Ellis, with music by Roberto Carlos Lange. Notable in the special-effects department is 2008's giant ice-skating robot advertising the Citroën R4, developed at Euro RSCG London, its soundtrack a fast-paced song, "Walking Away" by The Egg. And the 1999 music video for French musician Alex Gopher, *The Child*, is an urban tale told in typographical language, made by the small Parisian agency H5 and now a classic.

More and more hybrid animated graphic styles are emerging. Their overbearing audio presence is their most critical feature, though: press mute and the mesmerizing visual effects seem to die away with the sound. ■

The light fantastic

IDEA № 52
NIGHT SPECTACULARS

The City of Light, as Paris is sometimes called, was not only the first metropolis to install street lamps on its main boulevards, it was also the birthplace of commercial neon signs. In the 1920s, Dada poets, jazz musicians, and avant-garde writers were inspired by lighted advertising billboards and saw in them a vivid manifestation of modernity.

In 1932, when François Kollar was commissioned to photograph the Paris street signs for a book celebrating the wonders of electricity, neon illuminations were still a novelty. Kollar had to layer five different images to capture the excitement produced by the accumulation of bright signs against the night sky. The skewed angles of the glittering signboards and marquees emphasized the complexity of the urban landscape.

Comparing the Kollar image with night photographs of the Las Vegas strip taken 20 years later demonstrates how the design of lighted billboards evolved to accommodate their audience. Whereas the Parisian night spectaculars were conceived to be admired by pedestrians walking in dark streets, American signs, for the most part, were conceived to be seen by travelers sitting behind the wheel of a car. Accordingly, the names of the casinos in Las Vegas were displayed on horizontal panels facing the incoming traffic, stacked so as to be easily legible at a glance. Bright silhouettes against the pitch-black desert sky, they were easy to identify from afar.

Today the Las Vegas hotels and casinos, with their extravagant shapes, are replacing the lighted signs as visual landmarks. They have become giant illuminated billboards, their architecture more radiant by night than by day. Around the clock, the strip is now a blinding eyesore. But in Barcelona, Yann Kersalé has proved that night spectaculars can be flashy without being tacky: he designed the illumination of French architect Jean Nouvel's pinecone-shaped Torre Agbar so that after sunset it is transformed into a pixelated beacon.

In 2002, Paris was once again at the forefront of nighttime innovations. It staged an overnight event to showcase the work of conceptual artists for whom darkness is a preferred medium. Called "Nuit Blanche" ("All-nighter"), it drew crowds who ventured after sunset to unlikely venues where they admired installations by the likes of Sophie Calle, Claude Lévêque, or the Chaos Computer Club. It proved so successful it has become a popular yearly happening in Brussels, Madrid, Bucharest, Amsterdam, Rome, and Riga, among other European cities. Today graphic designers the world over join video artists, avant-garde architects, street performers, and lighting mavericks to illuminate the night. ∎

OPPOSITE: Les lumières dans la ville *(1932), by Hungarian photographer François Kollar, captures Paris by night and the wonders of electricity as perceived by the popular imagination.*

BELOW: Arcade *(2003), an installation by German Chaos Computer Club (CCC) for a "Nuit Blanche" art festival, turned one of the façades of the Paris Bibliothèque Mitterand into a giant, interactive, low-resolution monochrome computer screen.*

ABOVE: Agbar Tower *(2005), by Yann Kersalé, a self-described "night architect," transforms the celebrated Barcelona skyscraper by Jean Nouvel into a liquid surface of abstract colored forms.*

Entering the third dimension

IDEA № 53
SHADOW PLAY

One of graphic designers' most enduring obsessions is to try to escape from flat land. They would like to free images and text from the confines of the two-dimensional plane. Hungarian-born László Moholy-Nagy worked all his life to solve this vexing problem. Using photography and controlling light and shadows by means of lenses, mirrors, and filters, he imparted a sense of depth but also movement to otherwise static graphic elements.

In 1929, for the cover of a brochure titled *14 Bauhausbücher* (14 Bauhaus Books), Moholy-Nagy photographed metal type on a composing stick at various angles and collaged the prints together in such a way as to create a strange visual amalgam. Not only did the words pop up, they also defied the laws of perspective. Pairing letterforms with their distorted shadows, he realized, could transform the surface of paper into a window opening on an otherworldly realm.

Moholy-Nagy would have loved the work of American artist Ed Ruscha, whose monochromatic "word compositions" are often associated with an odd play of light and shadows. Inspired by the typographical environment of Los Angeles, his paintings are a cross between **film title sequences** and roadside advertisements. *Mighty Topic*, painted in 1990, is set in blocky capital letters, while its slightly fuzzy shadow appears on the wall behind in upper- and lowercase italic. In addition, it is projected at a steep angle, an optical absurdity. Yet, strangely enough, the image does not give the impression of being erroneous. On the contrary, it comes across as a faithful rendition of the kind of visual incongruities that give so much character to the southern California land-

scape, its billboards, motel signs, and oversized gas station marquees.

In 2004, for a poster for the Châtelet Theater in Paris announcing a production of Richard Wagner's *Tannhäuser*, Rudi Meyer created a ghostly illusion involving type and shadows. A large cutout "T," seen in perspective, projects across the page a long forbidding shadow in the form of a cross. The angle of the "T" and that of the cross do not match, a detail one might not consciously notice yet which contributes to the eerie impression of the composition. Shadow play is often used in scenography, so it is not surprising that during his seven-year tenure designing posters for the Châtelet Meyer created many such graphic illusions. His poster for *Le Fou*, in which bold letters cast crazy shadows on the page, makes a passing reference to *14 Bauhausbücher*, with some of the words arranged on what looks like a composing stick—as they are in the Moholy-Nagy topsy-turvy photograph. The overall impression is both bizarre and wonderful. ■

TOP: 14 Bauhausbücher *(1929) is a photographic* trompe l'oeil *by László Moholy-Nagy, who liked to "manipulate light" using photograms, collages, montages, mirrors, multiple exposures, and strange patterns with projected shadows.*

ABOVE: Mighty Topic *(1990), by American artist Ed Ruscha, can be interpreted as a wry commentary on the "mighty" distortion between what we think we see and what's really there.*

OPPOSITE: Tannhäuser *(2004), by Swiss graphic designer Rudi Meyer for the Châtelet Theater in Paris, uses odd vantage points and an ethereal glare to give the impression that the poster is illuminated by moonlight.*

CHATELET

THEATRE MUSICAL DE PARIS

DIRECTION MUSICALE ▶ Myung-Whun Chung
MISE EN SCÈNE ▶ Andreas Homoki
DÉCORS ET COSTUMES ▶ Wolfgang Gussmann
LUMIÈRES ▶ Franck Evin | Peter Seiffert ▶ TANNHÄUSER
Ildiko Komlosi ▶ VENUS
Petra-Maria Schnitzer ▶ ELISABETH
Ludovic Tézier ▶ WOLFRAM VON ESCHENBACH
Franz-Josef Selig ▶ HERMANN, LANDGRAVE DE THURINGE
Finnur Bjarnason ▶ WALTHER VON DER VOGELWEIDE

Robert Bork ▶ BITEROLF
Nikolai Schukoff ▶ HEINRICH DER SCHREIBER
Nicolas Courjal ▶ REINMAR VON ZWETER
Katija Dragojević ▶ UN JEUNE PÂTRE
Orchestre Philharmonique
de Radio France
Chœur
de Radio
France

Tannhäuser

NOUVELLE PRODUCTION

AVEC LE SOUTIEN DE Pierre Bergé

Richard Wagner

9

13

17

21

28 avril

19 h 30

25 avril

16 h

Design Rudi Meyer — mars 2004

Measuring excellence in design

IDEA № 54
GOOD DESIGN

Like artists, graphic designers struggle to define "Good Design." Who's the judge of the quality of the work they produce? The clients? The public? The critics? Or a jury selected by professional institutions? Art academies, in France in particular, have traditionally promoted and enforced official standards of excellence, as defined by a body of eminent artists. Needless to say, their decisions were often controversial, with antiacademism becoming a genre in its own right.

The concept of "Good Design" was pioneered by the Union des Artistes Modernes (UAM), a Paris organization founded by Robert Mallet-Stevens in 1929 in the aftermath of the watershed 1925 Arts Décoratifs exhibition. The UAM counted among its members Paul Colin, Jean Carlu, A.M. Cassandre, and Charles Peignot. Influenced by Cubism, and advocating a minimalist approach to decoration, these graphic designers were translating, in graphic language, the values and tastes of Modernist architects such as Pierre Chareau, Le Corbusier, and Charlotte Perriand—also UAM members. The anti-ornamentation stance of the UAM artists paved the way for what would soon be called "graphic design" as opposed to "graphic arts." Among poster designers, illustrators, and typographers, clear communication became a benchmark of excellence.

The expression "Good Design" was coined in 1940 by architect Eliot Noyes, who defined it for the *Useful Objects of American Design Under $10* exhibition at the Museum of Modern Art in New York. For him, functionalism and respect for materials were key issues. Between 1950 and 1955, under the curatorial direction of Edgar Kaufmann Jr., MoMA developed the concept of "Good Design" with a series of exhibitions that promoted pure form and equated over-indulgent styling with morally inferior taste. Though critically acclaimed, the shows are seen today as an attempt to institute an "official" aesthetics that celebrated a strict less-is-more sensibility but ignored other important European and American trends, from Streamlining to Surrealism.

The American Institute of Graphic Arts (AIGA), founded in 1914, was one of the first design academies to award medals for excellence in design, but no longer pretends to have the last word on aesthetics. One of the objectives of this professional association is to demonstrate the value of design to the business community.

Poles apart from the AIGA is the Alliance Graphique Internationale (AGI). A club rather than a guild, it is perceived as the arbiter of Good Design worldwide. Founded in Paris in 1951, its members include 400 of the world's leading graphic designers. Yet, like the AIGA, it tries to avoid the moralistic high ground, and distances itself from academism. Its mission statement declares that it "provides for friendship, mutual respect and the enjoyment of the company of the like-minded— even reassurance in the face of a sceptical world." ∎

365:
AIGA Annual Design Exhibition 29

December 11, 2008–February 20, 2009

AIGA National Design Center
164 Fifth Avenue, New York
212 807 1990

www.aiga.org

ABOVE: AIGA 365 poster (2008), designed by K.J. Chun, announced the yearly show that "extends a legacy that began more than 90 years ago and is widely recognized as the most selective statements on design excellence today."

OPPOSITE: Union des Artistes Modernes (1931), a poster designed by Paul Colin, shows a painter's palette as well as an architect's T square to symbolize the alliance of artists and architects who shared early Modernist principles.

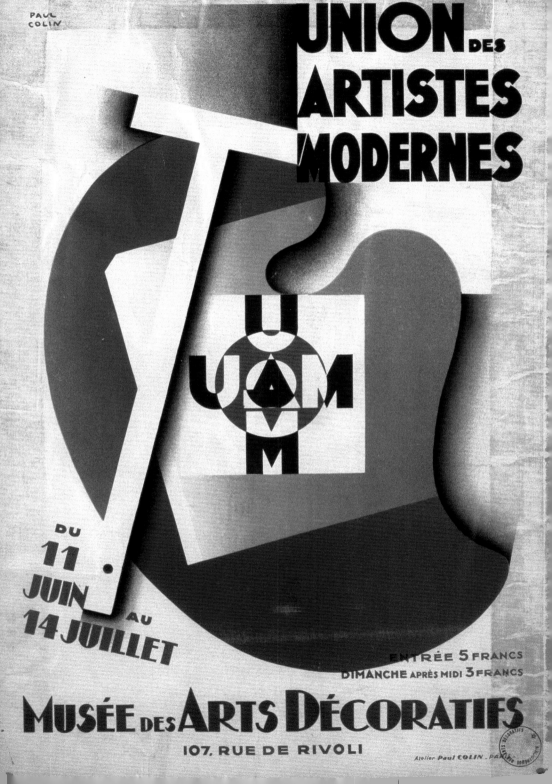

Keeping up to date

FORCED OBSOLESCENCE

The goal of what in the 1920s was called "style engineering" —better known to us now as "forced obsolescence"—was to increase consumer interest and make products more stylish through modern design. Marketers, promoters, and commercial artists believed that profits could be increased with packaging and promoting merchandise given a modernistic veneer. The advertising artist and industrial design pioneer Raymond Loewy referred to the notion as MAYA (Most Advanced Yet Acceptable)—that is, avant-gardisms that did not too shockingly defy popular tastes.

The MAYA principle rejected orthodox modern austerity while promoting colors and shapes that telegraphed a sense of the new and improved. It sought out forms that would not repel the predictably skeptical mass audience yet took the next step. It was a safety valve, of sorts, to prevent, as advertising pioneer Earnest Elmo Calkins stated, the potentially "distressing results in

suddenly attempting to make over a thousand products in new shapes and shades ... that did not harmonize with our ideas of luxury."

The New York World's Fair of 1939–40 was the epicenter of style engineering, with its Trylon and Perisphere centerpiece, at once futuristic yet accessible, modern yet styled to incorporate elements of the past. Modern art elevated advertising art to a higher aesthetic level. For most American designers Modernism was a bag of tricks the artist could use to set an ordinary product apart. Spearheaded by Calkins, artists posed commonplace objects (toasters, refrigerators, coffee tins) against new patterns and at skewed angles; contemporary industrial wares were shown in surrealistic and futuristic settings accented by contemporary typefaces with fashionable names such as Cubist Bold, Vulcan, Broadway, and Novel Gothic.

Modernism offered the aura of cosmopolitan culture and avant-garde style. Combining aspects of psychology with market research, the idea was to control consumers' behavior by feeding them perpetually changing, new,

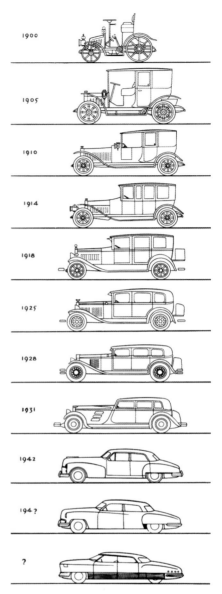

mouthwatering styles. Forced obsolescence was essentially a trick that encouraged redundancy and artificially stimulated growth.

The concept continues. Old is made new. New is made newer. Sometimes new is made old, to give a sense of history or heritage. Coca-Cola, one of the oldest international brands, has retained its original color and logo, but routinely alters its style—sometimes returning agressively to the past, at others switching gears to the future, but, following the MAYA creed, never too avant-garde.

Forced obsolescence is not without inherent flaws, then or now. "We see

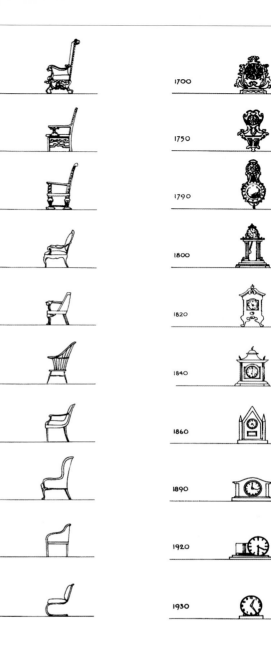

advertisements so 'arty' and artificial, that they neglect to sell the goods," wrote Harry A. Batten, vice president of the first advertising agency in the United States, N.W. Ayer & Son, in 1931. It is risky designing for the future. Technology may make a product obsolete without a second's notice. To engineer style, designers have to toe a fine line between the allure of the unknown and the fear of the unwanted. ∎

OPPOSITE: *La Revue Ford (1928), the cover of a periodical issued by the Ford Motor Company in Paris, was designed to evoke the fashion of the day.*

ABOVE: *Evolution charts (1934) created by Raymond Loewy to show the changes of style in everyday objects and fashion— from elaborate to streamlined.*

Throbbing colors demand attention

IDEA № 56
VIBRATING COLOR

Vibrating color is a derivative of 1960s psychedelic style, which was an ecstatic blend of sex, drugs, rock and roll—and the Bauhaus artist Josef Albers. Albers was leader of courses at Black Mountain College in North Carolina and head of the design program at Yale University in the 1950s. Through his "Interaction of Color" classes he unwittingly helped to launch the vibrating color trend that would typify the psychedelic poster and tie-dye graphic concepts.

Victor Moscoso, who studied under Albers at Yale and was one of vibrating color's founding fathers, claimed that he "likened Albers's famous Color Aid paper exercises to the futility of learning algebra in high school." Yet although color theory drove him crazy, it proved to be an invaluable resource. "Albers's impact really didn't show until the psychedelic poster, when I found myself in a situation where all I had to do was reach back to my dusty shelf, so to speak, and pull out what I had learned."

The dicta Moscoso attributed to Albers were not, however, set in stone. Rather, they were meant to be broken. "Don't use vibrating colors," for example, became "use them whenever you can and irritate the eyes as much as you can." The tenet that lettering should always be legible was changed to "disguise the lettering as much as possible and make it difficult to read."

If Albers was aware of what he had wrought, he might have been nonplussed. Yet Moscoso's use of vibrating color was not too far from Albers's original work. One significant element of Albers's theory was his concept of the relativity of color—that color changes in direct relation to its surroundings and the condition of the viewer. "Until one has the experience of knowing that he is being fooled by color," Albers wrote, "one cannot be expected to be very careful to look at things inquiringly." Color is responsible for producing deceptive and unpredictable effects, with multiple readings of the same hue possible depending on what colors surround it. Vibrating color was an affront to the senses, but was certainly unpredictable and deceptive.

Albers never mixed his colors; they went directly from tube to canvas. He forced his audience into a changing and dynamic relationship with his painting, rather than accepting one visual truth. Moscoso's vibrations forced the viewer into a throbbing and kinetic relationship with the two-dimensional picture surface that fostered a more dynamic relationship than flatness could achieve.

Vibrating color is now one of many tools in the colorist's kit. Evolving from **psychedelia**, jarring color combinations that simulate optical dimensionality are still common in imagery suggesting a youth culture aesthetic. ∎

Interaction of Color   **Josef Albers**

Unabridged text and selected plates
Revised edition

ABOVE: Interaction of Color *(1963), by former Bauhausler Josef Albers, is a seminal book in design practice and a clear influence on Op art. "Never vibrate color" is one of Albers's mantras.*

OPPOSITE: The Doors *(1967), designed by Victor Moscoso, was produced for the Avalon Ballroom in San Francisco, and busted the taboos against using vibrating color.*

mono

Why the language of comic books has been called an invisible art

IDEA № 57

STRIPS AND PANELS

The best storytellers are those who do not tell all, but allow their audience to fill the gaps in the narrative. It is the same with pictures. Comic books are a powerful media because the panels, strung together with a space in between, encourage readers to be mentally alert as they follow the action from frame to frame. The narrow strip of **white space** separating each scene is the invisible track that keeps the plot going.

In the late 1930s, American strips or "funnies," regularly published in newspapers, were occasionally bundled into books that sold at the newsstands for pennies. Though success was not immediate, laying out the individual strips to fill entire pages turned out to be a quantum leap. It took a couple of years for publishers to understand the potential of this new form of pulp fiction. Soon, action heroes fighting homegrown villains and jungle queens wrestling with Nazi spies came to life, jumping in and out of trouble the same way the intrigue was jumping in and out of frames. There was always an exciting variety in the way the action was portrayed, with an **extreme close-up** juxtaposed next to a down shot, or a deep perspective followed by a play of contrasting silhouettes against a solid background. Kids, always impatient to find out what happens next, loved the immediacy of it all.

Unlike storyboards that describe the continuous motion of a camera, comics fly around a scene, showing it from every possible angle. Take away the contrast between the panels, and you no longer have the same medium. It is exactly what Roy Lichtenstein did in the early 1960s when he copied individual panels from comics and turned them into large paintings. He altered the images by depriving them of their original context—a technique used by most Pop artists. Had he kept two panels next to each other with a gutter in between, he could have been accused of plagiarism. What he did was brilliant because he changed everything about the pictures by changing practically nothing. "The gutter plays host to much of the magic and mystery that are at the very heart of comics," wrote Scott McCloud, author of the 1993 cult manual *Understanding Comics.*

There are many enlightened comic book fans among graphic designers, Chip Kidd among them. His infatuation with Batman—more of an obsession, really—is one of the reasons his book covers are so compelling. He knows how to contrast the elements of his layouts in such a way as to create a space between them. Obvious or not, a separa-tion is always present. Kidd likes to pit two visuals against each other, or, more shrewdly, two concepts. The invisible line he draws across the cover of a book is the beginning of the long yarn that runs between the pages. ■

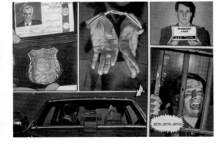

OPPOSITE: *Tarzan (1973), from DC Comics Vol. 26 No. 224, written and illustrated by Joe Kubert. The drastic change of scale between panels is one of the most important characteristics of this graphic language.*

BELOW: *Wild Palms (1990), a comic strip by British illustrator Julian Allen, was a sci-fi murder mystery combining comic-book action with cinematographic imagery. First published in Details magazine, it became a cult miniseries.*

ABOVE: *Chip Kidd's 2002 cover of* Great Neck *by Jay Cantor juxtaposes two images in a manner reminiscent of comic strips. A collector of Batman artifacts and books, Kidd has researched and analyzed why panel-to-panel narratives are so effective.*

A sequential narrative in pictures

IDEA Nº 58

FRAME BY FRAME

The sequential visual narrative is an established tool for storytelling. One of the earliest sequences can be seen on Trajan's Column (113 CE) in Rome, which is also the wellspring of Roman typography, telling a tale of the emperor Trajan through inscribed pictographs and words. Imagery of this kind is, however, ubiquitous throughout antiquity and later history, from Egyptian hieroglyphs to the Bayeux Tapestry in the eleventh century.

A much later evolution of sequential narration can be found in the work of the father of the modern comic strip, the nineteenth-century Swiss author and cartoonist Rodolphe Töpffer, whose short stories were conveyed through word and picture.

Yet the true forerunner of the modern sequence is found in El Lissitzky's *About Two Squares: A Suprematist Tale in Six Constructions* (1922), a picture book

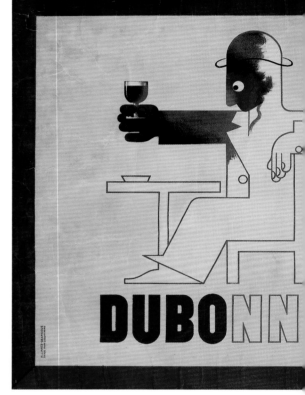

for children published by the De Stijl press of Theo van Doesburg. The narrative centers on the struggle of (literally) a red square to rebuild a new social city in defiance of a threatening black square. The red square symbolizes the new revolutionary order with unlimited possibilities and is in conflict with the black square, which signifies the old order. Their turmoil represents the Russian Revolution of 1917 and the triumph of Bolshevism.

With a more commercial goal in mind, A.M. Cassandre's 1932 sequential advertisement for Dubonnet, *Dubo Dubon Dubonnet* is an image that, while ostensibly static, urges the mind's eye to animate it. Credited with being the first poster designed to be read from a moving vehicle, it was consistent with Cassandre's broader embrace of the serial poster: a group of posters to be viewed in rapid succession to convey a complete idea. In this way the viewer engages more actively with the message than with a single, static image.

Most sequential images are supported by words, but designers have frequently used the wordless (or pantomime) sequence to express a concept—or make a graphic joke. Milton Glaser's *Mozart Sneezes* poster for a music festival at the Lincoln Center in New York makes

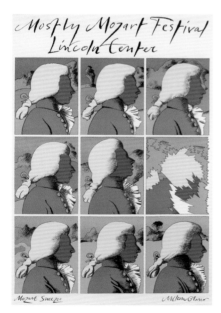

light of the typically serious portrait of Mozart. The sequence of motionless deadpan profiles begins to move gradually in the fifth panel and erupts as a sneeze in the sixth, only to return to the static state in the final three. The absurdity of the concept demanded the form, for a single sneezing Mozart might have been amusing but would have lacked the drama of a crescendo that then returns to stasis. ■

"Designers have frequently used the wordless sequence to express a concept."

The geometry of ideal proportions

IDEA № 59

PERFECT RECTANGLES

Graphic artists have long sought a formula that would help them design perfect rectangles, as elegant as the façade of a beautiful building. Frustrated by standardized page sizes that limit their design solutions, designers have tried in vain to find the graphic equivalent of the "golden ratio," which is allegedly the reason the Parthenon looks so sublime.

Unfortunately, the proportions of a regular poster or book cover are very much squatter than the idealized Renaissance rectangle. The 1:4 ratio (the length divided by the width) of most paper sizes worldwide is a far cry from the taller 1:6 golden ratio. To make a rectangular layout appear slender, German typographer Jan Tschichold suggested that the height of the main copy block be the same as the width of the page. He applied this formula to the design of the inside of his 1935 land-mark book *Typographische Gestaltung* (Typographic Design). But its cover, a masterpiece of understatement, did not follow this rule. By contrast, the cover of the 1974 English translation, issued as *Asymmetric Typography*, was designed by Tschichold almost 40 years after the German edition and showed a greater understanding of how to enhance the beauty of a rectangle.

Tschichold had figured out at last that a perfect rectangle includes an invisible square. The cover of *Asymmetric Typography* came close to perfection because it had not just one but two hidden squares. The distance from the baseline of the first word of the headline to the top of the cover was the same as the width of the book. This square area was practically blank—it was the keystone of the composition. A second square, a couple of inches below, rested on the baseline of the second word of the headline, its upper limit a red bar on the upper right-hand corner. These two interlocking squares subdivided the rectangle into overlapping areas of exquisite proportions.

Square keystones give rectangles monumental proportions. Josef Müller-Brockmann's 1960 *Der Film* poster was a bolder—and earlier—version of Tschichold's cover. Resting on the baseline of the headline, a black square soared upward. The lower portion of the poster served as a solid pedestal for this handsome minimalist layout. In a more recent example, a 2001 poster by Catherine Zask for a production of *Macbeth*, the headline is placed above an ominous black area, like the crenellation on top of a fortress. At the bottom, lines of type form steps leading the eye toward this mysterious black façade as unwelcoming as Macbeth's castle. ∎

OPPOSITE: Der Film *(1960), by Josef Müller-Brockmann, is an imposing use of the Helvetica typeface. Some experts attribute its pleasing design and elegance to the mathematical proportions of its grid, based on the golden ratio.*

BELOW: Asymmetric Typography *(1974), cover of the English translation of Jan Tschichold's* Typographische Gestaltung, *published in 1935. The diminutive "i" in "asymmetric" gives this otherwise severe cover flair.*

ABOVE: Macbeth *(2001), a poster for the Hippodrome Theater in Douai, France, was designed by Catherine Zask, who is known for her ability to suggest drama with simple letterforms. Here the space between the "M" and the "A" is sharp as a dagger.*

Creating a landscape inside our head

IDEA № 60
ABSTRACT GRAPHS

Graphs are by definition abstract: they do not pretend to depict a realistic picture. Their purpose is to project in the mind an image that supports our imagination. Unlike geographical maps, which are based on physical evidence, graphs are simply mental diagrams. However, the boundaries between graphs and maps are progressively blurring. Computer algorithms that allow us to visualize data are turning information into concrete forms that challenge the very notion of abstraction.

It is unclear whether Harry Beck, the creator of the 1933 London Underground map, had heard Alfred Korzybski's famous axiom "The map is not the territory." The two men, both trained engineers, were working thousands of miles apart, the former in London and the latter in America, yet their work was on parallel tracks: independently, yet concurrently, they were interested in charting abstract information.

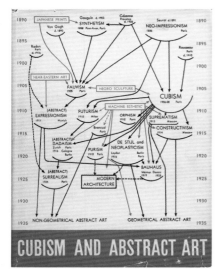

While Polish philosopher and engineer Korzybski charted the way we think, Beck, an Underground employee, charted the way we commute. In his spare time, he devised a topological diagram of the London Underground system that ignored geographical distances and instead proposed an elegant geometrical construct—a lattice-work of straight lines studded with diamonds representing interchanges. Train travelers loved it and adopted it instantly. In fact, they identified so much with the abstract representation of what had been until then a tangled web that the map *became* the territory.

Some graphs are so seductive that they can create their own reality. In 1936 Alfred H. Barr Jr., the young director of the Museum of Modern Art in New York, did just that when he sat down to draw a diagram tracking the various avant-garde movements that had influenced Cubism and Abstract art. A black-and-red vertical timeline that started at the top with the death of Van Gogh in 1890, his chart made the previous 50 years look like a clash of "isms." Downward arrows, connecting the various groups, suggested that art history was moving only in one direc-

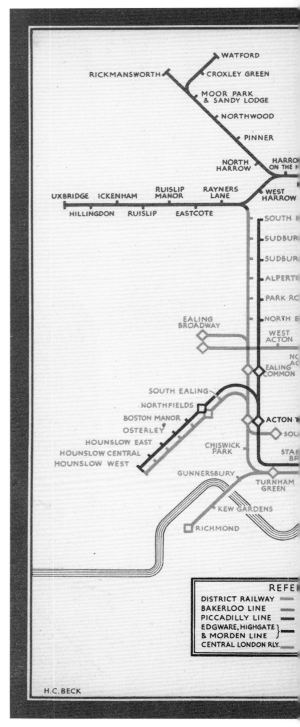

tion, toward the kind of Modernism championed by the museum. Yet it was not a futile exercise: the series of causes and effects that Barr had invented for his graphic demonstration has only been challenged recently.

Thanks to design software, one can now accurately "map out" abstract information. In 2006, to illustrate an article on the complex webs of spy

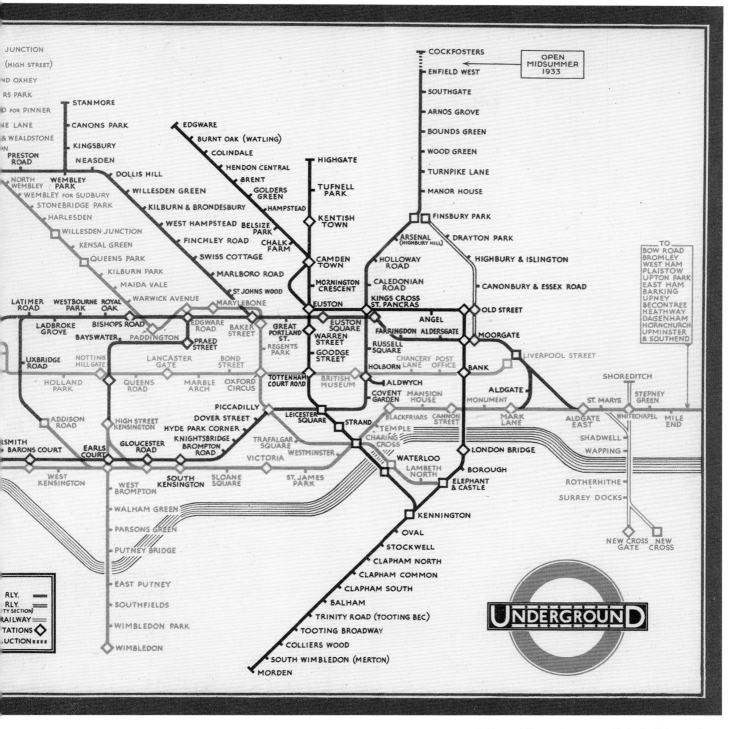

networks for the *New York Times*, Lisa Strausfeld and James Nick Sears, both from Pentagram UK and USA, were able to visualize in 3D the ever-changing relationship between terrorists, events, locations, and attacks. Creating accurate graphs that make it possible to analyze and interpret information is fast becoming a critical skill for graphic designers today. ∎

OPPOSITE: Cubism and Abstract Art *(1936) represents a gallant attempt by Alfred H. Barr Jr., the first director of New York's Museum of Modern Art, to explain how intricate avant-garde art movements influenced each other.*

ABOVE: The London Underground *map (1933), by Henry C. Beck, was the first modern map to treat a complex network of trains and stations as an abstract graph, easy to navigate mentally.*

Pitching right or left gives layouts "that swing"

IDEA № 61
DYNAMIC DIAGONALS

Nineteen-thirty was a tipping point in the history of graphic design. Russian avant-garde graphic artists, who had embraced the Revolution wholeheartedly, began to face persecution by Stalin's regime. Their champion and friend, the Constructivist poet Vladimir Mayakovsky, had committed suicide as a result. Their ideals were crushed and their creativity curbed. Yet 1930 was also the year the Constructivist movement produced one of its last and most celebrated masterpieces.

ABOVE: Pulchri Studio *(2006), a poster by Studio Dumbar for a celebrated art institution in The Hague, Netherlands, uses drops of paint as a metaphor to promote one of the studio's renowned art shows.*

BELOW: Stijl *(2005), logo for a Japanese company by Tota Hasegawa and Simon Taylor, members of the London-based Tomato design collective, makes reference to the Dutch art movement of the same name.*

OPPOSITE: Let's Fulfill the Plans for the Great Projects *(1930) began as a collage of original photographs and newspaper clippings, a technique favored by Constructivist designer Gustav Klutsis. His* Workers *poster is similar.*

Gustav Klutsis's election poster *Workers*, featuring a photocollage of raised hands against a red background, summed up the period in the most spectacular way, while also anticipating the next thing. Dangerously tilted, the pyramid of stacked hands looked as if it would have fallen down were it not for the headlines set at a 45-degree angle. Braced diagonals were a Constructivist trademark, and Klutsis was well acquainted with this type of composition. His design solution for the *Workers* poster was nonetheless innovative, because it did not treat the various graphic elements as building blocks. This was not a highly engineered layout, with all the pieces propping each other up, as was the case in the work of Rodchenko or Lissitzky. In Klutsis's 1930 poster, the thrust of a new vision—one that no longer needed to be tethered to an ideology—paved the way for a freer form of expression.

The dissolution of the Constructivist movement heralded a new era for Modernism. Diagonal layouts were still favored, but they no longer required a graphic infrastructure. In 1935, to illustrate the cover of a type manual for the famous Deberny & Peignot foundry, Maximilien Vox drew the silhouette of a man charging ahead, the movement of his body emphasized by dynamic bands of color slanting across the page. One feels that there was no turning back. In fact, from then on, most designers would choose right-leaning compositions. Unlike Klutsis's poster showcasing workers raising their hands toward the left, Modernist graphic designers, bent on celebrating the future, seemed to be reluctant to pitch lines backward, though some managed to do both.

Recently Studio Dumbar, in the Netherlands, designed a striking poster announcing an annual painting show with a pattern of fat paint drops splashing diagonally across the page. Tipped forward, the tear-shaped drops drip toward the lower back of the poster. Combining up–down with right–left is a technique that gives layouts an irresistible swing. ∎

From Stenso to street

DER WEINER STENTZEL

ABCDEFGHIJKLMNOPQR
STUVWXYZÄÅÂÁÀÃÆÇÇ
ÉÈÊËÏÏÍÑÖÓÔÒÕŒÙÚÛÜ
1234567890""''",,Ş¢ƒ£¥€
%#!¡~*()÷/<=>?:;[\]♥Fi
FL.ABCDEFGHIJKLMNOP
QRSTUVWXYZ¡§¨☺☻♥¿
Ø‰™‹›/—·«»˜

IDEA № 62
STENCIL TYPE

The stencil lettering style has long influenced sophisticated typography and graphic design. In the 1940s Ruth Libauer Hormats and her brother Robert Libauer developed an easy-to-use stencil system, making lettering for signs and displays much easier. Hormats did not invent the stencil (it goes back centuries), but her Stenso guide sheets on heavy cardboard were state-of-the-art long before the computer.

Stensos came in various sizes and families, including Gothic, Old English, Frontier, Modern Script, Art Deco, and even Hebrew. It was a significant departure from the brass stencils used for marking bales and crates in the eighteenth century. Complex paper stencils were also used during the Victorian period, applied to wooden boxes and other surfaces. Stencil lettering, characterized by breaks of negative space between portions of each letter, has never gone out of fashion, and today is one of the tools of the graffiti artist.

During the 1920s Modernist type designers adopted stencil lettering as suggestive of the machine age. Paul Renner's 1929 Futura Black, a variant of his original Futura, was a stylized stencil face. Bauhaus member Josef Albers constructed an avant-garde geometric, lowercase stencil face, while in the 1950s American logo-meister Paul Rand introduced a stencil logo for El Producto cigars based on the stencils printed on burlap tobacco sacks.

The stencil style often signifies something raw or urban. Saul Bass's 1961 *West Side Story* logo, with its silhouetted fire escapes, evokes the look of a tenement. This logo is the inspiration for the trademark of another urban musical, *Rent*, designed by Drew Hodges in 1994. The logo for the 2009 sci-fi film *District 9* helps to suggest the oppression of an off-limits refugee camp for extraterrestrials. A highly visible example is the logo for rappers Public Enemy, designed to suggest a violent urban aesthetic.

Stencil fonts can be high and low typographic art. Milton Glaser's Glaser Stencil, a clean, contemporary, geometric sans serif, has been used on everything from jazz posters to art books. Matt Desmond's Bandoleer is not as pristine as Glaser's, but evokes an alluring coolness. Eben Sorkin's No Step is inspired by lettering he saw on an airplane wing.

The majority of stencil faces are sans serif, but classic serif faces, such as Caslon and Garamond, have been adapted as stencils. Some stencils are gags, like Der Weiner Stentzel, which employs frankfurter-shaped characters cut into pieces (a play on "Wiener sausages" or frankfurters). An authentic stencil is usually a little rough around the edges, but new computer-generated stencils are flawless, except by design. ∎

ABOVE: *Der Weiner Stentzel (2000s) is a contemporary face available through Fontalicious/Font Bros. It consists of uppercase, frankfurter-shaped characters sliced with vertical lines.*

OPPOSITE: *West Side Story (1961), movie poster designed by Saul Bass using stencil lettering to suggest the veneer of a brick tenement building and the kind of type used on the city streets.*

BELOW: *Stenso (1956) was created by the Stenso Lettering Company. These "Roman" and "Gothic" lettering guides were common in elementary schools in the 1950s and 1960s.*

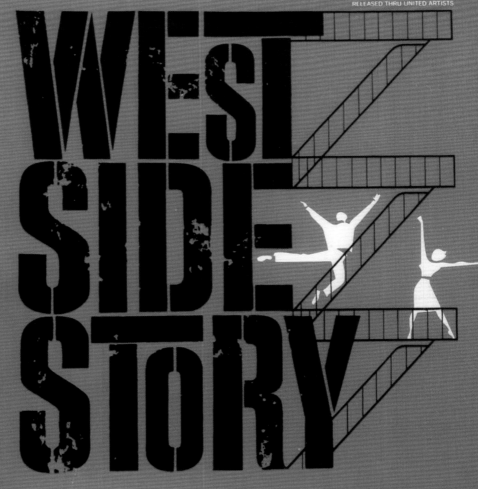

THE SCREEN ACHIEVES ONE OF THE GREAT ENTERTAINMENTS

IN THE HISTORY OF MOTION PICTURES

MIRISCH PICTURES PRESENTS

"WEST SIDE STORY"

A ROBERT WISE
PRODUCTION

STARRING NATALIE WOOD

RICHARD BEYMER   RUSS TAMBLYN
RITA MORENO   GEORGE CHAKIRIS

DIRECTED BY ROBERT WISE AND JEROME ROBBINS   SCREENPLAY BY ERNEST LEHMAN
ASSOCIATE PRODUCER SAUL CHAPLIN / CHOREOGRAPHY BY JEROME ROBBINS
MUSIC BY LEONARD BERNSTEIN   LYRICS BY STEPHEN SONDHEIM
BASED UPON THE STAGE PLAY PRODUCED BY ROBERT E. GRIFFITH AND HAROLD S. PRINCE
BOOK BY ARTHUR LAURENTS
PLAY CONCEIVED, DIRECTED AND CHOREOGRAPHED BY JEROME ROBBINS
PRODUCTION DESIGNED BY BORIS LEVEN   FILMED IN PANAVISION* 70   TECHNICOLOR*
PRESENTED BY MIRISCH PICTURES, INC. / IN ASSOCIATION WITH SEVEN ARTS PRODUCTIONS, INC.
RELEASED THRU UNITED ARTISTS

WEST
SIDE
STORY

The cartoon aesthetic comes of age

IDEA Nº 63
COMIC LETTERING

A splash panel is an introductory frame to a comic strip, designed to announce the visual narrative. Invested with more graphic bravado than a normal title page, it derives from the contoured letters of nineteenth-century sign painting, with their bold, colorful drop shadows. Circus poster alphabets made from ornamented bold slab-serif typefaces, such as Tuscans and Egyptians, are also an influence.

ABOVE: Man from Utopia *(1972), written, drawn, and designed by Rick Griffin, employs all the conventions of classic comic lettering, but also features a made-up language handwritten in a comic style.*

OPPOSITE: Cheap Thrills *(1968), the cover for the Janis Joplin and Big Brother album illustrated by Robert Crumb, is actually the back cover. The front was scrapped and the splash panel title was added to the back.*

In 1936 Howard Trafton designed a fat brush-lettered typeface he called Cartoon, which is accepted as the seminal comics font—it effectively introduced comic lettering to advertising and graphic design. There is a theatrical quality to this style of lettering. It jumps off the page—or stage—with all the melodrama of an acrobat on the high wire. It has the exaggerated quality of an operatic scene. Comic lettering is meant to "splash" on the consciousness with quirky allure: that is its goal.

Comic lettering usually parallels the drawing style and underscores the look of a specific comic strip. Robert Crumb's unmistakably bawdy lettering draws inspiration from the 1920s and 1930s comic strips that inform his absurdist tableaux. Rick Griffin's has the mystical aura of an illuminated manuscript. And Chris Ware builds on the foundation of hand-lettered advertising typefaces usually found in the back of vintage comics (see p.176). Each method is different, yet ultimately derives from similar roots.

Comic lettering is also genre-specific. For example, superhero comics use alphabets suited to the subject-matter that are loud, demonstrative, and masculine. The same is true for war, horror, and sci-fi, while romance comics use more "feminine" letters with swashes and curlicues. Certain lettering styles are emblems for their themes, but since the advent of "**underground comics**" (with their counterculture themes) in the late 1960s, comic lettering has drawn from all sources in a mixmaster of styles.

Comic lettering almost always pays homage to the past. The San Francisco underground artists were passionate about slab-serif wood type and curvilinear Art Nouveau motifs. These applications were not simply copied verbatim, but massaged into a comic form. Rick Griffin was among the most innovative of all these letterers. In addition to designing the original psychedelic curlicue swash logo for *Rolling Stone* (no longer used), he developed hand-drawn typography that reflected a calligraphic eccentricity, page after page of drawn letters with symbolic references and meanings. British comic artist and type designer Rian Hughes incorporates the comic aesthetic into his raucous display faces. In his hands type is both retro and forward-looking (see p.75).

With hand lettering making a steady comeback as a reaction to digital precision, comic-derived faces are ever more available to designers looking for a quirky character. Quirkiness will never come bundled or straight from the box: it must come from the hand. ∎

"Superhero comics use alphabets that are
loud, demonstrative, and masculine."

Nothing is sacred

BELOW LEFT: Der Spiegel (2002), illustrated by Jean-Pierre Kunkel, titled "The Bush Warriors—America's Crusade Against Evil," was designed as a critique of the decision to go to war in Iraq. It was accepted as a heroic characterization.

BELOW RIGHT: Der Spiegel (2008), titled "The Bush Warriors—End of the Performance," was a parody of a parody, and commentary on the disastrous outcome of the heroics.

OPPOSITE: Red Monarch (1983), a film poster designed by John Gorham with Howard Brown and photographed by Tony Evans, barbs a classic official portrait of Josef Stalin.

IDEA № 64
PARODY

Parody is arguably the most common form of visual satire. Although it dates back centuries, the act of altering a well-known image into a **visual pun** or other type of graphic witticism has largely been practiced during the second half of the twentieth century. The rise of consumerism sparked advertising campaigns that were at once embraced by the public yet became the butt of jokes.

One of the seminal purveyors of "modern" parody was American comic magazine *Ballyhoo*, published during the late 1920s and '30s, which was entirely devoted to send-ups of national advertising and brand campaigns. In addition to popular culture, the most common parodies are of famous images— art, photography, sculpture—that have universal recognition.

It is necessary that the audience be acutely aware of the original to appreciate the ironic transformation. Parodic wit is a fragile balance of recognition and surprise. When *National Lampoon* ran a virtually exact replica of Van Gogh's famous severed-ear self-portrait on its cover, the viewer at first saw the original with the bandage over the ear. On second glance it was clear that Van Gogh was holding the ear, which is not, of course, in the original.

Parodies are not always designed to insult the target but often, rather, to trigger recognition among the audience —the satisfaction that they are in on the joke. Few things are riper for parody than illustrious works of art, and few works of art are more well known than Leonardo's *Mona Lisa*. Her iconic smile is the subject of such intensive, often comic, homage that the image has been catapulted into the vernacular. When Rick Meyerowitz created "Mona Gorilla" as a cover of *National Lampoon* he launched a mini-fashion for famous figures in art as animals.

Great works of avant-garde design are also in the parodist's cross-hairs. Dozens of works from El Lissitzky's Constructivist *Beat the Whites with the Red Wedge* of 1919 (see p.68) to Milton Glaser's 1966 *Dylan* poster are probably as frequently satirized as Picasso and Dalí.

The German magazine *Der Spiegel*'s 2002 parody of the then U.S. President George W. Bush and his war advisers placed Bush in the role of Rambo, and transformed his cabinet into other mythic warriors. But parody here was a double-edged sword. What the German editors intended as a satirical insult on the eve of the Iraq War, which they opposed, was perceived as a high compliment by the maker of that war. Parody, therefore, is often in the eye of the beholder.

Parody seems easy—just copy something famous and give it a twist—but is one of the most difficult methods to achieve successfully. If the parodist takes too many liberties, then the parody will suffer; conversely, if the material is not tweaked enough, the result could read as plagiarism. ∎

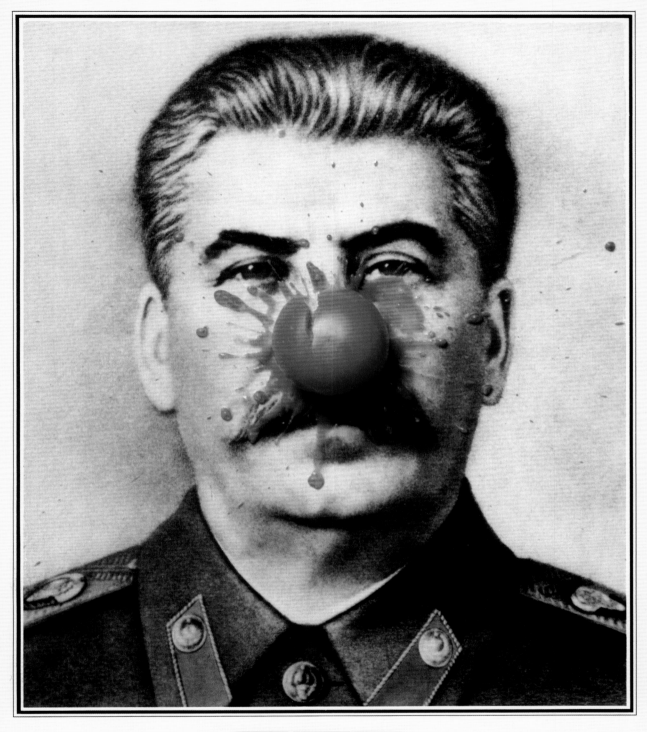

AN ENIGMA PRODUCTION
FOR GOLDCREST
★
COLIN BLAKELY
★
DAVID SUCHET
★
SPECIAL APPEARANCE BY
CARROLL BAKER

EXECUTIVE PRODUCER
DAVID PUTTNAM
SCREENPLAY BY
CHARLES WOOD
BASED ON THE STORIES OF YURI KROTKOV
★
PRODUCED BY
GRAHAM BENSON
DIRECTED BY
JACK GOLD

Create more, waste less

SUSTAINABLE PACKAGING

Paper production and printing are among the largest and most polluting industries in the world, affecting not only trees and land use but also air quality and water resources. For printers, pollution prevention is good business and can save a lot of money by reducing waste; their guidelines often recommend that graphic designers come up with more efficient layouts, pick nontoxic inks, and specify recycled stock. Yet these are only palliative measures. Sustainable thinking is a different story.

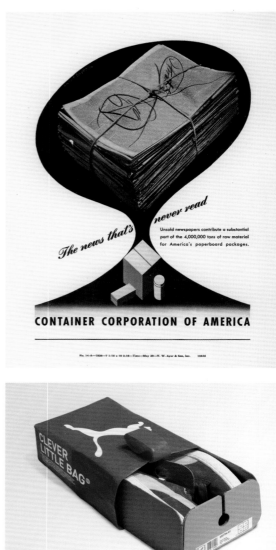

The real challenge is much more complicated than making sense out of environmental paper labels or de-inking recycled newsprint. One of the main causes of pollution is packaging. Reducing packaging will reduce environmental damage, but it requires rethinking the way we consume.

Packaging as we know it—convenient yet wasteful—was foisted on the U.S. housewife in the aftermath of World War II by corrugated-carton manufacturers looking to convert what had been a lucrative war industry into a peacetime business. Container Corporation of America (CCA) played a crucial role in this restructuring of our consumer habits by convincing businessmen that single items presented in graphically arresting boxes would be more profitable than unpackaged goods sold in bulk. Unfortunately, a side effect of the manufacturers' profits is the vast quantity of trash that packaging produces.

The best chance we have of reducing pollution from packaging might be to bring to bear the very same technique that was used by CCA: introduce a new aesthetic. CCA's art director, Herbert Bayer, had championed modern design. We need to propose as revolutionary a creative approach. Corrugated cardboard and molded paper pulp, unbleached, are some of the materials that most inspire graphic designers; today's art students come up with eco-friendly packaging that turns mailing packages into clever products.

A number of established designers are already coming up with alternative products that not only minimize waste but also turn trash into treasure: biodegradable cotton-based paper with seeds in it that you plant instead of throw away; light fixtures packaged in cardboard boxes that become lamps; tiles made of recycled paper mixed with postindustrial crushed glass or fly ash from coal.

Another approach is to design packages so that style- or fashion-conscious people cannot bear to throw them away, a tactic used by design-aware companies such as Puma or Apple: opening the various containers for the products is a gratifying process of discovery that is an integral part of the brand experience. For its Kindle e-book reader, Amazon combined two concepts: a product whose purpose is to do away with paper altogether packaged in a slender, minimal, polished cardboard box. ∎

TOP: The News That's Never Read (1939), an advertisement by Bayer for Container Corporation of America, one of the first U.S. companies to sponsor a newspaper recycling scheme.

ABOVE: Puma's Clever Little Bag (2010), by San Francisco designer Yves Béhar from Fuseproject, reduces the waste in traditional shoeboxes by wrapping a single-folded sheet of cardboard in a reusable PET bag.

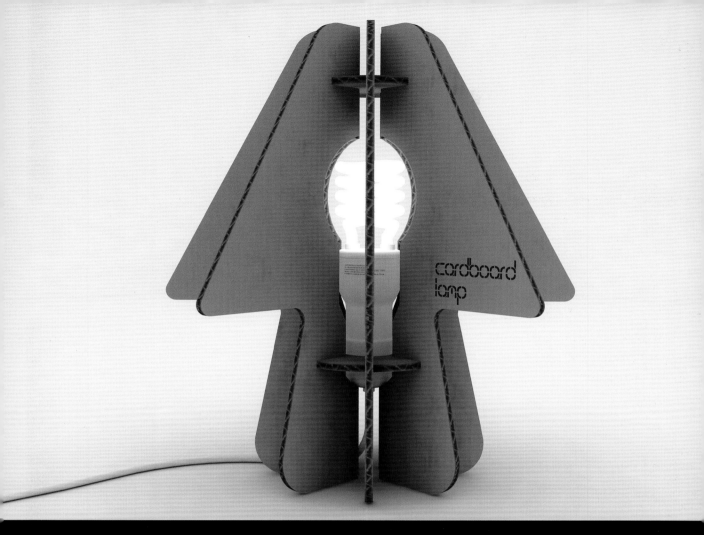

"Alternative products that not only minimize waste but also turn trash into treasure."

Cardboard Lamp (2010), by Mexican designer Luis Morales, is assembled from cutout shapes from the box itself. It holds an eco-friendly lightbulb.

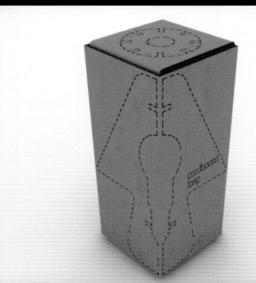

PARCE QUE LA PAUVRETÉ et LA PRÉCARITÉ SONT INADMISSIBLES AIDEZ-NOUS AGISSONS

www. secourspopulaire.asso.fr

MERCI

SECOURS POPULAIRE FRANÇAIS

Atelier de création graphique, Pierre Bernard 2005

Making a difference

IDEA № 66
PUBLIC SERVICE CAMPAIGNS

Noncommercial causes can prompt brilliant advertising campaigns, evidence that most creative individuals are eager put their talents at the service of the public good.

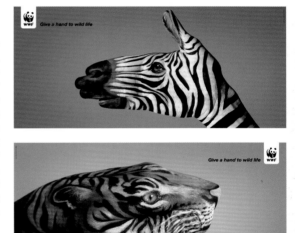

In the United States, the Advertising Council (Ad Council), founded in 1941 to support war propaganda, has become a powerful organization that coordinates and distributes public service announcements of national relevance. With the same flair with which it sponsored the wartime "Rosie the Riveter" crusade, the Ad Council has since masterminded such high-profile campaigns as "Keep America Beautiful" against pollution and litter, and "Smokey the Bear" to fight forest fires.

Whether or not these now historic campaigns made a real difference is hard to tell, but many of the phrases and characters they used have enriched the American vernacular. Such slogans as "The toughest job you'll ever love" (Peace Corps) or "You can learn a lot from a dummy" (crash-test dummies for Buckle Up For Safety) came from ad men and women who were able to unleash their inventiveness to elevate the public debate.

In 2009, to support the United Nations conference for Climate Control in Copenhagen, international advertising agencies such as Ogilvy, Ketchum, and Havas collaborated to create the campaign "Hopenhagen." Combining color photography with smart, manic graffiti, the posters suggested that the initiative was a grass-roots movement, even though it was paid for by advertising agencies.

Indeed, not all "noncommercial" advertising falls into the public service category. "Cause marketing" is a strategy that links a brand to an altruistic pursuit, such as Breast Cancer Awareness or Voter Registration, and results in ad campaigns that look as if they are performing a public service though they are in fact promoting a label or a trademark. Most of the for-profit businesses that choose this advertising tactic are linking their effort to a not-for-profit organization, giving part of their proceeds for a particular promotion to a legitimate charitable concern, like the Statue of Liberty Restoration project (American Express) or the American Heart Association (Cheerios).

A third kind of public service campaign is sponsored directly by charitable organizations, which commission graphic designers or advertising agencies of their choice. Among the most arresting is the French Secours Populaire campaign, whose visual identity is the work of Pierre Bernard, and the stunning ads for the World Wide Fund for Nature (WWF). ∎

OPPOSITE: Secours Populaire *(2010), the poster for an ongoing campaign to promote a French antipoverty charitable institution, is the work of Pierre Bernard, one of the founding members of the Grapus collective.*

ABOVE: Give a Hand to Wild Life *(2008), by Saatchi & Saatchi Simko agency in Geneva, is a series of clever and beautiful photographs of human hands camouflaged as wild animals by bodypainter Guido Daniele.*

If there be a country
which cannot stand
any one of these tests—

a country where *knowledge* cannot be *diffused*
without perils of mob law and statute law;

where *speech* is not *free;*

where the *post office* is *violated,* mail bags
opened, and letters tampered with;

where *public debts* and *private debts* outside
of the state are *repudiated;*

where *liberty* is attacked in the primary
institution of social life...

where the *laborer* is not *secured* in the earnings
of his own hand;

where *suffrage* is not free or equal—

that country is, in all these respects, not civil,
but barbarous; and no advantage of soil,
climate, or coast can resist
these suicidal mischiefs.
(*Civilization,* 1862)

R Waldo Emerson

Artist: herbert bayer

CONTAINER CORPORATION OF AMERICA

A company's image goes beyond its products

IDEA № 67
BRANDING CAMPAIGNS

Graphic design does not always serve lofty ideals. Often cited as being one of the most inspired and high-minded branding exercises, the "Great Ideas of Western Man" campaign was in fact an indoctrination program to convince American manufacturers that packaging was their most persuasive sales tool. A breakthrough in terms of marketing strategy, it demonstrated that promoting the image of a company rather than its products or services is sometimes the smartest business decision.

OPPOSITE: **Great Ideas of Western Man** *(1942–72) was a campaign designed to establish CCA as an innovative packaging company. In this example, Herbert Bayer illustrated a quote by Ralph Waldo Emerson. These were called "institutional" ads because they did not sell a specific product.*

ABOVE: *TRW (c. 1990), designed by Don Ervin. Simplicity yet recognizability is the key to an efficient corporate logo and identity system. Using two colors, this is the mark of an aerospace company that was defunct in 2002.*

Launched by packaging giant Container Corporation of America (CCA), the campaign, which ran for more than 30 years, was the brainchild of its president Walter Paepcke and design director Herbert Bayer. From 1942 to 1972, its full-page advertisements were a regular feature of upscale magazines such as *Life* and *Fortune*. Readers, many of them businessmen, were treated to dazzling examples of graphic designers' and illustrators' work. The ads were created by the likes of Cassandre, Alvin Lustig, Lester Beall, Herbert Matter, Alexey Brodovitch, Paul Rand, and Leo Lionni, as well as famous artists such as Ben Shahn, James Rosenquist, Joseph Cornell, and Leonard Baskin. Bayer had invited them to illustrate quotes by writers, politicians, and philosophers (a prestigious list that included Saint Paul, Thomas Jefferson, Benjamin Disraeli, and John Ruskin). Committed to the idea that great packaging design could boost sales and increase profit, the company used this oblique yet fantastically effective campaign as part of a wider marketing offensive.

At around the same time, another major packaging and printing company, Westvaco, used a similar strategy to grow its market share. Art director Bradbury Thompson was commissioned to design the company's in-house magazine, *Westvaco Inspirations*. Instead of relentlessly flaunting the accomplishments and technical expertise of the company's clients, Thompson was allowed to turn the publication into something of a personal project, one that reflected his Modernist taste and unorthodox graphic sensibility. His quirky inventiveness, which he demonstrated with brio in more than 50 issues of *Inspirations*, served to illustrate Westvaco's unique brand positioning and innovative vision.

A comparable marketing strategy today is the "Different Values" campaign of HSBC, a banking institution with a global footprint. In 2007, it launched a series of concise ads that smartly alluded to the complexity of doing business internationally. The same photographs were captioned with different, and sometimes opposing, one-word interpretations. Deployed in major airports worldwide, the campaign highlighted the fact that nothing should ever be taken for granted, an unconventional message for a bank. But the key to establishing a brand—any brand—is to be explicitly different. ∎

Transparent colors add depth

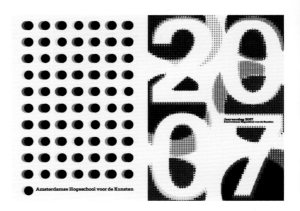

IDEA № 68
LAYERING AND OVERPRINTING

The smell of ink can act as a creative trigger. Stepping into a printer's shop or doing a press check is not only a heady sensory experience, it also spurs the imagination. Gooey, creamy, sticky—inks seem finger-licking good. Recently a number of designers have been taking ink-stained printer's proofs and reusing them as background to print unrelated artwork. The result is known as a palimpsest.

ABOVE: The Amsterdam Hogeschool's art school identity system (2007), developed by Thonik, uses overlapping colored dots to differentiate its various departments, a concept that allows for endless kaleidoscopic combinations.

BELOW: The Second Man (1956), a book jacket by Paul Rand for Alfred A. Knopf, portrays a man and his shadow as two overlapping silhouettes, creating an impression that both figures are ghosts.

OPPOSITE: La Fête de la Musique (2009), a poster by French graphic designer Fanette Mellier, advertises a yearly worldwide musical event with a playful jumble of notes—an allusion to the fact that many of the performers at this popular festival are amateurs rather than professionals.

Layering images to create a complex picture is not a new fad, though. Prehistoric painters, using their hands as stencils, often created colorful palimpsests on the walls of caves.

Making a graphic arts publication for a paper company is the closest thing to being invited to play with inks. When, after World War II, Bradbury Thompson was given the assignment to design *Westvaco Inspirations* for the West Virginia pulp and paper company Westvaco, he set out to demonstrate the versatility of

the four-color process by layering images in yellow, magenta, cyan, and black. Sometimes he would show progressive proofs to exemplify how each additional layer worked when superposed over the preceding one. Other times he would repeat the same silhouette in each of the four basic colors, either tilted or overlapping, to form strange and intriguing patterns. His most memorable compositions are visual palimpsests, such as his "Liberty Bell" layout, where he printed color cutouts of the bell swinging over an old engraving of the cross-section of a campanile.

Thompson was capitalizing on the brilliance of transparent inks. Other designers create the illusion of layering with opaque color blocks that change color where they overlap. Such is the case of an illustration by Paul Rand for Edward Grierson's 1956 novel *The Second Man*, a minimalist design representing the white outline of a man encountering his black shadow. The area where the two figures coincide is an ominous red. The more you stare at the image, the more complicated it looks: you can never figure out which of the two figures is in front, or which one casts a shadow on the other.

Mixing transparent and opaque ink is yet another way to create a sense of depth. In 1998, Paris-based designer Malte Martin launched *Agraf*, a limited-edition magazine printed on discarded printer's proofs whose original design was only partially obliterated by a murky brown ink. Clearly visible under a thin color-wash, other parts of the older background were allowed to stand out and interact with the newly printed matter. Some pages were varnished, others were not. The result is a publication so saturated with layered imagery that it looks, years later, as if the ink is still drying. ■

Fête
de la
musique
21 juin
2008

Graphisme: Rudolfe Pollier. Impression: Imprimerie Moderne de l'Est.

www.fetedelamusique.culture.fr

Define the problem, design the solution

IDEA № 69
DESIGN THINKING

How to tackle creative problem-solving is a problem in itself. In the mid-1950s, leading ad man Alex Faickney Osborn wrote a book about brainstorming, *Applied Imagination*, that described how to generate more productive design ideas by harnessing the imagination of a group of professionals. Today, designing in teams—but not by committee—is still a challenge, even though new names such as "design thinking," "concept design," or "integrated design strategy" show a new approach.

BELOW: The Integrated Studio *(2010) is one of the ways Richard Eisermann, strategic director for Prospect, a London-based design consultancy, explains to his clients how to create "great customer experiences."*

ABOVE: The Power of Your Mind *(1952), cover of a booklet by Alex F. Osborn, an advertising executive who is considered the inventor of the brainstorming technique.*

OPPOSITE: Design Thinking Digest *(2010) is the cover of the program for a symposium of the National Library Board in Singapore, in which designers, journalists, and business executives were invited to evaluate the various benefits of Design Thinking.*

For brainstorming to be effective, a very specific problem must be identified in advance, before being presented to the group. Rational as it seems, this turns out to be a thorny issue. Who has the expertise to isolate the "problem" to be solved, the client or the agency? Even though brainstorming techniques, which involve a number of stringent rules to keep the group focused, can produce interesting ideas, the ideas are little use if the problem they address is the wrong one. In the 1990s, a new discipline, called "design strategy," proposed that creative teams sit down with a number of experts to discuss not *how* to solve a given problem, but *what* problem should be solved.

Around the world, a new breed of design studios began to offer strategic services, including large agencies in the UK such as Live/Work, Arup, and Prospect Design. In the Netherlands, Fabrique, Total Identity, and EdenSpiekermann initiated "dialogues" with companies about their brands, communication, and product development opportunities. All over Europe and in North America, studios large and small working at the intersection of design, business, and social science became the norm.

Roger Martin, dean of the Rotman School of Management, Toronto, is a pioneer of "integrative thinking." He advocates new cross-disciplinary tactics requiring that experts from various fields be hired as research consultants on specific design "missions," "audits," or "evidence-gathering" tasks. Talent is outsourced in order to study every aspect of a project. One of the advantages of this Design Thinking approach is to demystify, for clients, the creative process, and help them feel comfortable with the resulting proposals.

Recently, using the Design Thinking approach, a number of American companies (among them Gap, Pepsi, and Tropicana) have attempted to upgrade their logos—with disastrous results. Although backed by often compelling arguments and market research, the changes were ridiculed by customers who felt that they were arbitrary, and evidence of corporate banality. They had a point: excellence in design cannot be achieved by a formula. The logo debacles threatened to undo the work of years during which graphic designers and creative agencies persuaded clients to think of design as a collaborative process.

Design Thinking is a great tool as long as one remembers that it defines *what* should be done, not *how* to do it. Group creativity techniques, though critical in the preliminary design phase, cannot replace a moment of inspiration in the making of an original work. ■

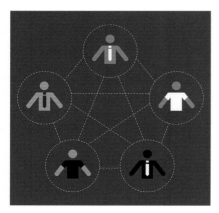

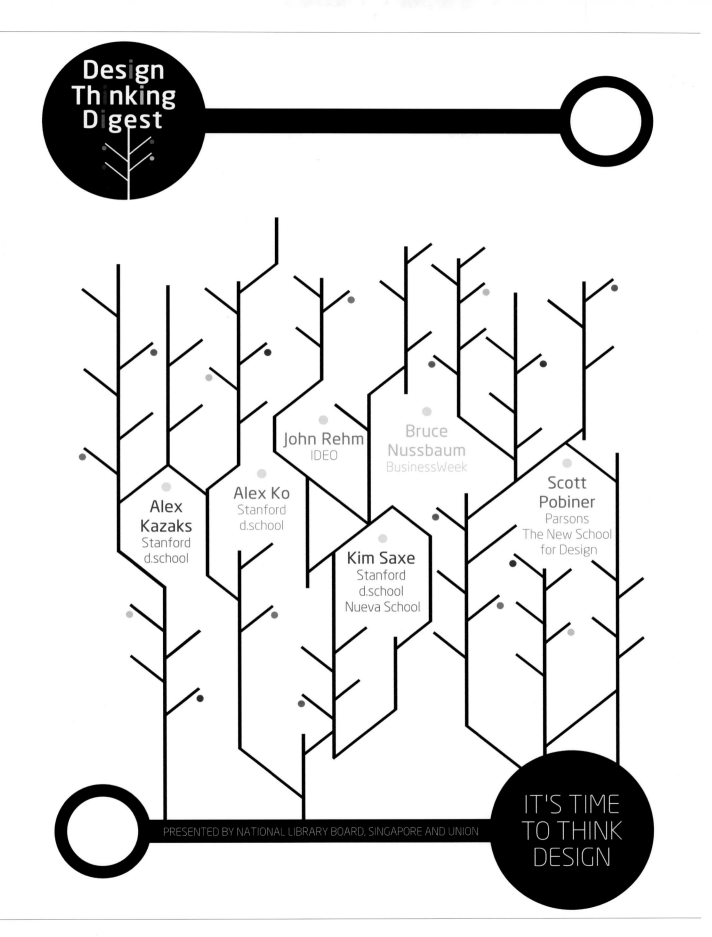

Design Thinking Digest

John Rehm
IDEO

Bruce Nussbaum
BusinessWeek

Scott Pobiner
Parsons
The New School
for Design

Alex Ko
Stanford
d.school

Alex Kazaks
Stanford
d.school

Kim Saxe
Stanford
d.school
Nueva School

PRESENTED BY NATIONAL LIBRARY BOARD, SINGAPORE AND UNION

IT'S TIME
TO THINK
DESIGN

Artistic alignment

IDEA № 70
THE GRID

Grid structures arguably date back millennia to narrative inscriptions in Egypt, where hieroglyphs told a visual story. But that is ancient history. In the annals of twentieth-century Modern design, the grid has been afforded a sanctified status—the design invention of the age. Its foremost platform, the Swiss International Style of grid-locked design and typography, defines the postwar 1940s and 1950s.

ABOVE: Grid Systems in Graphic Design *(1961), written and designed by Josef Müller-Brockmann, is one of the manuals for the Swiss Style method of grid systems.*

BELOW: 10 Zürcher Maler *(1956), art catalog cover designed by Emil Ruder, is typographically constructed on a grid that is at once readable and abstract.*

OPPOSITE: Vormgevers *(1968), poster for the Stedelijk Museum in Amsterdam designed by Wim Crouwel, builds its entire typographic structure on a tight grid.*

During the early twentieth century, even before the Bauhaus (the birthplace of the Modern grid), grids were found on everyday printed matter, including invoices, ledgers, and other materials used for tabulation. Yet once introduced as the panacea for graphic design clarity, rather than a simple organizational and compositional tool, the grid became a target of both love and hate. It was loved for bringing order to disorder and hated for purportedly locking designers into rigid confines.

The truth lies somewhere in between. Swiss designer Josef Müller-Brockmann, author of *Grid Systems in Graphic Design* (1961), warned: "the grid system is an aid, not a guarantee. It permits a number of possible uses and each designer can look for a solution appropriate to his personal style. But one must learn how to use the grid; it is an art that requires practice." The notion of "art" is key. To avoid using the grid as a template for conformity, aesthetic and conceptual choices must be made. To trigger excitement using the grid it is not enough to line things up: active design decisions are required. "The grid, like any other instrument in the design process, is not an absolute. It should be used with flexibility, and when necessary it should be modified or abandoned completely for a more workable solution," wrote Allen Hurlburt, in *The Grid: A Modular System for the Design and Production of Newspapers, Magazines, and Books* (1982).

Among Müller-Brockmann's many grid-based posters is his 1960 *Der Film* poster for the Kunstgewerbemuseum Zürich (see p.124), a very minimal typographic design that shows how locking the basic informational type to the grid anchors the more demonstrative display typography. The grid invisibly holds all the elements together in a precise way, not in a stranglehold but as adhesive.

Functionality was the hallmark of grid system design, and few designers used it more effectively than Czech-born Ladislav Sutnar, who as design consultant for the Sweets Catalog Service was tasked to bring clarity to usually unruly hardware catalogs. His distinct grid structures allowed the user easily to locate items and corresponding details such as prices and sizes. In this way the grid is as versatile as the designer who uses it, and as graphically vibrant as the message that is presented. ∎

Making the brand bigger than the product

IDEA № 71

BRAND NARRATIVES

Creating a brand is not the same as designing a corporate identity program, though the confusion still persists. A brand is a great deal more than a logo, more than a graphic universe, more even than the sum total of all its visuals, slogans, and ancillary products. A brand is an invisible entity, a story in the mind of consumers, a sense of excitement at the prospect of seeing, touching, or acquiring a particular thing. In other words, a brand is a compelling story.

In the mid-1950s, the tobacco company Philip Morris decided to change the "gender" of its Marlboro cigarettes in order to appeal to a male audience. After a couple of episodes of trial and error, it selected the cowboy as the quintessential Marlboro smoker. Advertising agency Leo Burnett commissioned a series of photographs of a handsome cowboy on location in the western United States, subliminally linking the cigarette to the powerful myth of the American frontier. The Marlboro Man was cast as a rancher with movie-star appeal, and the ads looked like stills from a major motion picture. Eventually advertisements were aired on television, with the theme from *The Magnificent Seven* as the soundtrack. Sold worldwide until 1999, the red-and-white cigarette pack was synonymous with rugged masculinity.

For brands to be successful, they must entertain as much as motivate. In 1984, Apple introduced its first personal computer with an advertisement inspired by *1984*, George Orwell's novel that described a world dominated by Big Brother, and by *Metropolis*, the 1927 futuristic film by Fritz Lang. For its college-educated target audience, the short clip was a parable that needed no explanation. It did not have to spell out

that Big Brother represented IBM, or that the hammer-swinging female who had come to liberate the drones was Apple's new personal computer. Brand stories like this one, which tap into our shared cultural references, can save the trouble of constructing complex and costly advertising fantasies.

The mandate of a brand is also to get people to the cash register. The experience of spending money is one that must complete the story—that must be perceived as its happy ending, whether it is in a store, where you can interact directly with the brand, or online, where the denouement of a brand scenario is expressed in a couple of clicks. The Google logo, which is morphed regularly to reflect local holidays or world events, can be construed as a live chronicle of what is happening around the globe. Its brand functions as a vast social network, as the gossipy center of the online community. ■

OPPOSITE: *Marlboro Man (1954–90s), the iconic figure for Marlboro cigarettes, was conceived by Leo Burnett as a symbol of rugged masculinity to counter the impression that filtered cigarettes were "feminine."*

ABOVE: *Google Doodles (1998), variations of the official Google logo, celebrate special events. The first doodle was in honor of the Burning Man Festival in 1998. Since, numerous competitions have provided endless entertaining variations. From top: Albert Einstein's 124th Birthday (2003), Dizzy Gillespie's 93rd Birthday (2010), 50th Anniversary of Understanding DNA (2003), and First Day of Summer (2010).*

The luxury of less

IDEA № 72
WHITE SPACE

In art as in life, white space is the ultimate luxury. The most recent architectural addition to the Museum of Modern Art in Manhattan is a superb example of the way acres of empty white walls can be used to make a superlative statement. On the page, white space works the same way. It signifies that you have plenty of room to spare. It frames images with an aura of inaccessibility. The less crowded a magazine layout, the more elitist its attitude.

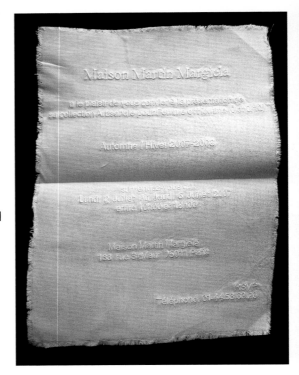

One of the first magazine art directors to realize that a blank surface could have as much impact as a printed one was Alexey Brodovitch. His *Harper's Bazaar* layouts in the 1950s treated white paper as if it was an electromagnetic field, with blocks of type and photographs charged with positive and negative energy. But never was white space as saturated with gravitational pull as in his layouts for *Observations*, a book of Richard Avedon's photographs. The arrangement of black and white electrons across each spread was so powerful that it prompted Truman Capote to describe the book's design as "boldness bordering on revolution."

Because of its upscale connotation, white space was vilified in the 1970s as too elitist. Editorial design strived to look trashy to emulate the British Fleet Street tabloids that were thriving on mass-market celebrity gossip, packing every square inch of space on their pages with garish headlines and lurid paparazzi shots. The Postmodernists had yet another reason to spurn white space: they associated it with the radicalism of purist architect Le Corbusier, the less-is-more diktat of International Style advocates, and the ideological minimalism of graphic designers such as Jan Tschichold or Sandberg. Only in the late 1980s did a handful of art directors, Neville Brody and Fabien Baron among them, dare to reintroduce white space in magazines, chiefly on opening spreads, to show off their typographical wit.

White space has yet to make a comeback in the popular press. It is now principally restricted to art books, where it is supposed to provide a respite for the eye. Yet some prominent European graphic designers use it not to soothe but on the contrary to subvert the "spectacle"—to undermine the sustained assault of commercial messages. Irma Boom's all-white cover for *Sheila Hicks: Weaving as Metaphor* is embossed with a deep texture that prepares readers to experience the

book as an object as sensual as the fiber sculptures shown inside. Here, white space is an overt invitation to replace visual stimulation with tactile pleasure.

Even though it is often described as "blank," "colorless," or "empty," white space is anything but neutral. It is about to be challenged yet again as being too costly for the environment. The high energy consumption of a white page, as opposed to the gray page on a computer screen, might force us to revise our relationship with this precious achromatic commodity. ∎

"His *Harper's Bazaar* layouts treated white paper as if it was an electromagnetic field."

ABOVE: **Observations** *(1959), here featuring John Huston and Alfred Hitchcock, a book featuring the work of photographer Richard Avedon and designed by Alexey Brodovitch, formerly of* Harper's Bazaar.

LEFT: **Harper's Bazaar,** *September 1992, art-directed by Fabien Baron and photographed by Patrick Demarchelier. An admirer of Brodovitch, Baron has appropriated his dramatic use of white space as his own signature style.*

Q

falls refined appeal

uiet luxury, considered line, beautiful fabrics: These are the qualities that epitomize the new elegance that underlies fall's flashier changes. These are clothes beyond the seasonal vagaries of fashion, yet within their timeless appeal show real, substantive changes that are absolutely of the moment. A sweeping black evening dress that bares only the shoulders is a statement of subtle exposure. A soft gray coatdress worn with matching trousers, in a completely original variation on the suit. "Elegance is understatement," says Calvin Klein. "The woman should stand out; the clothes should not overtake her." There's an integrity of design that allows these pieces to stand on their own: They don't need the glittery camouflage of a wristful of bracelets or strands of necklaces to look finished. "That ethic of jeweled, fussy, scalloped, and teased is just not in my world anymore," says Isaac Mizrahi. "Now a sweep, a defined eyebrow, is all you need." Impeccable in balance, cut, and proportion, these are the clothes that, by virtue of their practicality, their lack of pretension, are the foundation of a great wardrobe. A new grace comes to evening. Opposite page: Black viscose/Lycra turtleneck, drop-waist dress, about $1375, by Donna Karan.

Herman
Miller
Collection

Verkauf ab
9. März
Contura SA
Basel
Aeschen
vorstadt 4
Passage

Möbel unserer Zeit

Entwurf: A. Hofmann / Druck: Wassermann A.G.

A pared-down postwar aesthetic

IDEA № 73
LESS IS MORE

In Europe after World War II, "Ulm" was a magic word for anyone interested in graphic design. Referring to the Ulm School of Design (Hochschule für Gestaltung), a prestigious German design school founded in 1953 by Max Bill, it symbolized a new aesthetic so radical, so unencumbered, so flawless, that it felt like the dawn of a new age.

What came to be known as the "International Typographic Style" turned out to be the linchpin that would hold together the history of graphic design in the twentieth century. Though some of the tenets that the Ulm School promoted had been developed in the Netherlands before the war, its practical applications had never been clearly formulated. A Swiss architect, sculptor, and designer who had studied at the Bauhaus in Dessau, Max Bill spelled it out in no uncertain terms. He established strict norms regarding typography and design with the exactness of a watchmaker. To minimize waste and enhance read-ability, he advocated using a grid; avoiding symmetrical layouts; using only sans serif letterforms; setting narrow columns of text flush left, ragged right; and systematically choosing photography over illustration. His method was reductive, yet the posters, book covers, and brochures he designed were so inspired that they instantly changed the graphic design landscape.

The International Typographic Style was a misnomer of sorts. It was not a wide-ranging international movement, but one rooted in the bookish Protestant tradition of Northern Europe; it was not very popular in the Mediterranean countries, such as Spain, France, and Italy. More to the point, it was never meant to be a "style"; quite the contrary. Max Bill and his followers despised the streamlined styling of postwar American design. "Good form" and "moral purpose through design" were expressions they used to describe their philosophy. Emil Ruder, Armin Hofmann, and Josef Müller-Brockmann were Swiss designers who, like Max Bill, did not confuse design with style and felt comfortable occupying the moral high ground. Yet, as with Max Bill, ideology never got in the way of creativity. Müller-Brockmann's posters for *Musica Viva* are playful eye charts, Hofmann's 1962 poster for Herman Miller shows a stack of abstracted sofa shapes spilling across the page, and the cover of Ruder's 1967 *Typographie* (Typography) flaunts every rule of readability. In America, Swiss typography was much admired by such designers as Rudi de Harak, Ivan Chermayeff, Tom Geismar, and Massimo and Lella Vignelli, and by its pragmatic rationality influenced many. Unfortunately, the kind of typographic excellence that was, for Max Bill, the essence of "good form" soon became synonymous with "good taste," and was rejected by the next generations of designers as too conventional. The International Typographic Style is experiencing a revival of interest today—the 2007 documentary *Helvetica* by Gary Hustwit is now a cult film. ∎

OPPOSITE: Armin Hofmann's 1962 poster for Herman Miller shows how information complexity can be reduced to graphic simplicity through color and shape.

BELOW: The cover of Typographische Monatsblätter (1961), designed by Emil Ruder, a Swiss magazine about printing and typography. This design is minimalist in spirit, relying on the repetition of the title in various sizes.

ABOVE: This poster for Musica Viva (1962) by Josef Müller-Brockmann is a prime example of the Swiss style of economy and simplicity, allowing the type composition to be the illustrative element.

Clarifying the cases

IDEA № 74
MONOALPHABETS

In Germany in the 1920s, type reformers railed against the illegibility of the spiky black-letter alphabets that had been traditional since the age of Gutenberg. Seeking to replace the unwieldy alphabet, the designers turned to simpler, sans serif letters known as gothic or grotesque. But the heavy black-letter faces were not the only problem.

"Why should we write and print in two alphabets?" wrote Bauhaus member Herbert Bayer. "We do not speak in a capital 'a' and a small 'a.' A single alphabet gives us practically the same result as the mixture of upper- and lowercase letters, and at the same time is less of a burden on all who write."

With this in mind, Bayer produced the first designs in 1925 for a sans serif typeface void of capital letters. His contribution to what he called "a one letter type"—an all lowercase type family—the "universal alphabet," was originally designed for exclusive Bauhaus use, while his "bayer-type," produced by the Berthold Type Foundry, was commercially available.

Bayer based his alphabet on simple lowercase letterforms, merged in a way that would aid linguistic clarity, but at the same time stay true to existing traditions. The universal alphabet "represents a practical attempt to give a modern expression to classical Roman type by means of geometrical construction of form," he wrote. Moreover, it must not suggest handwriting; it must have uniform thickness of all parts of the letter; it must be a "renunciation" of all up and down strokes. Simplification was a foregone assumption.

Alphabet 26 was a subsequent simplified English system created in 1950 by the American designer Bradbury Thompson. After observing his son experience difficulty in recognizing the similarity between the words "Run" and "run" in "Run pal. See him run," he decided that the two-letter system hampered the experience of learning to read. Confusion occurred because of the change from a capital R to a lowercase r—two different letters with the same phonetic sound. Thompson counted 19 other instances of dissimilar upper- and lowercase letters.

While Bayer believed capitals were extraneous, Alphabet 26 was not as doctrinaire. It was, however, a system of *only* 26 characters, some upper- and some lowercase, typeset in Baskerville. Thompson's scheme was to keep a lowercase and discard the uppercase version of the seven characters of the alphabet that are the same across both cases (Cc-Oo-Ss-Vv-Ww-Xx-Zz). Of the remaining 19 dissimilar characters, he kept the uppercase version of 15 of them—Bb-Dd-Ff-Gg-Hh-Ii-Jj-Kk-Ll-Pp-Qq-Rr-Tt-Uu-Yy—and the lowercase version of four—Aa-Ee-Mm-Nn. The intention of a monoalphabet was to make the written language function on the same plane, more or less, as the spoken tongue. It has not yet been adopted as the designer hoped. ∎

a B C D e
F G H I J K
L m n O P
Q R S T U
V W X Y Z

● Upper-case design is used for these characters
● Lower-case design is used for these four characters
● Only one design exists for these seven characters

HERBERT BAYER

399

defghi

nopqr

vwxyz

Beispiel eines Zeichens
in größerem Maßstab
Präzise optische Wirkung

sturm blond

Anwendung

THE QUICK BROWN FOX JUMPS OVER THE LAZY DOG

ABOVE: *Universal Alphabet (1925) was Herbert Bayer's experiment at an alphabet that combined upper- and lowercase letters into a more phonetic system.*

LEFT: *Monoalphabet (2006) by Manfred Klein is among the most recent in this tradition, making reading easier by combining upper- and lowercase letters—particularly where the two cases are at odds with each other.*

OPPOSITE: *Alphabet 26 / monoalphabet (1950), by Bradbury Thompson, was created to simplify the English language for early readers, who have to memorize 26 capitals and lowercase letters, which are often not the same.*

Cutting-edge credits

FILM TITLE SEQUENCES

Unlike film trailers, which are edited with marketing objectives in mind, film title sequences are not under commercial constraints: they are designed to appeal to people who have already bought their ticket. As a result, graphic designers who work in this genre can enjoy a freedom that few other commercial artists possess. Saul Bass was the first filmmaker to take full advantage of this creative loophole. He transformed what used to be a dull typographical exercise into a graphic art form.

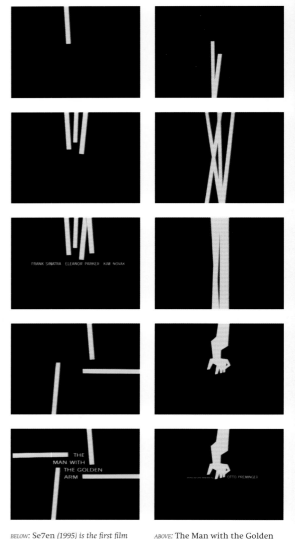

Saul Bass's credits for *The Man with the Golden Arm* (1955), a controversial film about drug addiction by Otto Preminger, were a landmark event in film title history. The short abstract animation, a tight orchestration of white bars against a black background, was a sophisticated display of graphic virtuosity. The final image, a **paper cutout** representing the distorted arm of a heroin addict, was a powerful icon. It stayed on the screen for less than five seconds, yet that single moment defined the way filmmakers would conceive the opening credit sequence from then on. Rather than just a directory of names, it became an arresting visual experience.

Saul Bass created countless sequences, including for *Vertigo* (1958), *Psycho* (1960), and *West Side Story* (1961), and dominated the scene for nearly five decades. Among his many emulators were Maurice Binder

and Robert Brownjohn, who worked on the James Bond film credits. Edgy and sexy, Binder's and Brownjohn's animations made the most of black backgrounds, female forms, extreme cropping, and abstracted geometry—visual codes all established by Bass.

During the 1970s, a number of opening sequences eschewed narrative elements altogether and used type exclusively. Three examples stand out: *Monty Python and the Holy Grail*, a hilarious spoof of Swedish films; Woody Allen's *Annie Hall*, a no-nonsense directory set in elegant Windsor letterforms; and the opening sequence of *Alien*, a minimalist typographical puzzle of chilling exactness. Meanwhile, live-action openers were gaining popularity. Referencing Orson Welles's 1958 single-take sequence for *Touch of Evil*, Robert Altman's tracking shot for *The Player* (1992) was a brilliant, almost eight-minute overture.

However, a second revolution in film titles was in the making. Starting in 1995, Kyle Cooper reinvented suspense with a series of cinematographic masterpieces that used the opening credits as a ploy to display disturbing **collages** of ominous images, manipulating, digitizing, colorizing, and reengineering original mate-

BELOW: Se7en (1995) is the first film title sequence of Kyle Cooper, who has made a career in this genre, bringing the level of creativity, technical prowess, and imagination to heights unknown before.

ABOVE: The Man with the Golden Arm (1955) is known for its opening sequence by Saul Bass as much as for the acting of Frank Sinatra, playing a heroin addict whose "golden arm" is the subject of Bass's striking black-and-white animation.

rial. Cooper is the author of more than 100 film titles including *Se7en* (1995), *The Island of Dr. Moreau* (1996), and *The Incredible Hulk* (2008).

Some remarkable filmic moments happen while the credits are rolling. In the past decade, deserving an Academy Award for best picture under three minutes are *Catch Me if You Can* by Kuntzel Deygas (2002), *Kiss Kiss Bang Bang* by Danny Yount (2005), *Casino Royale* by Daniel Kleinman (2006), *The Fall* by Stefan Bucher (2007), *Juno* by Shadowplay Studio (2008), and *A History of Scotland* by Iso Design (2009). ∎

The Fall

PRODUCTION DESIGNER
GED CLARKE

EXECUTIVE PRODUCER
TOMMY TURTLE

LEO BILL
SEAN GILDER
JULIAN BLEACH

SCREENPLAY
DAN GILROY
AND NICO SOULTANAKIS
& TARSEM

MARCUS WESLEY
ROBIN SMITH
JEETU VERMA

PRODUCED and
DIRECTED by
TARSEM

Big, bold, buy me

IDEA № 76
BIG BOOK LOOK

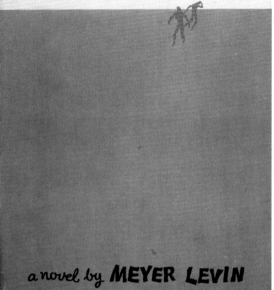

In the mid-1950s the American designer Paul Bacon defined a literary design genre known as the "big book look," in which a book cover was characterized by a large title, a large author's name, and a small symbolic image. The look was conceived as a matter of commercial pragmatism in 1956 when Bacon designed the **dust jacket** for *Compulsion* by Meyer Levin, a book based on the real-life story of two young men who murdered a boy to see if they could get away with it.

The publisher wanted the jacket to evoke the case without sensationalizing it. Bacon sketched out a number of ideas until he came up with the notion of positioning the rough, hand-scrawled word "Compulsion" at the top of the jacket, taking up a fifth of the space. Under that, two tiny, nervously rendered figures running on the vacant expanse toward the title were printed in red. The art is reminiscent of Saul Bass's 1955 Expressionistic film poster and titles for *The Man with the Golden Arm* (see p.156), but was influenced by the jazz albums Bacon had designed starting in the late 1940s. The book became a huge best-seller and the jacket caught the U.S. publishing industry's attention. Other publishers wasted little time in contacting Bacon to design jackets for their potential bestsellers.

Bacon's jacket *oeuvre* embodies the history of late twentieth-century commercial book cover design—a legacy of eclectic lettering, illustration, and typography before the digital revolution. Perhaps more importantly, he made books sell. Marketers liked using an icon or a logo on a jacket rather than conventional treatments of type or literal illustration. Bacon was good at, as he put it, "finding something that would be a synthesis graphically of what the story was about."

While he was no traditionalist, neither did he follow the Modernist notions of Paul Rand, Alvin Lustig, and Leo Lionni, who imbued their covers with more subtlety. While Bacon admired these designers, their book covers were generally designed for works of criticism, analysis, and literature with small print runs, enabling them to do virtually anything they wanted with little interference. Bacon's more commercial orientation required that he navigate sales and advertising requirements.

Though most of Bacon's covers were built on some conceptual idea or image, the cover for Philip Roth's *Portnoy's Complaint* (1969) was uncharacteristic. It was solely type against a yellow background, with no fancy touches, except for the **swashes on capitals** (with flowing or curlicue serifs) in the title and the author's name. Asked why he avoided his signature conceptual image, Bacon said it was because of the difficulty in portraying the book's most prominent element—masturbation.

Ambiguity—fragmented and vague pictorial jackets with skewed type—is much more frequent in present-day book covers, which may explain why the big book look, though not precisely obsolete, is no longer a design code. ∎

OPPOSITE: Catch-22 *(1961), jacket design by Paul Bacon, epitomizes the big book look with a large title and almost as large author's name. In some cases, the author is even larger than the title.*

ABOVE: Compulsion *(1956), jacket design by Paul Bacon, was arguably the first to lead toward the big book look. The title was large, but the cover itself was spare, forcing the eye to look at the title.*

Retro classics remade

IDEA № 77
NOSTALGIA

Fashion and graphic design have one thing in common: they are ephemeral art forms. Both disciplines create artifacts that are transient, even though some exceptional garments—and some special books—become treasured classics. Like fashion trends, graphic design trends are periodically rediscovered, their revival often as much of a cultural event as their original introduction.

Nostalgic fads are good indicators of what excites new generations. In the 1970s, under the influence of Push Pin Studios, graphic designers in the United States (and also overseas) began to adopt ornamental typefaces from the past, redrawing them occasionally to update their contours. Seymour Chwast and Paula Scher were, and still are, passionate lovers of vintage type, but their use of it is anything but stale. Chwast's delightful 1974 *Water Torture Escape* poster for a television show is evidence of how much fun nostalgia can be.

In the next decades, retro styles turned into engines for innovation. In San Francisco, **psychedelic** poster designers were revisiting Art Nouveau. In France, Roman Cieslewicz spearheaded a Constructivist revival. In England, Neville Brody explored the graphic sensibility of Dada artists. At Cranbrook in Bloomfield, Illinois, Katherine McCoy encouraged her students to reference the typographical approach pioneered by early Modernist movements. By the early 1990s, when Scott and Laurie Makela began to take their cues from the 1950s avant-garde movement Fluxus, their richly layered "Living Surfaces" aesthetic was hailed as a precursor of a new media communication genre.

The digital revolution created a longing for handmade things. Letter-press printing made a comeback with David Pearson. His "Great Ideas" covers for Penguin Books, launched in 2004, reproduce the tactile quality and slight irregularities of old-fashioned metal typesetting, in perfect sync with the concept of the series, which publishes new editions of classics. His designs, however, are contemporary interpretations of the historical period in which the texts were originally written.

Nostalgia these days is turning up an interesting crop of graphic artifacts. When Polaroid discontinued its instant camera in 2008, geeks had to find a replacement: today, iPhone applications allow shutterbugs to make their digital pictures look as if they just popped out of a vintage SX-70. Also nostalgic are Lego bricks; in 2009, Christoph Niemann celebrated their comeback as cult emblems in his *I Lego NY* graphic feature published in the *New York Times*. Garish 3D logos from the early days of computer graphics are now hot background animations to music videos. More quaint, but just as hot, pop-up books, cardboard figures, and **paper cutouts** are revisited by **motion graphics** animators. But for anyone who hung around video arcades in the 1980s, Space Invaders are today's supreme sentimental icons. The classic video game inspired Patrick Jean from OneMorePro-

ABOVE: Pixels *(2011), a short animated film directed by Patrick Jean and photographed by Matias Boucard, describes the destruction of New York City by 8-bit creatures, space invaders, and Lego bricks.*

OPPOSITE: Water Torture Escape *(1974), by Seymour Chwast, advertised a Mobil Showcase television special by approximating a Victorian magic-show poster common in Harry Houdini's time.*

duction in Paris to create *Pixels*, a striking animation in which New York City is attacked and eventually destroyed by voracious 8-bit creatures intent on rasterizing the universe. ■

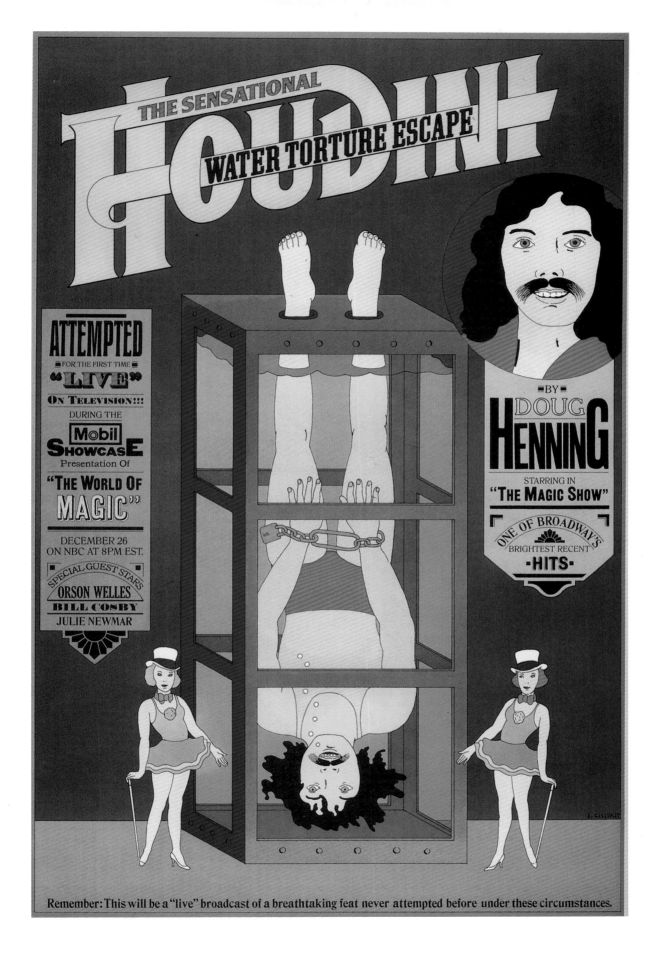

Surprisingly effective communication

IDEA № 78
ILLEGIBILITY

The human brain can decipher words without actually reading them. It scans letters to see if they add up to spell a word that is already known. This time-saving neurotransmitter method, which allows us to recognize words at a glance even if, perhaps, all the letters are not present, is a godsend for designers.

Designers have taken advantage of this phenomenon to twist, compress, section, tangle, cube, distort, maim, and mangle written text, happily defying the ordinary precepts of "readability." An early example of this technique is a mid-twentieth-century poster for a French cordial called St. Raphaël. A red, black, and white calligraphic exercise, designed by Charles Loupot, it made mincemeat of the product name by chopping it up into three parts, St.Ra/pha/ël, and jumbling them up every which way. Yet, when reassembled into a crazy-quilt patchwork, the new typographical configuration was invariably easy to unscramble, even though it was technically illegible. So popular was this Cubistic and dynamic logo that it became an icon for postwar economic recovery in France. The St. Raphaël patchworks were painted on walls, pasted on palisades, posted on billboards, turned into ashtrays, coasters, and clocks, always triggering in the mind of onlookers the full name of the product.

Illegibility per se was not a new idea. The Futurists, the Dadaists, and principally the Lettrists had experimented with it, often turning calligraphic gibberish into an art form that teased the brain into its deciphering mode.

However, recently, with the flowering of the digital age, illegibility has gained popularity as an effective means of communication. Designers who have capitalized on the ability of scrambled text to stimulate brain activity are David Carson, Ed Fella, Rick Valicenti, Pierre di Sciullo, David Niessen, M/M (Paris), and Irma Boom, to name a few. So fascinating is this phenomenon that more and more contemporary artists are venturing into illegibility to create installations that stop spectators in their tracks and compel them to take a deep breath before deciphering texts that are barely legible. Jenny Holzer is probably one of the most prolific conceptual wordsmiths of this generation. She makes her aphorisms spin, swarm, stream, fade, and disappear, reaffirming, in the process, the restorative power of the written word. ∎

ABOVE: St. Raphaël (1955), an abstract composition, was in fact a modular system that could be adapted to fit surfaces of various sizes. The more "readable," horizontal version of this logo was traced by Charles Loupot in 1947.

OPPOSITE: Upside Down (2008), a silkscreened poster by Dutch graphic designers Niessen & de Vries, for a lecture in Ulm for the 23rd Forum Typografie, spells "AESTHETES" one way, and "MORALISTS" when you hang it the other way up.

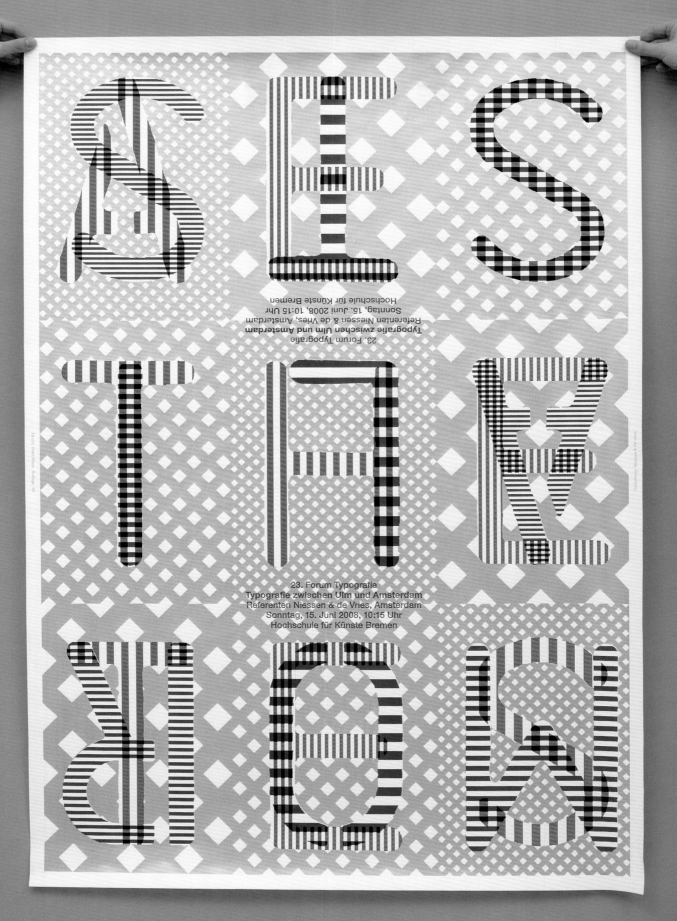

23. Forum Typografie
Typografie zwischen Ulm und Amsterdam
Referenten Niessen & de Vries, Amsterdam
Sonntag, 15. Juni 2008, 10:15 Uhr
Hochschule für Künste Bremen

Lines of distinction

IDEA № 79
SCAN LINES

Why are there lines running through the IBM logo? If the logo's designer, Paul Rand, were alive he might answer with one of a litany of rationales depending on his mood. He had a few reasons. One centers on what has become the common theory that they are "scan lines," the magnetic kind used to safeguard official documents, such as checks and stock certificates, from forgery or theft.

This motive makes sense, since back in 1956, when Rand was commissioned by Eliot Noyes to redesign the IBM logo, this type of technology was common. It was not until 1960 that Rand added the stripes to the logo, and his primary reasons were at the same time to lighten up the City Bold typeface (designed by Georg Trump) and to create a mnemonic element, which has not only permanently lodged in people's minds but is also often perceived as scan lines.

There are various ways to represent a technological future symbolically. Scan lines are to the digital age what motion lines, often made with airbrush,

were to the machine age. The latter signify speed, the former computer technology (a different dimension of speed). However, there is something old-fashioned about speed lines as opposed to scan lines. Rand's striped IBM logo is more than 50 years old, but it is still in use, and not in the seminostalgic way associated with some vintage products. IBM is not timeless, but up-to-date.

The scan lines make it so. They transformed a typeface designed in 1930 at the height of the machine and Stream-line ages into a logo that suggests computer technology that is current today. Rand understood that without the lines the heavy weight of City Bold could weigh heavy on public perception—in other words, get old over a short period of time. But the lines provided both distinction and a symbolic charge. They made the logo now, not then.

Yet not all scan lines are created equal. In 1983 Saul Bass designed the AT&T logo, a globe cut by scan lines of varying thickness to evoke a sense of weight and volume. Earlier, in 1978, he had used four such lines cutting across a circle for the Minolta logo. Eventually, scores of other industries followed suit, and scan lines became the corporate identity trope of the 1980s. ∎

ABOVE: IBM logo (1972) designed by Paul Rand, was the second iteration of the City Bold logotype. The first, solid, version was created in 1956. Rand added the lines to give the logo a mnemonic and push back the black.

BELOW: AT&T Bell System logo (1983), called the "globe" logo, designed by Saul Bass after the breakup of the Bell System. Scan lines, giving the impression of high technology, were used frequently as a graphic conceit at the time.

OPPOSITE: This Book is a Seesaw (1994) by Hans Knuchel and Jürg Nänni (Lars Müller Publishers), a book of optical illusions using shapes and forms to subvert conventional sight patterns.

seesaw

Dieses Buch ist eine Schaukel   This Book is a Seesaw

Hans Knuchel / Jürg Nänni

Lars Müller Publishers

Identifying a new market

TEEN MAGAZINES

Before World War II "teenagers" did not exist. The group aged between 13 and 19 were youngsters, young people, or young adults. Trapped between childhood and adulthood, teenagers were ignored as a viable market, except perhaps as consumers of music. But even their album and sheet music graphics were not designed with them in mind the way they were in the 1960s. After the war, when advertisers sought to mine new markets, the teenager came into existence.

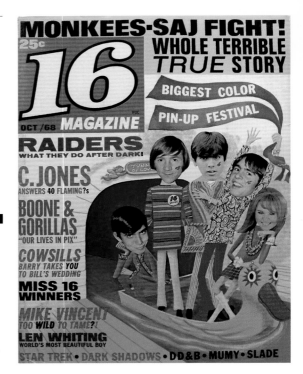

ABOVE: 16 Magazine (1968). The teeny-bop magazine emerged just as the British invasion hit American shores. This clarion of teen boys and girls developed a distinctive look with silhouette heads of stars on drawn or painted comic bodies.

BELOW: Teenagers Ingenue (1962) capitalized on the developing female teenage commercial market for fashion, cosmetics, and other beauty aids. Teens were now treated as young adults.

The American magazine *Seventeen*, first published in 1944, was the first magazine to define and target teenage girls, and started the marketing ball rolling. It was art-directed by Cipe Pinelas, who imbued it with an elegant typographical style that complemented the sophisticated conceptual illustration and fashion photography. Yet the real thrust behind teenage ascendancy was a marketing consultant named Estelle Ellis. She persuaded advertisers to address this group by employing the first market-research studies to distinguish teenage girls from working women and then see them as an economically powerful market.

Once teenagers were installed as a true demographic, there was no stopping the graphic codes and messages aimed at them. During the mid-1960s the celebrity-focused *16 Magazine*, which targeted starstruck adolescent girls, was the teenage version of *Photoplay*, *Silver Screen*, *Movie Star*, and other pulp fan magazines of the 1920s. It was designed as a typographic and pictorial midway, not elegant like *Seventeen* but full of varied and discordant colorful typefaces and eye-catching headlines. Edited by former fashion model and pop idol-maker Gloria Stavers, *16* was the first bona fide American teenage fan magazine and hype engine for the popular music and television juggernaut thrusting its way into the hearts and minds of America's baby-boom, teeny-bop generation. *16* was a voyeur's cornucopia replete with "oodles" of "wowee" publicity pictures of "adorable" blemish-free stars and candid canned gossip about pop's leading heartthrobs—presented without an iota of irony.

With the floodgates thus opened, *Junior Bazaar*, *Teenagers Ingenue*, and *Teen*, among other mainstream magazines, advised adolescents how to be "in," glamorous, and desirable—recommending the best deodorant (Arrid), hair color (Toni), and acne cream (Clearasil), and offering tips on how to meet the right guys and get modeling jobs.

Yet an alternative, *Rolling Stone* magazine, was the diametrical opposite of *16*. It helped remove the artifice from the teen demographic, replacing it with rebellious "youth culture." It treated the baby boomer as a distinct entity and reported on its eccentricities. It gave rise to more risqué, though still resolutely slick, teen-oriented magazines, such as *Zoo* in the UK, that pushed the boundaries further. ■

OPPOSITE: Honey (1969) reveals one of the graphic ways in which teens were being taken seriously as a fashion and lifestyle market.

Young, Gay and Get-Ahead   *February '69*

2'6

honey

The who's who of the young genderation...

where you can't tell the girls from the guys.

Subversive spoofing

BELOW: Do women have to be naked to get into U.S. Museums? (1995). The infamous campaign by the Guerrilla Girls, based on Ingres's Grande Odalisque, was refused by most media as too "suggestive" on the pretext that "the figure appeared to have more than a fan in her hand."

IDEA № 81
CULTURE JAMMING

Today, disrupting the dominant culture takes wit. Causes whose radical agendas are perceived as humorous rather than simply inflammatory are more likely to inspire. But while delivering a subversive message requires humor and ingenuity, it also entails a solid understanding of the way visual codes function in our media-controlled society.

In the late 1950s, members of Situationist International, a short-lived but influential political movement, tried to expose what they called "the spectacle"—the relentless display of media images. Although they never produced truly "breakthrough" visual interventions, the idea that modern life is nothing but a spectacle staged by powerful interest groups has since inspired a number of avant-garde artists to find ways to counter the stifling effect of corporate capitalism. Whether spontaneous or elaborate, the hijacking or appropriation of media images is now common practice. Billboards are often commandeered for these graphic counteroffensives.

In the mid-1980s, a group of anonymous feminist artists who called themselves Guerrilla Girls began to speak out against sex discrimination in the art world. They pasted yellow billboards around New York on which the head of a gorilla was **collaged** onto the body of Ingres's *Grande Odalisque*. A luridly styled heading asked, "Do women have to be naked to get into U.S. museums?," lampooning the sensationalist headlines of supermarket tabloids. The posters not only decried sexism, they did so in the visual language of lowbrow culture.

In the 1990s, commenting on the increasingly strident consumer culture by mocking its tropes became a popular activity among artists and graphic designers alike. The Canada-based magazine *Adbusters* made an editorial policy out of "culture jamming," a satirical technique that consisted of spoofing logos, advertisements, and media images to sabotage their messages. In 1992, the magazine promoted a day of protest, Buy Nothing Day, that tried, with a series of imaginative posters, to convince people to refrain from purchasing anything on the Friday after Thanksgiving (one of the biggest shopping days in the United States). The campaign, repeated annually and in various countries, never worked as such, but it was fun to ridicule acquisitiveness with clever **visual puns** while restating a serious message about over-consumption.

The convergence of activism and artful irony found a spokesperson in Shepard Fairey, an American skateboarder and street artist whose perversely mischievous brand, OBEY, was a covert invitation to rebel against the powerful capitalist political and monetary system. Using a strategy that is now a hallmark of many contemporary artists, he appropriated marketing techniques to disseminate his message, distributing a wide range of stencils, stickers, and posters in order to allow his fans to plaster his fractious OBEY message on walls from Baltimore to Berlin and beyond. ∎

Stay Away from Corporations That Want You to Lie for Them *(1999)*, *a billboard designed by Jonathan Barnbrook to illustrate a quote by Tibor Kalman. It was produced to coincide with the launch of the reedition of the* First Things First *manifesto (see p.57) —a call for more meaningful design.*

"The hijacking of media images is now common practice."

High impact

IDEA № 82
HIGH CONTRAST

Eastman Kodak's Kodalith photographic paper was invented in 1931 to facilitate the reproduction of ultra-high-contrast images, or line art. It removed all the middle tones in conventional photographs, leaving only the darkest masses and brightest highlights. These areas could be manipulated using either darkroom methods or by hand, eliminating the need for time-consuming airbrush retouching. Kodalithing, as it was called, made art and design more dramatic.

BELOW: The Medium is the Massage *(1967) by Marshall McLuhan and Quentin Fiore, who also designed the book, is a collection of factoids, bromides, and theories of postwar media and its "inventory of effects."*

ABOVE: Dubnobass with My Headman *(1993), album cover for electronic band Underworld. Multiple layers of high-contrast black-and-white imagery give it the aura of DIY artwork.*

OPPOSITE: Stadt Theater Basel *(1963). This poster for a municipal theater focuses on high-contrast hand play to give the sense of drama in motion.*

Kodalithing was initially used to hold down production expenses, yet during the 1960s it also spawned a counter-culture aesthetic. At first it was simply cosmetic—a means to goose-up a layout with bold graphics. Much like the German Expressionist woodcut, however, Kodalith enabled artists to capture on paper what was deemed primitive. Just as the Expressionists built a new art on the foundation of naive arts, Kodalith allowed a new Expressionism to be built out of naive technology.

During the politically charged 1960s Kodalith became synonymous with polemical communications. Kodalith aided graphic subversion. High-contrast images effectively masked the obscene or lurid parts of halftone photographs. Portraits of such left-wing leaders as the Black Panther Eldridge Cleaver or Latin American revolutionary Che Guevara were Kodalithed for stickers, posters, and T-shirts. High-contrast reproduction made blatant sexuality more ambiguous and libelous depictions less tangible. Removing all tonal information transformed realism into abstraction. Truth could be fiction and fiction could be taken as fact. Kodalith further made mundane imagery more "artistic." Other screen techniques, including mezzotint, scratch, and continuous line, might render a halftone into line art, but only Kodalith had transformative powers.

Designer Quentin Fiore used Kodalith to heighten graphic intensity in the books he collaborated on with media philosopher Marshall McLuhan, *The Medium is the Massage* (1967) and *War and Peace in the Global Village* (1968). Similarly his design of Youth International Party

founder Jerry Rubin's *Do-It!* (1970) combined high-contrast and halftone photography in a veritable orgy of counterculture images. But the most dramatic use was Fiore's cover of *The Medium is the Massage*, a high-contrast depiction of the face of a burned Vietnamese child. At first glance it appears abstract, with just a few identifiable characteristics signaling a human form, but as the viewer's eyes begin to absorb the visual information the tortured visage becomes more vivid. A conventional halftone might be more easily recognizable, but not as dramatic once it is perceived. This high-contrast form forces the viewer to pause before opening the book, and as the image is revealed the viewer comprehends the critical message about how images are processed in a media-glutted information age. ∎

A new visual language

IDEA № 83
PYSCHEDELIA

Gebrauchsgraphik International Advertising Art November 1968 B3149E

Hippies reigned, hallucinogenic drugs flowed, and rock filled the air during the late 1960s in San Francisco. Victor Moscoso, Rick Griffin, Stanley Mouse, Alton Kelly, and Wes Wilson were the vanguard of the distinctly American youth culture design mannerism known as psychedelia. Characterized by decorative typefaces, **vibrating color**, and vintage illustrations, psychedelic art was a rebellious graphic language that communicated with a select community and for a brief time excluded all others (until co-opted by the mainstream and exported throughout the world).

BELOW: "The Peacock Skirt" (1894) from Salomé, illustrated by Aubrey Beardsley, who was one of the influences for the drug-inspired psychedelic work that arose in the 1960s.

ABOVE: Gebrauchsgraphik (1968). The youth style influenced by drugs and rock and roll quickly became a commercial visual vocabulary. Founded in San Francisco, this German version smoothed out some of the rough edges.

RIGHT: Grateful Dead (1966), created by Stanley Mouse for the Avalon Ballroom, draws upon lettering of the Jugendstil period and artwork of the Symbolists.

Each of the principal artists had a distinct personal style, yet the overall psychedelic visual language comprised an assortment of images in the public domain, including engravings, old photos, labels, postcards, and other commercial ephemera. Custom psychedelic typefaces were hand-drawn based on Victorian, Art Nouveau, and Vienna Secessionist models, including faces derived from one of Alfred Roller's emblematic Vienna Secessionist alphabets and an ethereal face called Smoke. The artists drew the letters by whiting out all the areas between the bodies of the letterforms rather than drawing them directly. Color was made to vibrate. Slightly off-register trapping gave images and letters a three-dimensional look.

A major influence was the nineteenth-century English illustrator Aubrey Beardsley. The so-called "dandy of the grotesque" was posthumously recalled from his exile in the artistic wilderness. His excessive curvilinear style and chiaroscuro sexual fantasies were a potent antidote to austere Modernist design. His style was also a particularly apt influence on the drug-inspired hippie aesthetics of the day. French Symbolists, such as Odilon Redon and Félicien Rops, played influential roles in the illustrative approaches, as did the Czech Alphonse Mucha.

Despite the layers of graphic effluvia common to all psychedelic art, the compositions were always strategically arranged and obsessively sketched—nothing was left to chance—and serendipity was in the eye of the beholder, not the maker. While being stoned may have contributed to the enjoyment of these posters, it was not altogether necessary for achieving poster nirvana.

Certain art and design tenets were rejected to attain maximum visual sensation. It took some getting used to, but once the new ostensibly **illegible** conceits were absorbed the work was quite accessible.

Predictably, psychedelia became a cliché, viewed by some design critics as a brief commercial aberration. Much of the art was lumped under the umbrella of 1960s kitsch. But like that of the great turn-of-the-century poster masters Lautrec, Cheret, and Bernhard, the original psychedelic work transcends its stylistic era. ■

TICKET OUTLETS: *SAN FRANCISCO* THE PSYCHEDELIC SHOP; CITY LIGHTS BOOKS; BALLY LO; CEDAR ALLEY COFFEE HOUSE; MNASIDIKA; DISCOUNT RECORDS (North Beach); SANDAL MAKER (North Beach)

SAUSALITO TIDES BOOK SHOP; SANDAL MAKER
BERKELEY RECORD CITY, 234 Telegraph Avenue
MENLO PARK KEPLER'S BOOK STORE

Mixing a rainbow

IDEA Nº 84
SPLIT FOUNTAIN

Split (or rainbow) fountain printing was a mundane technique commonly used by job printers during the late nineteenth and early twentieth centuries to give the illusion of four or more colors on a printed piece. The process, which is still used, involves adding two or three colored inks in the ink well (or fountain) of a press or smeared on a silkscreen. As the press rollers turn, or the silkscreen squeegee is pulled, the colors mix to make additional hues, like a rainbow.

The most common print genre for split fountain was cheaply produced carnival and circus posters—the kind that were nailed to telephone poles—since the rainbow luminosity suggested fun and games and grabbed the eye. Split fountain was employed much later during the 1960s in underground newspapers, such as the *San Francisco Oracle*, and on rock posters, to save expensive four-color printing costs.

Like most underground publications, the *Oracle* was economically printed on a

web offset press on porous newsprint. Four-color process printing almost quadrupled the basic expenses, so the split fountain allowed for numerous chromatic variations that would otherwise have been prohibitively expensive. Yet, more importantly, this process highlighted the editorial content of the publication, which was devoted to hippy culture—in other words, sex, drugs, and rock and roll. The *Oracle* helped to define the **psychedelic** look of the age, but was also more primitive-looking than the psychedelic posters produced around the same time.

Although split fountain was an unsophisticated method reserved for run-of-the-mill printing jobs, it earned its place among the emblematic techniques of the era. The rainbow was identified with the alternative culture and hippy movement. Eventually it was co-opted by those who marketed the alternative youth culture as a commodity. In fact, on some mass-produced hippyesque products the split fountain was accomplished by cheating, using four-color process printing.

For the French book designer Massin, however, the technique was not a youth code at all, but rather one of many venerable printing techniques that he used to add verve to his designs. His

1954 cover for *L'Or* by Blaise Cendrars predates the hippy movement by more than a decade, but his application of the split fountain as a background for the bold nineteenth-century typography is used both to suggest the past and at the same time to remove the book metaphorically from the musty stacks. Its brightness was totally contemporary.

Bill Cahan's 1994 poster advertising a lecture he gave at the AIGA and Eric Heiman's 2002 cover for *Rock My World* both pay homage to—and are **pastiches** of—the carnival posters that launched the trope rather than the hippy culture that adopted it. Despite the nod to the past, the prismatic color scheme projects an even more contemporary association—the distinctive shine of a compact disc or DVD, symbols of the computer era. ∎

L'Or (1954), book jacket designed by Massin using three colors that blend to form a rainbow effect.

"The rainbow luminosity suggested fun and games and grabbed the eye."

Der Berufsphotograph (1938), poster designed by Jan Tschichold. The split fountain is used in the type—three colors from yellow to blue to red.

Taboo tales move to the mainstream

UNDERGROUND COMICS

In 1968 underground "comix" began to attack the conservative values of a moribund postwar society. A decade and a half earlier, in 1954, the comics industry had agreed to police itself through the Comics Code Authority, which applied strict standards regarding "appropriate material" in comics prior to bestowing its seal of approval—without which a comic would not be stocked by distributors. Yet neutering comics fomented rebellion.

ABOVE: Acme Novelty Library #12 *(1999), created by Chris Ware as one in a series of comic books, all drawn and handwritten by the artist.*

BELOW: Gothic Blimp Works #4 *(1970), cover illustrated by Spain Rodriguez. This early underground comic newspaper was published by the* East Village Other, *prefiguring comic books.*

OPPOSITE: Zap (1967), *created by Robert Crumb for Apex Comics, was the first actual underground comic book. Zap #0 was the third in the series, even though it was drawn before #1, published in 1968.*

Early underground comics appeared in underground newspapers, such as New York's *East Village Other* and its sister publication, *Gothic Blimp Works,* where Robert Crumb, Kim Dietch, Gilbert Shelton, S. Clay Wilson, and Spain Rodriguez launched assaults on convention. While they looked like comics and read like comics, in fact they were "comix," a combination of a conventional visual language and taboo story lines.

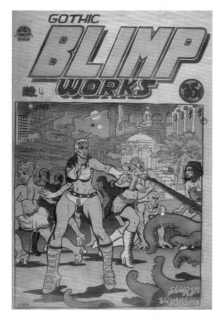

The spearhead of the comic book revolution was *Zap* #1. Under the advisory "Fair Warning: For Adult Intellectuals Only," Robert Crumb introduced a selection of tales, including the now-classic "Keep on Truckin," that had their spiritual roots in *MAD* magazine's irreverent satire. In retrospect, these tales were tame compared to later underground raunchiness. But at the time even comical jibes at frontal nudity, recreational drug use, and racial stereotyping tested the tolerance of accepted standards.

Victor Moscoso and Rick Griffin were among the most prominent graphic artists of the San Francisco scene. Crumb invited Moscoso, Griffin, and S. Clay Wilson, who was already well known in underground paper circles, to join in *Zap* #2.

Problems with the Comics Code Authority were avoided by bypassing the traditional sales outlets and selling directly via the poster and head shops that had sprung up in hippy strongholds of big cities and college towns. By the time *Zap* #3 and #4 were published sales were as high as 50,000 copies each for the first printing. The first two issues of *Zap* were fairly innocuous compared to *Zap* #3, which rocked the boat with its risqué content that lived up to its "Adults Only" advisory. The Moscoso-designed center spread featured drawings of Daisy and Donald Duck engaged in comic-book hanky-panky. By the 1970s, raucous raunch was a staple of underground comix and arguably had opened the door in other media as well.

Zap is today a textbook study of the way in which fringe ideas when unleashed are no longer mysterious or threatening. Undergrounds have settled into the mainstream, having evolved into graphic novels and movies. ∎

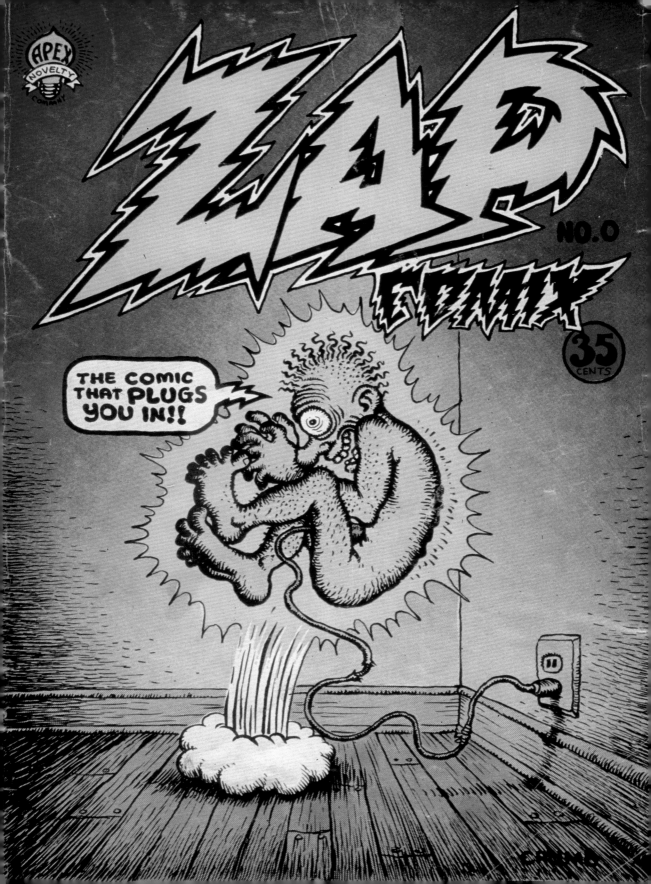

Cover versions

IDEA № 86
RECORD ALBUM COVERS

Sheet music covers from the late nineteenth and early to mid-twentieth centuries were often beautifully illustrated, but early recording cylinders and records were bereft of art. Shellac records were protected in kraft-paper sleeves printed with the record company's trademark and collected in a bound "album" of sleeves, differentiated by colored bindings. Some albums were adorned with preexisting artworks, but most were not.

In 1939 Alex Steinweiss designed the first original cover art for the 78 rpm record album, thereby inventing a major design genre that added an entirely new dimension to the musical experience and to the sales of recorded music. Steinweiss was art director for Columbia Records, headquartered in the industrial city of Bridgeport, Connecticut. For the first six months he was the entire art department and designed ads, posters, booklets, and catalogs. "I put some style into it," he said about his European modern design influences, including Lucian Bernhard and A.M. Cassandre. Then he had an epiphany: he experimented, designing a few covers with original art. Although manufacturing costs increased, Columbia took the risk. The very first album was for a Rodgers and Hart collection, for which he rendered a theater marquee with the album title appearing in lights. Sales rose dramatically on albums with the new covers.

Steinweiss also helped to invent the physical LP record sleeve as well, but it was the younger generation of art directors and designers that emerged as design innovators throughout the 1950s and 1960s. Creatively, progressive rock LPs exploded with unconventional cover art. Robert Crumb's cover for Big

Brother and the Holding Company's 1968 album *Cheap Thrills* (see p.133) launched an anything-goes ethos, which evolved into cover images that both busted and perpetuated sexual taboos as it expanded the definition of what a cover should depict as promotion and identity for the music.

With the advent of CDs, the LP was shrunk from its generous size to a smaller scale. Some original special-effects work was done for CD covers, especially in the boxed-set genre, but the verve of the 12 x 12 inch cover was gone.

Today, with MP3 players the primary conveyance for music, covers have been miniaturized even further. They have become little more than icons, fitting for the computer or iPhone screen. Vinyl records are making a comeback, but this is akin to quaint letterpress printing as a vintage alternative to digital reproduction. The album cover is effectively dead. ■

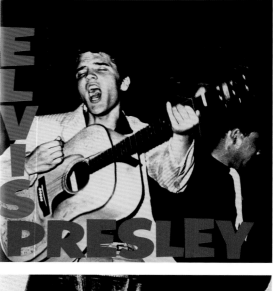

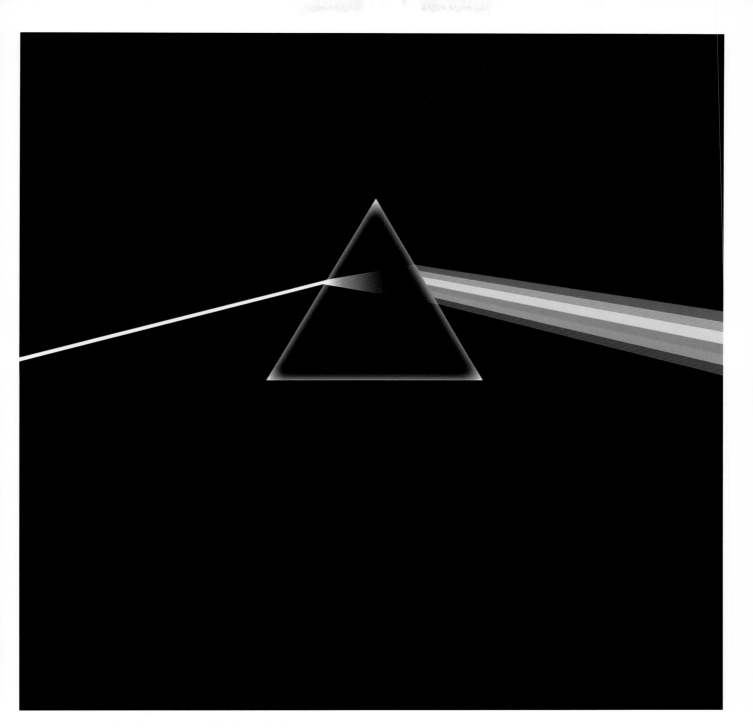

OPPOSITE ABOVE: Concerto in F *(1948) by George Gershwin was designed and illustrated by Alex Steinweiss, the first person to create unique artwork for 78 rpm recordings.*

OPPOSITE CENTER: Elvis Presley *(1956) was Elvis's debut album. The cover looks like it might have been designed today, but it was the first rock and roll album to reach number 1 on the Billboard charts.*

OPPOSITE BELOW: Sticky Fingers *(1971) by the Rolling Stones was conceived by Andy Warhol, photographed by Billy Name, and designed by Craig Braun. The photo is of Factory member Joe Dallesandro's crotch in tight blue jeans, not Mick Jagger's.*

ABOVE: Dark Side of the Moon *(1972) by Pink Floyd, designed by Hipgnosis, a design group that specialized in surreal and abstract record imagery. Their work defined 1970s conceptual music.*

Signs of the times

STREET SLOGANS

What we read in a distracted state—while crossing the street, for example—is not necessarily less memorable. In fact, what we see with our peripheral vision might be more striking, because it is perceived by receptor cells in the eye that are more sensitive to black-and-white figures and to unexpected motion. Furtive slogans scrawled on walls, plastered on top of scaffolding, or stenciled on the sidewalk are just as likely to be seen as colorful advertisements prominently located at the center of our field of vision.

ABOVE: Il est interdit d'interdire *(1968), a Situationist slogan that was painted on the walls of Paris during the May 1968 students' revolt. Meaning "It's forbidden to forbid," it became a rallying cry for the insurgents.*

OPPOSITE ABOVE: Private Property Created Crime *(1985) is one of American conceptual artist Jenny Holzer's better known site-specific art installations. This statement was displayed in New York's Times Square when the area was still considered a sleazy neighborhood.*

In France in 1968, during the student uprising, disruptive slogans were written all over the city, on walls but also on stairs, on sidewalks, on cars, on parapets, on barricades, on fences. "It's forbidden to forbid" and "Be real-istic—demand the impossible" were some of the most poetic and ubiqui-tous pronouncements. They were hard to ignore because they popped into view at the oddest angles, when least expected. Handwritten, spray-painted, they were untidy, the hurried quality of their letterforms suggesting haste, momentum, speed—characteristics that are meant to raise a red flag in our brain and make us extra vigilant.

Jenny Holzer is one contemporary artist who understands how slogans function in the urban environment and is using public art not to create yet another spectacle but to activate in viewers a less guarded vision. Her 1985 light installation in New York's Times Square, *Private Property Created Crime*, placed at the intersection of Broadway and Seventh Avenue, did not look very different from the other signs. It was meant to trigger a double-take, a "wait a minute!" moment in those who saw it. It was sneaky, not openly confrontational.

In Spain, Marti Guixé used the street slogan approach with striking results as well, often applying scratchy messages on top of his own designs, their disrup-tive presence a form of social criticism. In 2002, for the shoe manufacturer Camper, he created a campaign titled "If you don't need it don't buy it." Its delib-erately awkward calligraphic style became an integral part of the Camper image.

In France, German-born graphic designer Malte Martin perfected the technique for a season's posters for the Théâtre de l'Athénée, Paris: a direct quotation from the play advertised is set in black and white inside a stylized "bubble." Busy commuters automati-cally glance at the words, their catchy design as compelling as a visual jingle.

Under the impression that a larger billboard in a prime location is the best way to get noticed, some clients still ask designers to "make it bigger and make it red." But in our age of mobility, distrac-tion is the new attention. ∎

"They popped into view at the oddest angles, when least expected."

En Attendant Godot (2009), poster by German-born Malte Martin for the Théâtre de l'Athénée in Paris. His distinctive, bold, black-and-white compositions—quotes from the theatrical productions being advertised—always attract the attention of busy subway commuters.

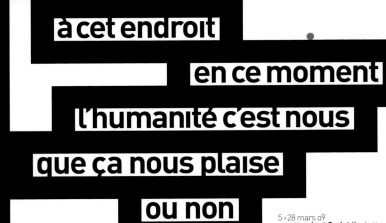

à cet endroit

en ce moment

l'humanité c'est nous

que ça nous plaise

ou non

athénée
théâtre Louis-Jouvet
o1 53 o5 19 19
athenee-theatre.com

5 › 28 mars o9
en attendant Godot Beckett
31 mars › 4 avril o9
cosi fan tutte Da Ponte/Mozart
8 › 11 avril o9
riders to the sea Synge/V. Williams

Taboo today, mainstream tomorrow

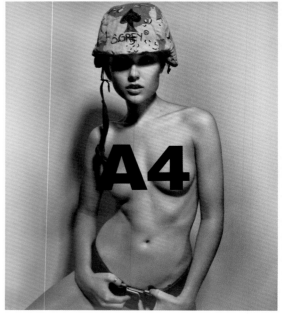

IDEA № 88

SEXUAL TABOO BUSTING

Every era has its share of visual taboos, cultural, political, or sexual. Graphic representations of sexual acts are taboo in some cultures and not in others (although sex itself is always taboo to some extent). In the graphic design arena sexual taboos came to the fore in a 1966 landmark opinion in the matter of Ginzburg v. United States, which jailed the publisher of the exquisitely designed *Eros* magazine, Ralph Ginzburg.

ABOVE: Richardson Magazine A4 (2003) is the brainchild of British fashion stylist Andrew Richardson. This issue focuses on "the female gaze" and charts the sexual encounters of some contributors.

BELOW: Playboy (1961), designed by Art Paul. The ingenuity of Paul's cover designs—using a dictionary as the background here—is what elevated the magazine from tawdry to smart.

OPPOSITE: Eros (1962), founded by Ralph Ginzburg and designed by Herb Lubalin, was an elegant "erotic" journal that challenged the mores of American postwar culture.

It was the first time in American history that a magazine publisher was sentenced to a prison term for producing and distributing a magazine that was judged to have abrogated the moral values and standards of society. *Eros* was much less salacious than today's *Maxim* or *FHM*. But in 1963, television moms and dads slept in separate beds and the word "pregnant" was forbidden on the airwaves. America, on the surface, was still unrepentantly puritanical and *Eros* dared to challenge those mores.

Yet *Eros* was neither a pornography magazine nor a semi-artsy nudist journal. The subscription-only quarterly was one of the most beautifully designed periodicals of the time. Graphic designer and typographer Herb Lubalin infused *Eros*'s pages with exquisite typography, and his elegant layouts were enticing rather than prurient.

Playboy, which began in 1955, used partial nudity, particularly women with ample airbrushed breasts, to lure male readers into its cosmopolitan lifestyle coverage. Conversely, *Eros* did not directly objectify women. There were no pinups or gatefolds, as in *Esquire* magazine (founded 1933). In its four issues, eroticism was addressed as an integral fact of life. The magazine did not take the name Eros, the god of love, in vain. The marriage of love and sex, routinely ignored in publications that pandered to voyeuristic appetites, were not divorced in *Eros*. Ginzburg explained, "The erotic in my life has always been richest, most fulfilling, when intertwined with love, with the romantic. The investigation and portrayal of this combination is what *Eros* was all about."

Sexual taboo busting began with *Eros*, which opened the doors to the boudoir for many others—including magazines, posters, record and book covers—to follow, sometimes in decid-

edly raunchier ways. It was the first national magazine to show intimacy between a black man and white woman, and the first to publish a nude layout of America's greatest sex goddess, Marilyn Monroe.

In the early 1960s sexual imagery was still taboo, but magazines like Hugh Hefner's *Playboy* and its clones fought to open the floodgates. Attempts to suppress them in court had failed. This led the way not only to the busting of sexual taboos, but the integration of a once taboo image-language into the quotidian visual vocabulary. ∎

EROS

Spring, 1962

From booklet to blog: showcasing new work

IDEA № 89
SELF-PROMOTIONAL PUBLISHING

"Festschrift," borrowed from the German, describes a booklet that celebrates a person or thing. Perhaps the first designer "self-promotional" festschrift was a monthly arts periodical by Will Bradley, the nineteenth-century American typographer and book designer who introduced Art Nouveau to the United States and founded in 1895 the Wayside Press in Springfield, Massachusetts. *Bradley: His Book* comprised mainly his own writing and examples of his latest work. He triggered a trend that continues to this day.

BELOW: The Next Call *(1923–26), conceived and designed by H.N. Werkman, was a personal journal in which he created experimental wood type compositions called* drucksels.

ABOVE: Bradley: His Book *(1896), conceived and designed by Will H. Bradley, an American type and book designer, was a compilation of stories and images he created as illustrations and advertisements.*

Other designers have published personal journals and broadsides, some lasting for only a few issues, others, such as *The Pentagram Papers*, appearing regularly for more than 20 years.

Although these festschrifts generally promote existing work by designers for the purpose of attracting clients, some were hothouses for experimentation. In the 1920s H.N. Werkman, a Dutch printer and typographer and a member of the artists' group De Ploeg (The Plough), produced an experimental journal titled *The Next Call*. This slim infrequent organ, composed in wood type, was a showcase for his typographic constructions, and used stenciling and stamping to achieve unique effects. Werkman distributed the eight-page magazine through the mail. Although it did not directly showcase his printing, it did provide a window on to Werkman's aesthetics.

The most ambitious of these publications, *The Push Pin Almanack* (from 1957 *The Push Pin Monthly Graphic* and lasting for 86 issues), published by the New York-based Push Pin Studios, was a miscellany filled with arcane facts and curious quotes that were elegantly typeset and illustrated with comical line drawings and chiaroscuro woodcuts by Seymour Chwast, Milton Glaser, Ed Sorel, and Reynold Ruffins. They had seized upon the almanac as a novel way to attract attention. The genteel subtitle on the otherwise quiet cover announced "The choicest morsels of essential information gathered for those persons in the graphic arts," indicating that the *Almanack* was not intentionally designed to disrupt mainstream commercial art with convention-busting avant-gardisms.

The *Graphic* was for Push Pin Studios what in 1967 *Sgt. Pepper's Lonely Hearts Club Band* was for the Beatles (see p.90). Although *Sgt. Pepper*, the first "high-concept" album of the 1960s, was a one-shot encapsulation of the Beatles' innovation to that date, while the *Graphic* was ongoing and cumulative, both were creative investigations that found acceptance outside the laboratory in the public arena.

A decade after Seymour Chwast ceased the *Graphic* he launched *The Nose* in 1997, which showcases his work in myriad forms, each issue based on a specific theme, including "Fear," "Crime," and "Dirty Tricks." Lately, blogs and other online "experiences" have become the popular venues for the festschrift. ∎

The Pentagram Papers *(1975–2011) are booklets, regularly published, on themes of interest—usually rooted in design and popular culture—to the Pentagram design partners, who select and design them.*

The spray can goes global

TAGS

To graffiti artists, the streets are nothing but big picture frames. In them, any surface that is baked by the sun and washed by the rain can serve as their canvas. Their tags, those large signatures that are works of art in their own right, are now sold in art galleries all over the world. They have come a long way since their humble beginnings in the 1970s in the streets of New York City.

Growing up in underprivileged neighborhoods in Brooklyn, Queens, or the Bronx, most teens could not afford the cost of a subway ride to Manhattan. But they figured out a way to get around: sign their names on the sides of subway cars that would be seen all over town. They spray-painted their names or nicknames in big freestyle bubble letterforms, boldly outlined and filled with bright colors. The bulging shapes of these tags were produced by the arm movements required to cover a large surface as quickly as possible. In subway train yards at night, the artists were able to develop individual styles and techniques that made their tags easily recognizable from far away. Described in the press as vandalizing offenders, the "style writers," as they sometimes called themselves, wanted to flaunt their skills in front of their friends. They were after "fame"—status in their community. Eventually, what many of them got was a different kind of fame—worldwide recognition in the rarefied art world.

In the 1970s, rare was the designer who did not dismiss these graffiti as simply visual pollution. Graphic designers too were trying to leave their mark in the urban environment, but they were creating geometric murals called **supergraphics**. Keith Haring was an exception. He had studied graphic design but understood the importance of the subway artists. He can be credited for bridging the gap between these two cultures. Meanwhile, taggers were cropping up in cities around the globe, many of them becoming fully fledged performance artists. The physical exertion necessary to create large-scale graphics has always been a differentiating factor between designers and taggers. As graffiti techniques evolved and became increasingly sophisticated, incorporating stencils, special effects, and cultural references to rap, comic books, skateboarding, and the club scene, graphic designers slowly joined in.

Today, taglike calligraphy is one more trope borrowed from street art. The twisted, puffed up typefaces, with their whimsical swashes, work well as eye-catching devices. On a layout, they function as a cool "tag"—as they did for Swiss-based designer Adam Machácek's candy wrapper for Lifebar, or for James Victore's poster for the New York School of Visual Arts. Once the signature of a handful of frustrated hip-hop artists, the aerosol strokes, paint drips, and 3D shadows of the hand-drawn letterforms have become universal graphic codes. ■

"The twisted, puffed up typefaces work well as eye-catching devices."

OPPOSITE: **Continuing Education Bulletin** *(2003), by James Victore for the School of Visual Arts in New York, makes reference to the popular culture of tags and graffiti that is so much part of the visual vitality of the city.*

THIS PAGE: *New York subway graffiti (c. 1972) spelled out the names of the street artists who could not afford the price of a ride into Manhattan, but who would apply their signature on the side of trains for all to see.*

A fingerprint for the digital age

IDEA № 91
UNIVERSAL PRICING CODE

ABOVE: Corporate Fascist *(2007), by Jonathan Barnbrook, uses the UPC to approximate Adolf Hitler's mustache in a satirical commentary on U.S. President George W. Bush.*

OPPOSITE: Print *magazine (1984), cover designed by James Cross, was issued around the time the UPC was getting mass recognition.*

BELOW: Spaghetti, *designed by Beach Packaging for a jar of pasta sauce, comically transforms the necessary scan lines of the UPC.*

The Universal Pricing Code (UPC), or barcode, is arguably the most significant design idea of the twentieth century. Originally developed in 1952 by Joseph Woodland, a mechanical engineer, the linear scheme was determined entirely on functional grounds, including how best to "read" it on a scanner and how efficiently it could be imprinted on products. In 1970 the U.S. Supermarket Ad Hoc Committee on a Uniform Grocery Product Code set guidelines for barcode development and standardized the approach.

With the consulting firm McKinsey & Co., an 11-digit code was created by which all products could be identified. By 1980 the barcode was launched in markets in the United States and Canada, and both savings and sales increased owing to this technically efficient graphic tool.

Today the barcode is ubiquitous. It is printed on virtually every product—from groceries to books, from automobiles to airplanes—and used as a calculating, trafficking, and measuring instrument for almost everything industrial and not, including personal information. The UPC is a digital fingerprint, and every product has a unique one.

While the human fingerprint is a random composition of contoured lines, which gives it a somewhat chaotic look, the UPC's repetitive vertical lines are decidedly more mechanized, which gives it a sinister air as well.

During the late twentieth century this iconic milestone nudged out the fingerprint as a primary symbol of identity and individuality (or the lack thereof); it has been used as a metaphor for such concepts as imprisonment, governance, and economy, and is symbolic of building a database of the citizenry's individual characteristics. Evoking the tattooing of concentration camp prisoners, depictions of it tattooed on the human body eerily evoke a specter of official surveillance. The UPC has been shown in illustrations as a brand—a high-tech slave bracelet. What is more, this grotesque notion is not implausible. The barcode is also used to represent a kind of cityscape symbolizing the overarching control of a faceless power over human life.

Not all depictions are so negative. The UPC is essentially a neutral device and a common fact of life. Since it must be prominently situated on almost every mass-produced object, it is sometimes necessary to camouflage it by decoration, ornament, or cartoon to better integrate it into a design. Barcodes are made into stems of flowers or barrels of guns, even occasionally squiggling the straight line. In this way the UPC is actually more versatile than it appears. ■

$5
AMERICA'S GRAPHIC DESIGN MAGAZINE
MARCH/APRIL 1984
PRINT XXXVIII:II

Print

0491004101

Anonymous designs become precious visual references

IDEA № 92

VERNACULAR

The Italian Renaissance was prompted by a rediscovery of the art of Greek and Roman antiquity. Ever since, artists have been mining the past for sources of inspiration. One genre is often overlooked: ubiquitous artifacts, done by local artists, that are so modest they do not attract attention. Impervious to nostalgia, they remain practically invisible until someone begins to collect them.

OPPOSITE: I Have a Dream (2010), a typical American motel sign, is the marquee of the Lorraine Motel in Memphis where Martin Luther King was shot, now the National Civil Rights Museum.

ABOVE: Relax (2010), one of a series of colorful posters designed by Anette Lenz and Vincent Perrottet for the local theater in Chaumont, France. The visual vocabulary is deliberately working-class to celebrate the blue-collar values of this small provincial town.

In the early 1970s, architect Robert Venturi took his Yale University students to Las Vegas to study the urban forms of that typically American phenomenon, the strip mall. They discovered the "forgotten symbolism" of the commercial structures along the main highway, and introduced in the process the idea that vernacular designs can be beautiful—even the marquees and signposts advertising cheap motels and gambling halls. His 1972 book, *Learning from Las Vegas*, turned the study of vernacular forms into a trendy academic topic. From then on, in the United States, vernacular designs were no longer safe from the scrutiny of graduate students, social anthropologists, and collectors. Treasure hunters prowled flea markets looking for once-commonplace objects, from gas-station enamel signs to cardboard store mannequins. The distinctive typographical features and design particularities of these humble commercial articles eventually found their way into the mainstream visual vocabulary. In New York, Tibor Kalman was their enlightened champion. In Minneapolis, Charles S. Anderson embraced the working-class aesthetic of naive industrial logotypes and made it his own. In the middle of Delaware, House Industries, a type foundry, has gathered an impressive collection of calligraphic fonts from labels, posters, cans, boxes, and architectural renderings of yore.

Outside of the United States, vernacular designs are just beginning to be exploited. Until now, innovations and new technologies, not cultural archaeology, were engines of creativity for young designers. But recently, avant-garde practitioners in France, Belgium, and Germany have discovered homespun treasures, some hiding in plain sight. Police badges, artless crests, naive logos, and industrial signs are favorite visual references of the award-winning Flanders team Randoald Sabbe and Jan W. Heespel. Their posters promoting cultural events make provocative use of forgotten graphic artifacts. Also trendy today are two-color posters and flyers in basic red and blue, their typographical signature reminiscent of cheap playbills from the 1940s. Florian Lamm in Leipzig, Germany, and Vincent Perrottet in Chaumont, France, are turning vernacular reproduction techniques, such as Ben-Day dots (enlarged screened patterns), blurry halftone reproductions, **split fountain** color printing, and new artworks inked on top of recycled posters, into sophisticated aesthetic statements.

Infatuation with arcane forms of advertising art is no longer restricted to a few connoisseurs. But French cheese labels, Irish road signs, cigarette packs from the USSR, German candy wrappers, Greek restaurant menus, and cigar boxes from Spain have yet to release the forgotten symbolism of their graphic codes. ∎

IDEA № 93
FRENCH THEORY

In the late 1980s in the United States, graphic design educators adopted the notions of deconstruction, as championed by the French philosopher Jacques Derrida, as a critical tool to reinvent visual communication. Coinciding with the advent of the digital age, the deconstructivist trend challenged accepted standards of legibility and turned graphic artifacts into exciting typographical ciphers.

BELOW: Holland Festival Programme *(1987), designed by Robert Nakata of Studio Dumbar, challenges the conventional definition of legibility and proposes instead a new form of intuitive perception.*

ABOVE: Paschal Candles *(1987–91), letterpress and silkscreen compositions from the college thesis of British typographer Phil Baines, is an example of what celebrated design critic Rick Poynor calls "alternative models of textual organization."*

OPPOSITE: The Cranbrook Graduate Program in Design *(1989) by Katherine McCoy is an early manifesto of the digital age. It champions multiple readings as a way to encourage readers to become active participants in the construction of the message.*

In the last part of the twentieth century, when a handful of French thinkers reflected on the fact that values we take for granted may be nothing but narrative constructs, they unwittingly started a cultural war. While some in the United States embraced the new ideas, conservative forces vilified the "French theory" as dangerous rhetoric contrived by anarchists. For the graphic design community, the controversy was a godsend. Adding the study of critical literary theories, deconstruction, linguistics, and semiotics to the curriculum "legitimized design by giving it its own meta-language," as graphic designer, curator, and educator Ellen Lupton wrote. It also gave those who embraced these abstruse intellectual disciplines an aura of rebellion that flattered their egos.

The work of avant-garde graphic designers during this period in Britain and America, and to a lesser extent in the Netherlands and France, looks fractured, splintered, shattered—challenging the reader's ability to decipher the overall message. Beginning in 1985, English type designer Phil Baines found intriguing ways to untether headlines and text and set them loose on a sheet of paper, as he did for the layout of his college thesis *The Bauhaus mistook legibility for communication.* By 1987, Edward Fella was treating typographical elements as windblown bits of information, Rudy VanderLans was turning *Emigré* into a festive eye chart, and Studio Dumbar was using photographic crazy quilts as background for its word **collages**. Katherine McCoy's 1989 poster advertising the Cranbrook Academy of Art's graduate program is a textbook example of how to "deconstruct" a text into elegant smithereens. Never mind that breaking down the structure of a page into its components was not exactly what Derrida had in mind when he coined the term "deconstruction."

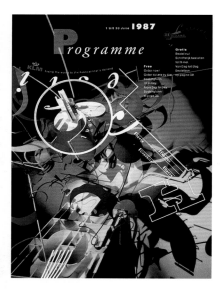

Graphic designers had appropriated the concept with Postmodernist zeal.

Only recently are former deconstructionists waking up to the fact that Derrida never advocated we dismantle a text and its message bit by bit. He merely suggested that what the message is *not* is just as important as what it is. Perhaps the best example of this reevaluation of deconstruction is a television trailer made by London-based Why Not Associates. Called "Unseen Gaza," it shows—without showing anything—the suppressed news about this war-torn territory. Headlines are crossed out before the viewer can read them and video images are systematically obscured by a white rectangle. Pointing to what is not there is sometimes the best way to explain it all. ■

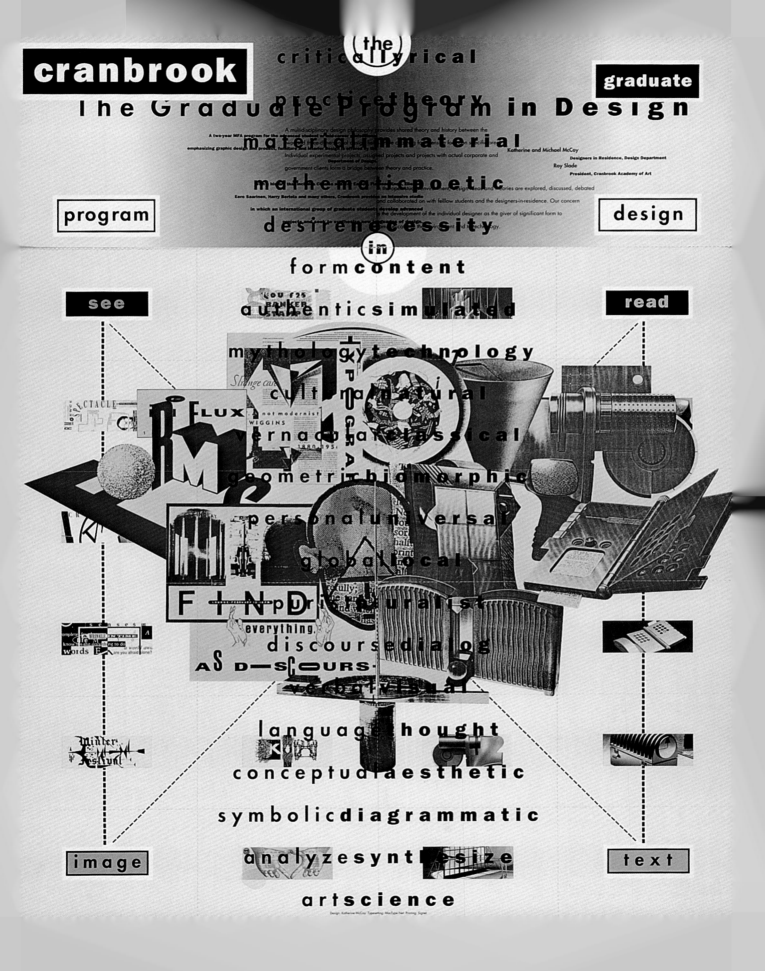

Be your own designer

IDEA № 94
DO IT YOURSELF

ABOVE: Sniffin' Glue (1977), a monthly illustrated punk zine, was instantly popular among British music fans and proponents of the DIY ethic, who applauded its anticonsumerism aesthetics and subculture ideology.

The word "design" was coined to describe the practice of mass-production. Handmade objects were in an altogether different category, considered to be finer, better-looking, and of greater value. In the 1970s, punks turned it all around and began to promote a clumsy, amateurish, do-it-yourself aesthetic. Their crude posters, fanzines, and T-shirts, with their **ransom-note** style typography, bad calligraphy, and poorly reproduced photographs, were a hit with bands and their fans. It was a funky and fun look that defined the spirit of an urgent, self-reliant, and pugnacious counterculture.

The British monthly publication *Sniffin' Glue* lasted only a year (1976–77), but had a circulation of 15,000. Designed, written, and published by punk musician Mark Perry, it had almost no running text, only commentaries and profanities scrawled by hand around black-and-white photographs of alternative rock and roll musicians. It was the graphic equivalent of the garages, warehouses, and basements where bands used to rehearse and perform. To its readers, *Sniffin' Glue* was an invaluable source of pictures of their idols but also a **manifesto** of their anticonsumerist stance. The instant success of fanzines such as this one was the expression of a cultural rebellion in part inspired by the Situationist movement.

The popularity of the DIY approach can also be explained as a consequence of the oil crisis of 1973–74 that signaled the end of postwar prosperity and spurred waves of rationing, strikes, and social unrest. The economic downturn of the 1970s motivated people to make do by being creative, fixing things, and figuring out inexpensive shortcuts. The French collective Grapus gave the DIY movement a new meaning: its members did everything together as a group, pasting bits and pieces of visual reference that they all agreed upon, and tying it all together with hand-drawn calligraphy. A 1988 advertisement for Polaroid, for a campaign organized by Pentagram in London, effectively combines a rough drawing of the front of an SX-70 camera, made to look like a face, spitting out a portrait of someone sticking his tongue out at the viewer. It was a perfect metaphor for the way advanced technology can create more spontaneity.

Perhaps paradoxically, computers today are empowering people who want to make things from scratch. Anyone can declare himself or herself a publisher, filmmaker, typographer, or recording artist. Do It Yourself has morphed into Design It Yourself, as technology allows for higher standards of design excellence. A recent book by the American designer and curator Ellen Lupton aims to teach this new generation of eager amateurs the basic principles of good design. As an educator, Lupton believes that an ability to learn from books is the most essential DIY tool. ∎

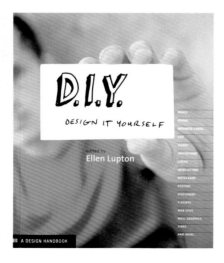

BELOW: Design It Yourself (2006), graphic designer and educator Ellen Lupton's answer to digital fatigue: capitalizing on the self-publishing and blogging trends, she inspires readers to put their personal imprint on everyday objects.

OPPOSITE: New Polaroid Impulse (1988) was an assignment from London-based Pentagram to the French collective Grapus. Deemed too radical, the poster was rejected by the client, evidence that even the most innovative corporations were reluctant to embrace the DIY approach.

Make sure you read the fine print

IDEA № 95
THE FINE PRINT

Text printed in very small type can be perfectly legible. People read best what they recognize, and if they know what to expect, they can decipher it. The choice of a typeface for train timetables, telephone books, footnotes, product warranties, or warning labels has as much to do with reading habits as with size, layout, or print quality.

In the 1970s, when Matthew Carter was asked by AT&T to improve on the existing typeface of the U.S. telephone book, he made the type smaller and tighter—yet infinitely more readable. The distinctive 1937 Bell Gothic font was not fit for the new high-speed offset lithography presses on which the phone books were printed. The letterforms broke apart, becoming either too light or too heavy.

Carter designed a new sans serif typeface, Bell Centennial, a miracle of clarity on a small scale: he provided notches in the creases of the letterforms to trap the extra ink that used to spread outward and make the words look fuzzy. Though hardly noticeable, these indentations gave the typeface an overall sharpness that made the long lists of names and numbers singularly easy on the eye. Other adjustments included getting rid of diagonal strokes, minimizing horizontal ones, and designing slightly fatter but more condensed letterforms.

What is written in small type is sometimes the most arresting part of a label. Customers these days scrutinize the information on the back of packaging the way detectives inspect a crime scene. Their mind becomes a magnifying glass as they evaluate lists of ingredients, side effects, or nutritional content. With safety regulations becoming more complex, additional legal jargon must be crammed into small spaces, a challenge that is usually handled in a 6 point (very small), condensed, sans serif typeface. Though conventional wisdom still holds that serifs (the tiny projections finishing off the strokes of a letter in some typefaces) make large blocks of text easier to decipher, they also make them blacker, a major disadvantage when letters are small and printed on inexpensive stock.

With information viewed on a computer screen rather than on paper, the loss of legibility of small letterforms is staggering. Advocating the readability of printed matter, Edward Tufte, an expert on analytical design, invented "sparklines," finely chiseled, wordlike graphics that convey a significant amount of data at a glance. Minute details, it turns out, are eye-catching devices. The slightest change in the texture of type is surprisingly noticeable. This is a phenomenon that British artist Daniel Eatock understood well when he designed a card for the Walker Art Center in Minneapolis, Minnesota, to celebrate the new millennium: by repeating the number 1999 one thousand nine hundred and ninety-nine times, and the number 2000 two thousand times, he created two very distinct blocks of tiny numbers, the microscopic variation between the two evoking the momentous shift into the next century. ■

ABOVE: What about that "fine type" compromise? *(1911),* a headache remedy advertisement that tried to lure consumers with small rather than large claims, aware that shouting is not the best way to establish one's authority.

OPPOSITE ABOVE: Millennium Card *(1999),* by British designer Daniel Eatock for the Walker Art Center in Minneapolis, was formed by repeating the numbers 1999 and 2000. The dividing line between the two blocks of numbers is barely visible.

OPPOSITE BELOW: Minutes Diary *(2003)* by Struktur Design illustrates the year broken down into its consituent minutes, all 525,600 of them set at 10-minute intervals. The days, weeks, and months are overprinted in black and gray.

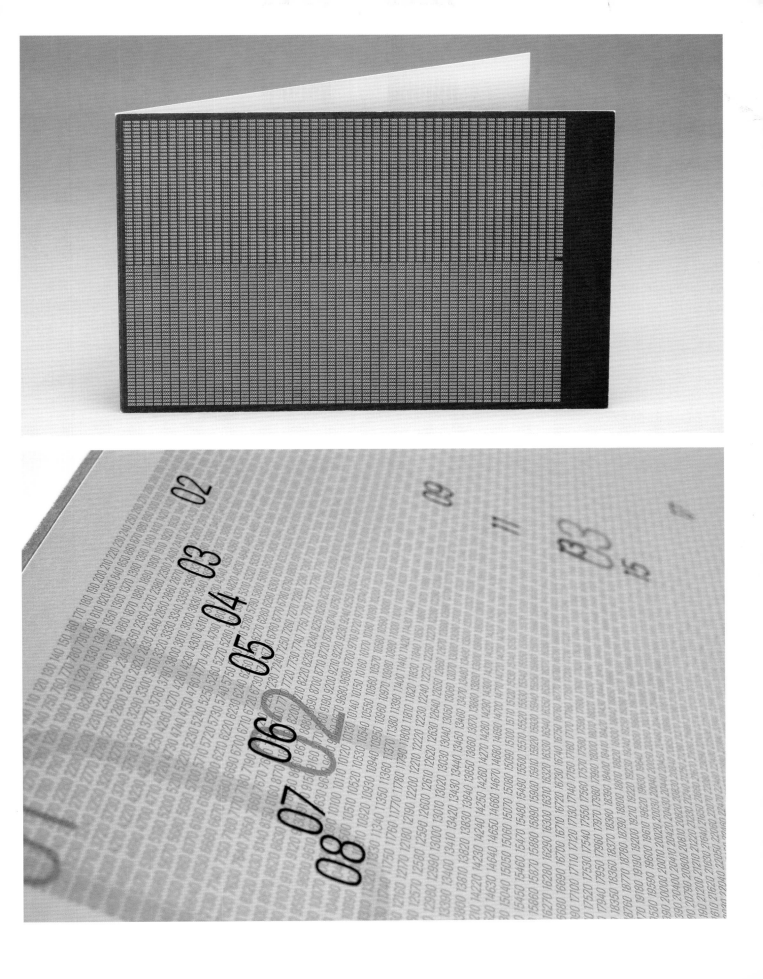

Taking over the cover

IDEA № 96
MAGAZINE COVERLINES

Which magazine was the first to place numerous headlines on its cover (coverlines) is not known, but the practice is a double-edged design sword. On the sharp side are poignant, pithy, and powerful headlines that transform a cover into a poster, highlighting editorial content and revealing an editor's standpoint. On the dull side, in recent years a plethora of coverlines billboards almost every page of magazine content.

Covers were originally designed with emphasis on strong images. In the 1930s magazines like *Vanity Fair*, *Vogue*, and *Harper's Bazaar* didn't even use coverlines. When newsstand competition became more intense in the 1950s and 1960s, they became more common. The practice of squeezing as much hyperbole as possible onto a cover started in the late 1970s when Condé Nast design czar, Alexander Liberman, ordered the designers of the fashion and lifestyle magazines in the group to adopt techniques common to tabloid newspapers. Liberman reasoned that fashion had become too fantasy-oriented, and required an injection of grit that could be accomplished through unsophisticated graphic design. Concurrently, marketing experts believed that coverlines would increase visibility and attract readers in a highly competitive field. In theory this approach mirrored changing social attitudes, but the shift from the old to the new style—from minimalist elegance to more-is-more information—marked a shift in magazine design practice, one that offers questionable results. Once the die was cast coverlines became a necessary evil.

There are plenty of examples of good practice. A powerful example is the all-black *Esquire* cover of October 1966 with its stark white headline "Oh my God—we hit a little girl," designed by George Lois, referring to a seminal article on the Vietnam War. *National Lampoon*'s January 1973 cover, "If You Don't Buy This Magazine, We'll Kill This Dog," well, speaks for itself. Other magazines treat coverlines as an integrated element of a cover's design. But sadly these are exceptions to a convention that has turned the most valuable piece of editorial real estate into a waste ground of intrusive typography.

Fashion and lifestyle magazines, which should be rooted in elegance, are now covered with forests of words. Many do not treat the coverline as a design element meant to draw attention to each magazine's unique message. Rather, the headlines act like scaffolding in front of a construction site, obstructing the effectiveness of the central image. The strategic benefit gained by having plenty of selling copy on the front cover can be argued: a startling headline will always attract attention. But a striking headline *and* an alluring image is the best combination. ∎

ABOVE: National Lampoon (1973), art-directed by Michael Gross for the "Death" issue, threatened to put down poor pooch if the customer failed to put down 75 cents.

OPPOSITE: Esquire (1966), designed by George Lois. During the throes of Vietnam War protests, this all-type cover hit a nerve that a photograph may not have found.

BELOW: BusinessWeek (1987) makes a point: with a cell phone (new at the time), anyone can be a Dick Tracy and talk from anywhere. Computers were getting faster, smaller, and more powerful, so jobs and work would never be quite the same.

Esquire

THE MAGAZINE FOR MEN

AUGUST 1966
PRICE 75c

"Oh my God —we hit a little girl."

The true story of M Company.
From Fort Dix to Vietnam.

Advertising by stealth

IDEA Nº 97

GUERRILLA ADVERTISING

"Guerrilla" suggests surreptitious warfare. In the late 1990s the word was applied to a genre of edgy urban advertising campaigns. Also known as "never been done before" (NBDB) or "ambient" advertising, guerrilla ads involve the semi-subversive planting of messages in venues and on objects ordinarily free of advertising, such as banana skins, body tattoos—even urinal disinfectant pucks. Other venues include sidewalks, taxi roofs, and graffiti on vacant storefronts.

The irreverent New York agency Kirshenbaum Bond Senecal + Partners, a pioneer in guerrilla pique, spray-painted New York sidewalks in 2007 with the line "From here it looks like you could use some new underwear" for a lingerie company. A year later the ad agency Creature, based in Seattle, Washington, created the so-called "Good Samaritan" campaign for Starbucks, affixing precarious red paper cups to the roofs of dozens of cabs: if a "Samaritan" warned the taxi's passenger about the cup before driving off, he or she was given a free Starbucks gift card. During the 2007 baseball season, Ogilvy & Mather applied thin plastic sheets to random car windows, to look as though a baseball had crashed through; promoting the New York Mets, they came with an apology note from the team's management.

Not all guerrilla campaigns are for commercial products. Guerrilla approaches were initially used by political groups that had little or no access to mass media. The German Amnesty International campaign against human trafficking—a transparent suitcase with a woman trapped inside—is an unforgettable way to remind people of the horror of the forced sex trade.

Guerrilla methods came into being for a very practical reason. As New York University historian Stephen Duncombe has noted, "Advertising, for all its immensity and importance, is in trouble." The advent of digital TV recorders, which allow viewers to eliminate advertising altogether, coupled with the downsizing of traditional advertising media (TV networks, newspapers, and magazines) because of competition from cable TV and the Internet, means that mainstream advertisers are finding it difficult to target audiences efficiently.

Exploiting new media is not original. Back in the 1930s, advertisers conquered the heavens with skywriting and blimps. Wherever there is new technology, advertisers are among the first to adopt it. The colonization of public space in many large cities is only the latest frontier. Digital display and printing technologies have made it easy to print onto fabrics and decal stickers in all sizes and shapes, as well as to project laser image messages onto almost any surface. But how much "never been done before" advertising will the public tolerate before they feel their space has been taken over? ∎

ABOVE: Yes We Can (2008), produced by will.i.am, uses Barack Obama's trademark words from his 2008 U.S. presidential campaign. This collaged video included over two dozen performers. The song went viral on the Internet.

OPPOSITE ABOVE: Woman in a Suitcase (2009), by Agency Serviceplan in Munich, was developed for an Amnesty International campaign against human trafficking. On second glance, travelers waiting for their bags realized that the woman in a transparent case was real.

OPPOSITE BELOW: AXE (2007) by Lowe + Partners, Belgium, riffs on the vernacular of exit signs to suggest crowds of girls chasing the man who uses AXE deodorant. The subversive idea is adding to existing signage.

"Wherever there is new technology, advertisers are among the first to adopt it."

Pixeleted images are emblems of the digital age

IDEA № 98
PIXELATION

A bitmap is an image-file format in computer graphics, a mapped array of pixels also known as a raster image. A pixel (from "picture element"), is a single point in a bitmap: a tiny single square, the smallest viewable unit on screen. Pixelation is a visual effect caused by enlarging a bitmap to such a scale that individual pixels are exaggeratedly visible to the eye.

Before the advent of high resolution, most on-screen images for graphics and type were pixelated; output printing was equally rough-edged. The pixel is to the computer what the halftone is to print photography; it is the means by which a digital image is displayed. As the symbol of computer-generated design, it is now used to conceptually represent and critically comment on media.

When the Macintosh computer was first introduced as a design tool in 1984, all on-screen imagery was black and white with a bluish tint and bitmapped. Dot-matrix printers produced 72 dpi rough-edged type and image. Rather than fight against the limitations of technology, in 1985, only a year after the Mac came on the market, Zuzana Licko, type designer and cofounder of Emigre Fonts, designed digital typefaces including Emigre, Emperor, Oakland, and Universal. Each pixelated font was built out of blocks on a grid structure and the resulting image was the bitmap. "The coarser the resolution, the more limited is the possibility of pixel placement, and the variety of representable font characteristics is limited accordingly," Licko noted in the Emigre type catalog. For a brief moment the bitmapped face was the emblem of the pixelated age.

During the late 1980s and early 1990s graphical applications, notably video games and other interfaces, appeared at very low resolutions, with a limited number of colors. The pixels were vivid, with sharp edges giving curved objects and diagonal lines an awkwardly stiff appearance. However, when the number of available colors increased to 256, even low-resolution objects looked smoother. Ultimately, high resolution eliminated the problem of unwanted pixelation.

But that remedy did not stop designers using pixelation as a stylistic conceit. Berlin-based eBoy create urban panoramas, made from brightly colored pixelated computer-renderings in a retro **parody** of vintage computer games. Similarly Christoph Niemann's sardonic personal computer icons are a comedic look at the abundance of clichés from the early digital era. They also prefigure the current growth of app icons.

Today pixels are on the screen, but so minimized that only a keen eye will see them. However, as an ironic feature, graphics are still made in low resolution for comic or aesthetic effect. ∎

OPPOSITE: Analog vs Digital *(2010), a pixelated mosaic by Charis Tsevis and Indyvisuals Design Collective for Design Walk 2010, one of the most important graphic design platforms in Greece.*

ABOVE: Pecol *(2008) is a laptop skin made from eBoy's Pecol vinyl toy series with "every member of Jackhammer Jill's extended family."*

Brain-teasing typographic compositions

AMBIGRAMS

An ambigram is a typographical composition that may be read as one or more words not only in the form as presented, but also from a different orientation—upside down, right side up, or back to front—or as a totally different word or words. John Langdon, an American typographer, ambigram expert, and author of *Wordplay*, says an ambigram is a decipherable puzzle, but it is also the basis for certain kinds of intricate logos.

The earliest known ambigram was designed in 1893 by the children's book illustrator Peter Newell (*The Hole Book*), who published various books of invertible images, whereby the picture turns into a different image entirely when turned upside down. The last page in his book *Topsys & Turvys* contains the phrase THE END, which, when inverted, reads PUZZLE.

As a logo, the ambigram is usually most effective when it is kept as simple as possible, and is thus instantly readable. With only three letters in each word, Raymond Loewy's 1969 "New Man" mark does not require a whole lot of perceptual gymnastics to comprehend it. Yet the combination of letters is still surprising and forces the reader to do a double take when seeing the mirror image of the words for the first time. The more a logo can be cognitively interactive, the greater the chance it will be a successful mnemonic. So the 1989 logo for the rock band Nine Inch Nails (NIN) designed by front man Trent Reznor and Gary Taplas, employing a backward "N" that can be read from right to left and left to right, offers just the right twist to ensure memorability—and the proverbial smile in the mind.

Langdon's ambigrams tend to be more complex. His use of gothic, black letter, and swash lettering adds both to the elegance and to the vexing nature of his compositions, but once they are turned around, the viewer's cognitive realization triggers a unique sense of accomplishment.

Ralph Schraivogel's *Evil/Live* is not the traditional ambigram, but it does convey the message that "evil prevails when good men fail to act." Like all ambigrams, this is a graphic lock that demands picking. In general, ambigrams are typographic tools—similar to a **visual pun**—for engaging the reader in a game and providing immediate cognitive payback. ∎

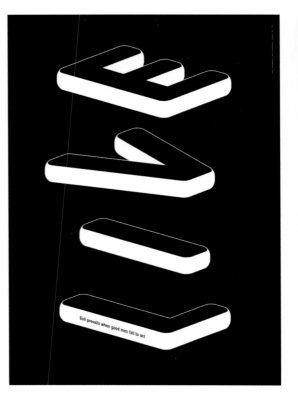

TOP: Evil/Live (2009), designed by Ralph Schraivogel, is not strictly an ambigram, but it does convey two key meanings through reversing the letters.

ABOVE: New Man (1969) logo, designed by Raymond Loewy, is described as the first logo to be created as an ambigram —and read in either direction.

BELOW: Pod (2007), designed by Darren Gordon of Volatile Graphics, is the quintessential topsy-turvy logo, reading left to right and right to left, and upside down.

Earth Air Fire Water *(2007) by*
John Langdon, who began creating
ambigrams in the early 1970s.
Wordplay, *his book of ambigrams*
and the philosophical essays he
wrote to accompany them, was
published in 1992.

"The combination of letters forces
the reader to do a double take."

Marking territory online

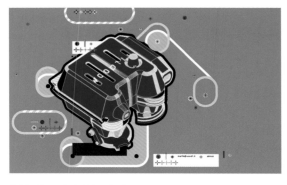

IDEA № 100
DESIGNERS' WEBSITES

Where is the grid when you need it? The computer screen is a blank surface that is too wide for the human eye to scan comfortably at a glance. On their websites, designers use every trick they know to turn this graphic no man's land into an intimate visual experience. For a prospective client, leafing through a designer's portfolio used to be as laid-back as looking at a magazine; for the owner of the portfolio, it was a brief and terrifying moment. Today, websites make the vexing interviews unnecessary.

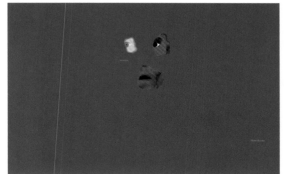

TOP: www.woodt.li/ (2011), the website of unconventional Swiss designer Martin Woodtli, is a locked puzzle that cannot be opened unless you figure out its code. It looks at first glance like a piece of machinery requiring an engineering degree to operate.

OPPOSITE: www.cyan.de (2010), the website of the Berlin-based studio Cyan, comes up as a seamless scroll of serendipitous images, each project organized by topics, with the "plakat" (poster) category the longest of all.

ABOVE: The website for poster legend Michel Quarez (2010) was a solid, flat green surface, the color of a billiard table, on which you were invited to shoot around bits of information about his life and philosophy.

Rather than try to fill all available space, most designers occupy only the upper left area of the screen, leaving the right side mercifully empty. Designing a website is not unlike designing a menu or a table of contents, with projects listed by clickable category or keyword. New York graphic designer Stephen Doyle has one of the most user-friendly, foolproof websites: on his pristine home page, keywords are presented twice, first as a list and second as a circle of small icons around a sundial. By contrast, Niessen & de Vries in the Netherlands have devised an opener that is deliberately confusing: it looks like a mesmerizing checkerboard of spaced letters, until you slide your cursor over the puzzle and realize that the keywords are listed vertically. Degrees of complexity on opening pages are inversely proportional to the years in business; well-established studios tend to eschew tricky presentations.

Mosaics are a popular approach, perhaps the most extreme example being the website of Cyan, a Berlin studio. The entire surface of the screen is wallpapered with close to 500 vignettes, each the entry point to a specific project. Creating comprehensive archives is another favorite design solution. Vertical timelines make it easy. Paul Sahre—a resident of New York, where space is at a premium—has managed to pack about 275 projects on a tight 8in square on the upper left-hand side of his screen. Among the most unexpected visual strategies found in designers' websites, from Vince Frost (Australia) to Reza Abedini (Iran), are diagrams, **collages**, graffiti, blackboards, bulletin boards, flash cards, flow charts, blinking icons, laundry lists, and random carousels of images.

Graphic designers tend to shun showy animations, sound effects, and video. Linear blog architecture, where projects are logged chronologically, has its fans, notably among people who want to avoid locking up their work in rigid categories. In this class are websites by radical French *graphistes*, who are first and foremost "authors." Vincent Perrottet has a seamless presentation of more than 100 candid photographs of work in progress, strung together as an endless scroll, with his cats as prominently featured as his gigantic posters. Pierre di Sciullo regularly updates his display, each window designed as a handsome abstract typographical "tableau." ∎

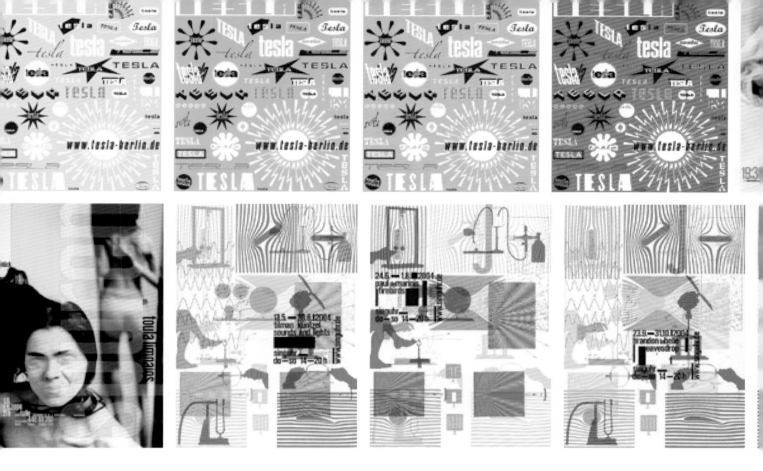

Glossary

AIGA
The American Institute of Graphic Arts, the foremost design advocacy and educational organization in the United States.

Art Deco or Art Moderne
International design style introduced after World War I and following Art Nouveau, developed in France as a combination of classical and Modern aesthetics. Known for its rectilinear forms as well as decorative conceits.

Art Nouveau
Known by different names in different nations (including Stil Liberty, Modernista, Vienna Secession, Jugendstil), this international design style started in the late 1890s, characterized by curvilinear forms and naturalistic motifs.

Arts and Crafts
An English late nineteenth century design movement led by William Morris, promoting handcrafts and celebration of medieval guilds, and protesting against industrial standardization.

Baroque
Architectural style from 1600 to 1750, characterized by melodramatic effects and theatrical perspectives. The term is used today to describe mannered or over-the-top decorative schemes.

Bauhaus
German state-run arts and crafts school and workshop that helped introduce orthodox Modernism to all design media from graphic design to architecture. Closed by the Nazis in 1933.

Color blocking
Flat patches of colors are assembled side by side to create an image that is either figurative or abstract.

Constructivism
Russian revolutionary visual language based on avant-garde art forms and philosophies, which was incorporated into orthodox Modernism in the 1920s. Ended by Stalin with the advent of Socialist Realism.

Cubism
Early twentieth century progressive art movement pioneered by Pablo Picasso and Georges Braque, mostly applied to painting and sculpture, but introduced to commercial graphic design to suggest modernity.

Dada
An antiart literary and art movement that began in Zurich and fanned out to Berlin, Paris, New York, and elsewhere. Graphically, Dada disrupted the printed page by ignoring balance, proportion, and the accepted rules of typography. It influenced what became known as grunge and punk type aesthetics in the 1970s and 1980s.

De Stijl or neoplasticism
Dutch for "the style," this art movement was conceived by Piet Mondrian and Theo van Doesburg. Its rigid geometries and limited primary colors helped set the stage for Modernist graphic design.

Deconstruction
A catchall term for any non- or anti-Modern method or practice. Built around French linguistic theory, in typography it was characterized by the discordant type styles and sizes smashed together in late 1980s and 1990s designs.

Expressionism
A Modernist art movement based on creating images from a subjective perspective, using distortion to achieve an emotional response. Graphically, it was noted for wood and linocut imagery and lettering.

Fauvism
A French art movement, peaking in 1905, which took the saturated palette of the Impressionists to the next level. During this period, Henri Matisse, André Derain, and Maurice de Vlaminck combined exotic colors with wild brushstrokes, a technique described as *fauve*, meaning "as wild as beasts."

Festschrift
A book or other publication, usually printed in limited numbers, celebrating an individual or thing. Such limited editions are common to graphic design as a means of informing and educating other designers.

Futurism
An artistic, cultural, and political movement founded by the Italian poet F.T. Marinetti in 1909 and adopted by rebellious artists and writers, many of whom supported Italian Fascism. Typographically, Futurist design, like Dada, was focused on kineticism, making "words in freedom" that screamed off the page, rather than communicated ideas neutrally.

Halftone
Technique used to reproduce photographs or continuous-tone artwork by breaking the image into rows of tiny dots, which to the naked eye provide an infinite range of gray tones.

Impressionism
Late nineteenth century French painting school, including Claude Monet, using colorful strokes to capture the fuzzy contours and ever-changing appearance of their visual impressions.

Jugendstil
German term for Art Nouveau, which in Germany was somewhat more rectilinear than the French curvilinear variety. Both relied heavily on ornamented flora.

Kodalith
Kodak high-contrast film, which eliminated all middle tones, leaving only the essential black and white information. Used frequently during the 1960s to enhance poor-quality graphics.

Lettrism
A Surrealist, post-Dada, avant-garde movement from the mid-1940s that celebrated letterforms as the expression of pure sounds. Its frontrunner, Isidore Isou, treated text as if it were a musical form.

Logo or logotype
A mark or typographic abbreviation used to identify a product, company, or institution. Logos can be simple or complex, but are always a shorthand for a larger thing or idea.

Mezzotint
A printing effect using a screen of random lines to break down a continuous-tone image into an Impressionistic or Expressionistic outcome. Also used to make poor-quality graphics look more artful.

Modernism
In the broadest sense, an art and cultural movement born of industrialization. In the design sense, a method and style applied to mass-production and mechanically produced objects. Many movements and schools contributed to Modernism, but graphically it is characterized by simplicity and function-ality—the absence of sentimentality.

New Typography
The typographic offshoot of Modernism, codified by Jan Tschichold in 1925, this is underscored by asymmetry, sans-serif lettering, and an emphasis on geometry.

Op art
Popular in the mid-1960s, this movement elevated optical illusions to an art form. Tightly wound geometric patterns, in colors or black and white, were graphically arresting visual conundrums.

Pop art
A reaction to late 1940s and 1950s Abstract Expressionism, this art celebrated the quotidian design found in supermarkets and elsewhere. Led by Andy Warhol, Claes Oldenburg, Robert Rauschenberg, Roy Lichtenstein, and others, the everyday was turned into cultural icons. Many of the artists started as advertising designers.

Punk
Graphically, like Dada, punk rejected all design standards in favor of deliberate amateurism. Ransom-note lettering and handwriting replaced "official" typography. A reaction to the flower-power generation, but also an expression of do-it-yourself aesthetics.

Sachplakat or object poster
A style developed in 1906 by German Lucian Bernhard, proto-Modern and anti-Art Nouveau, reducing advertisements to the essential component parts—the product and brand name.

Situationist International
A small subversive group, virulent critics of the consumer society, who tried to counter the belief system promoted by advertising messages by lampooning them.

Spectaculars
Broadway, New York (the Great White Way) was lit up with the invention of advertising "spectaculars," which employed multiple light sources and kinetic movement to give drama and energy to the signs seen from the street.

Spencerian
Handwritten script that was taught as "official" penmanship throughout the United States from 1850–1925, created by Platt Rogers Spencer. It found its way into many logos and trademarks, such as the Coca-Cola and Ford logos.

Streamlining
The machine-age design style that paralleled Modernism and Art Deco in the United States, developed by a new breed of indus-trial designers. It symbolized technological progress during the years between World Wars I and II.

Suprematism
A Russian avant-garde art movement that focused on essential geometric forms, the circle and square. Founded by Kasimir Malevich in 1915, it later influenced much of the Modern typographic aesthetic and later Swiss Modern mannerisms.

Surrealism
A more introspective offshoot of Dada, Surrealism grew into a movement of pseudo-science and influenced artists who reveled in unexpected figurative juxtaposi-tions. A major influence on "conceptual" illustration from the 1970s to the present.

Ukiyo-e
A Japanese woodblock style whose bold graphic motifs and minimalist color signature greatly influenced Toulouse-Lautrec. The trend, also called "Japonisme," became the favorite source of inspiration for Art Nouveau artists.

Vorticism
A literary and artistic movement in England, 1912–15, linked to Italian Futurism. Founded by Wyndham Lewis, it celebrated the energy of the machine and machine-made products and rejected nineteenth-century sentimentality. Like Futurism, it promoted the cult of violence. Graphically, Vorticist compositions were abstract and sharp planed.

Werkbund
The German Werkbund was an association of artists, architects, designers, and industrialists, leading the way to modernity before the advent of the Bauhaus school. Its goal was to establish a partnership of product manufacturers with designers and improve the competitiveness of German companies in global markets.

Further Reading

Recently Published (2006–11)

Baines, Phil and Catherine Dixon. *Signs: Lettering in the Environment* (London: Laurence King Publishing, 2008).

Bataille, Marion. *ABC3D* (New York: Roaring Brook Press, 2008).

Bergström, Bo. *Essentials of Visual Communication* (London: Laurence King Publishing, 2008).

Brody, David and Hazel Clark, eds. *Design Studies: A Reader* (London: Berg Publishers, 2009).

Burke, Christopher. *Active Literature: Jan Tschichold and New Typography* (London: Hyphen Press, 2008).

Chwast, Seymour. *Seymour: The Obsessive Images of Seymour Chwast* (San Francisco: Chronicle Books, 2009).

Donaldson, Timothy. *Shapes for Sounds* (New York: Mark Batty Publisher, 2008).

Dougherty, Brian. *Green Graphic Design* (New York: Allworth Press, 2008).

Erlhoff, Michael and Tim Marshall, eds. *Design Dictionary: Perspectives on Design Terminology* (Basel: Birkhäuser Verlag, 2007).

Freyer, Conny, Sebastien Noel, and Eva Rucki. *Digital by Design* (London: Thames & Hudson, 2008).

Glaser, Milton. *Drawing is Thinking* (New York: Overlook Hardcover, 2008).

Gordon, Bob, ed. *1000 Fonts: An Illustrated Guide to Finding the Right Typeface* (San Francisco: Chronicle Books, 2009).

Hayes, Clay. *Gig Posters: Rock Show Art of the 21st Century* (Philadelphia: Quirk Books, 2009).

Heller, Steven, ed. *Design Disasters: Great Designers, Fabulous Failure, and Lessons Learned* (New York: Allworth Press, 2008).

Heller, Steven and Gail Anderson. *New Vintage Type: Classic Fonts for the Digital Age* (New York: Watson-Guptill, 2007).

Heller, Steven and Seymour Chwast. *Illustration: A Visual History* (New York: Harry N. Abrams, 2008).

Heller, Steven and Louise Fili. *Stylepedia: A Guide to Graphic Design Mannerisms, Quirks, and Conceits* (San Francisco: Chronicle Books, 2006).

Heller, Steven and Mirko Ilic. *The Anatomy of Design* (Minneapolis: Rockport Publishers, 2007).

Heller, Steven and Mirko Ilic. *Handwritten: Expressive Lettering in the Digital Age* (London: Thames & Hudson, 2006).

Heller, Steven and Lita Talarico. *The Design Entrepreneur* (2nd edition) (Minneapolis: Rockport Publishers, 2011).

Himpe, Tom. *Advertising Next* (San Francisco: Chronicle Books, 2008).

Jedlicka, Wendy. *Packaging Sustainability: Tools, Systems, and Strategies for Innovative Package Design* (Hoboken, New Jersey: Wiley, 2009).

de Jong, Cees, Alston W. Purvis, and Jan Tholenaar, eds. *Type: A Visual History of Typefaces and Graphic Styles, Vol. 1* (Cologne: Taschen, 2009).

Jubert, Roxane. *Typography and Graphic Design* (Paris: Flammarion, 2006).

Klanten, R. and Hendrick Hellige. *Playful Type: Ephemeral Lettering and Illustrative Fonts* (Berlin: Die Gestalten Verlag, 2008).

Lois, George. *George Lois: On His Creation of the Big Idea* (New York: Assouline, 2008).

Lupton, Ellen and Julia Lupton. *Design Your Life: The Pleasures and Perils of Everyday Things* (New York: St. Martin's Press, 2009).

Müller, Lars and Victor Malsy. *Helvetica Forever* (Baden: Lars Müller Publishers, 2007).

Munari, Bruno. *Design As Art* (London: Penguin Books, 2008).

Pentagram. *Pentagram Marks: 400 Symbols and Logotypes* (London: Laurence King Publishing, 2010).

Perry, Michael. *Over & Over: A Catalog of Hand-Drawn Patterns* (New York: Princeton Architectural Press, 2008).

Poynor, Rick. *Designing Pornotopia: Travels in Visual Culture* (New York: Princeton Architectural Press, 2006).

Roberts, Lucienne. *Good: An Introduction to Ethics in Graphic Design* (Lausanne: AVA Publishing, 2006).

Sagmeister, Stefan. *Things I Have Learned in My Life So Far* (New York: Harry N. Abrams, 2008).

Shaughnessy, Adrian. *How to be a Graphic Designer Without Losing Your Soul* (2nd edition) (London: Laurence King Publishing, 2010).

Shedroff, Nathan. *Design is the Problem: The Future of Design Must be Sustainable* (New York: Rosenfeld Media, 2009).

Thorgerson, Storm and Aubrey Powell. *For the Love of Vinyl: The Album Art of Hipgnosis* (New York: Picture Box, 2008).

Vienne, Véronique and Steven Heller. *Art Direction Explained, At Last!* (London: Laurence King Publishing, 2009).

Visocky O'Grady, Jennifer and Ken Visocky O'Grady. *A Designer's Research Manual: Succeed in Design by Knowing Your Clients and What They Really Need* (Minneapolis: Rockport Publishers, 2009).

Vit, Armin and Bryony Gomez Palacio. *Graphic Design, Referenced: A Visual Guide to the Language, Applications, and History of Graphic Design* (Minneapolis: Rockport Publishers, 2009).

General Bibliography

Ades, Dawn. *Photomontage* (London: Thames & Hudson, 1986).

American Type Founders Company. *Specimen Book and Catalogue 1923* (Jersey City: American Type Founders Company, 1923).

Baines, Phil. *Penguin by Design: A Cover Story 1935–2005* (London: Penguin Books, 2005).

Barron, Stephanie and Maurice Tuchman, eds. *The Avant-Garde in Russia 1910–1930* (Cambridge, MA: The MIT Press, 1980).

Blackwell, Lewis. *The End of Print: The Grafik Design of David Carson* (2nd edition) (London: Laurence King Publishing, 2000).

Blackwell, Lewis. *20th Century Type* (revised edition) (New Haven: Yale University Press, 2004).

Bruce's New York Type-Foundry. *Specimens of Printing Types* (New York: George Bruce and Son and Co., 1882).

Crimlis, Roger and Alwyn W. Turner. *Cult Rock Posters: Ten Years of Classic Posters from the Glam, Punk and New Wave Era* (New York: Billboard Books, 2006).

DeNoon, Christopher. *Posters of the WPA 1935–1943* (Seattle: University of Washington Press, 1987).

Dickerman, Leah, ed. *Building the Collective: Soviet Graphic Design 1917–1937* (2nd edition) (New York: Princeton Architectural Press, 1996).

Eason, Ron. *Rookledge's International Directory of Type Designers* (New York: The Sarabande Press, 1994).

Freeman, Judi. *The Dada & Surrealist Word-Image* (Cambridge, MA: The MIT Press, 1989).

Friedman, Mildred, ed. *Graphic Design in America: A Visual Language History* (Minneapolis and New York: The Walker Art Center and Harry N. Abrams, 1989).

Glaser, Milton. *Milton Glaser: Graphic Design* (revised edition) (Woodstock: The Overlook Press, 1983).

Gottschall, Edward M. *Typographic Communications Today* (Cambridge, MA: The MIT Press, 1989).

Greiman, April. *Design Quarterly #133* (Cambridge, MA: The MIT Press for Walker Art Center, 1986).

Heller, Steven and Louise Fili. *Design Connoisseur: An Eclectic Collection of Imagery and Type* (New York: Allworth Press, 2000).

Heyman, Therese Thau. *Posters: American Style* (exhibition catalog) (New York: Harry N. Abrams, 1998).

Jaspert, W. Pincus, W. Turner Berry, and A.F. Johnson. *Encyclopedia of Typefaces* (55th anniversary edition) (London: Cassell Illustrated, 2008).

Kelly, Rob Roy. *American Wood Type 1828–1900: Notes on the Evolution of Decorated and Large Types* (New York: Da Capo Press, 1977).

Lasky, Julie. *Some People Can't Surf: The Graphic Design of Art Chantry* (San Francisco: Chronicle Books, 2001).

Lawson, Alexander. *Anatomy of a Typeface* (London: Hamish Hamilton, 1990).

Lewis, John. *Printed Ephemera: The Changing Uses of Type and Letterforms in English and American Printing* (Woodbridge, Suffolk: The Antique Collectors' Club, 1990).

Lewis, John. *Typography Design and Practice* (London: JM Classic Editions, 2007).

McKnight-Trontz, Jennifer and Alex Steinweiss. *For the Record: The Life and Work of Alex Steinweiss* (New York: Princeton Architectural Press, 2000).

McLean, Ruari. *Jan Tschichold: Typographer* (London: Lund Humphries, 1975).

Meggs, Philip B. and Rob Carter. *Typographic Specimens: The Great Typefaces* (Hoboken, NJ: Wiley, 1993).

Meggs, Philip B. and Alston W. Purvis. *Meggs' History of Graphic Design* (4th edition) (Hoboken, NJ: Wiley, 2006).

Mouron, Henri. *A.M. Cassandre* (New York: Rizzoli International Publications, 1985).

New Typographics (Tokyo: Pie Books, 2008).

Poyner, Rick. *Typographica* (New York: Princeton Architectural Press, 2001).

Purvis, Alston W. *H.N. Werkman* (New Haven: Yale University Press, 2004).

Purvis, Alston W. and Martijn F. Le Coultre. *Graphic Design 20th Century* (New York: Princeton Architectural Press, 2003).

Remington, R. Roger. *American Modernism: Graphic Design 1920 to 1960* (New Haven: Yale University Press, 2003).

Rothenstein, Julian and Mel Gooding, eds. *ABZ: More Alphabets and Other Signs* (San Francisco: Chronicle Books, 2003).

Rothschild, Deborah, Ellen Lupton, and Darra Goldstein. *Graphic Design in the Mechanical Age* (New Haven: Yale University Press, 1998).

Sherraden, Jim, Elek Horvath, and Paul Kingsbury. *Hatch Show Print: The History of a Great American Poster Shop* (San Francisco: Chronicle Books, 2001).

Spencer, Herbert, ed. *The Liberated Page* (San Francisco: Chronicle Books, 1991).

Spencer, Herbert. *Pioneers of Modern Typography* (revised edition) (Cambridge, MA: The MIT Press, 2004).

Thompson, Bradbury. *Bradbury Thompson: The Art of Graphic Design* (New Haven: Yale University Press, 1988).

Updike, Daniel Berkeley. *Printing Types, Their History, Forms, and Use: A Study in Survivals* (3rd edition) (Cambridge, MA: Harvard University Press, 1962).

VanderLans, Rudy and Zuzana Licko with Mary E. Gray. *Emigre: Graphic Design into the Digital Realm* (Hoboken, NJ: Wiley, 1993).

Vienne, Véronique. *Chip Kidd* (London: Laurence King Publishing, 2003).

Vienne, Véronique. *Something to be Desired: Design Essays by Véronqiue Vienne* (London: Graphis, 2000).

Wozencroft, Jon. *The Graphic Language of Neville Brody* (London: Thames & Hudson, 1988).

Index

Picture credits

a = above, c = center, b = below, l = left, r = right

8 courtesy of Bruce Mau Design; 9a © DACS 2011; 9b Museum fur Gestaltung Zurich, Graphics Collection. Franz Xaver Jaggy © ZhdK; 10a art direction Stefan Sagmeister, photography Tom Schierlitz, client AIGA Detroit; 10b Digital image, The Museum of Modern Art, New York/Scala, Florence; 11 Courtesy: Jenny Holzer / Photo: Alan Richardson / Art Resource, NY. © ARS, NY and DACS, London 2011; 12 Ich&Kar wall sticker *Trees* for Domestic; 13 Letraset Ltd / Ahmad Sha'ath; 14 © Disney; 15a Courtesy of Ogilvy & Mather Advertising; 15b Museum fur Gestaltung Zurich, Poster Collection. Franz Xaver Jaggy © ZhdK; 16a The Bridgeman Art Library; 17 lithographic print by David Lance Goines, Saint Hieronymus Press; 18a © Clare Acheson; 18b Library of Congress Prints and Photographs Division Washington, D.C. Copyright by General Cable Corporation; 19 Museum fur Gestaltung Zurich, Poster Collection. Franz Xaver Jaggy © ZhdK; 20 © Pierre Bernard; © 2011 Scala; 21b © Alexandre Orion, Ossario, 2006–2010 Urban intervention executed by selectively scraping off black soot deposited by car exhausts on tunnel walls; 23 Harvey Hacker, GSD Poster Coop; 24–25 The Museum of Modern Art, New York / Scala, Florence; 26bl art direction Pascale Renaux, photography Sofia Sanchez and Mauro Mongiello, make-up Sol Shurnan, model Anaïs @ Vision; 27 Digital image, The Museum of Modern Art, New York/Scala, Florence; 28a Cary Graphics Collection, Rochester Institute of Technology. Estate of Lester Sr. Beall. DACS, London/VAGA, New York 2011; 28b Photography © The Art Institute of Chicago; 29 art direction, design and photography Stephan Bundi; 30a akg-images / ullstein bild; 30b Courtesy of www.kusmitea.com; 31 Courtesy of Marian Bantjes; 32 creative director Matteo Bologna, art direction and design Andrea Brown, Mucca Design for Morandi; 34 akg-images; 35b Photo Scala, Florence. © Rodchenko & Stepanova Archive, DACS 2011; 37r design Piet Schreuders, cover printed in 3 colors by Drukkerij Mart. Spruyt bv, Amsterdam; 39 a Roosevelt Civil War Envelope Collection, Georgetown University Library, Special Collections Research Centre, Washington, DC; 39b art direction Stefan Sagmeister, design Stefan Sagmeister and Matthias Ernstberger, photography Matthias Ernstberger, client Art Grandeur Nature; 40a © 2011. Photo Spectrum/Heritage Images/Scala, Florence; 40b © Phil Baines; 42a Cary Graphics Collection, Rochester Institute of Technology; 43 Karel Martens, poster for the 21st International Poster and Graphic Design Festival, Chaumont; 44 © Dan Reisinger; 45a © Noma Bar / Dutch Uncle; 47ar © Pyramyd; 48a ADAGP, Banque d'Images, Paris 2011. © ADAGP, Paris and DACS, London 2011; 49 The Museum of Modern Art, New York/Scala, Florence; 50a © Shepard Fairey/ObeyGiant. com. Photo National Portrait Gallery, Smithsonian/Art Resource/Scala, Florence; 52b © DACS 2011; 53 © The Royal Society for the Prevention of Accidents; 54b Image copyright The Metropolitan Museum of Art/Art Resource/ Scala, Florence. © Succession H. Matisse / DACS 2011; 55 Reproduced by permission of the Henry Moore Foundation; 57a Written and designed by Ken Garland; 57b M/M (Paris): Altermodern World Map Poster for the Tate Triennial at Tate Britain, used through exhibition space 2009, 4 color offset, 120 x 176. Courtesy of mmparis. com; 60a 3 saisons, 2002, Antoine+Manuel for CCNT; 60b akg-images / ullstein bild; 61 © Marian Bantjes, Published by Thames & Hudson; 64 Photo Scala, Florence. © Rodchenko & Stepanova Archive, DACS 2011; 65a © New Statesman Ltd, 2011; 66a Digital image, The Museum of Modern Art, New York/Scala, Florence. © DACS 2011; 66b Willi Kunz for Columbia University GSAPP, printer Matrix Printing, New York; 67 akg-images; 68a © DACS 2011; 69 Alain Le Quernec; 70a Photo © The Fine Art Society, London, UK / The Bridgeman Art Library. © Estate of Edward Wadsworth. All rights reserved, DACS 2011; 70b A. R. Coster/Topical Press Agency/Getty Images; 71 © Margherita Spiluttini; 72a © DACS 2011; 72b Etienne Robial, ON/OFF Productions, client M6 Television; 73 creative director B. Martin Pedersen, designers Greg Cerrato, YonJoo Choi, B. Martin Pedersen; 75a © Seymour Chwast; 76 Private Collection / The Bridgeman Art Library. © DACS 2011; 77a © V&A Images; 77b © Dan Reisinger; 78 Think Small advertisement and trademarks used with

permission of Volkswagen Group of America, Inc; 79a © Oleksiy Maksymenko Photography / Alamy; 80b Animal Farm, 2008. Courtesy of Shephard Fairey/ObeyGiant Art; 83 © Jeffrey Tribe, Bedford College; 84a Jamie Reid / Isis Gallery; 84b Photo: akg-images / INTERFOTO / Bildarchiv Hansmann. © ADAGP, Paris and DACS, London 2011; 85 author Richard Wilbur, art Henrik Drescher, publisher Harcourt Brace; 87b book written and designed by Ellen Lupton, Princeton Architectural Press 2010 (2nd edition); 88 © DACS 2011; 89a designer Tod Lippy © *Esopus*; 90a © Apple Corps Ltd; 91 Collection Centre Pompidou, Dist. RMN. © ADAGP, Paris and DACS, London 2011; 92 Museum fur Gestaltung Zurich, Poster Collection. Franz Xaver Jaggy © ZhdK; 93a "I LOVE NEW YORK" is a registered trademark/service mark of the NYS Dept. of Economic Development, used with permission; 93b Museum fur Gestaltung Zurich, Poster Collection. Franz Xaver Jaggy © ZhdK; 95 © The Heartfield Community of Heirs/VG Bild-Kunst, Bonn and DACS, London 2011; 98a The Museum of Modern Art, New York/Scala, Florence; 99 Museum fur Gestaltung Zurich, Poster Collection. Franz Xaver Jaggy © ZhdK; 100 © 2011. Digital image, The Museum of Modern Art, New York/Scala, Florence; 101a Museum fur Gestaltung Zurich, Poster Collection. Franz Xaver Jaggy © ZhdK; 101b © 2011. DeAgostini Picture Library/Scala, Florence; 102 Digital image, The Museum of Modern Art, New York/Scala, Florence. © DACS 2011; 103a Courtesy of Paula Scher/Pentagram; 103b Bauhaus Archiv. © DACS 2011; 104 Digital image Mies van der Rohe/Gift of the Arch./MoMA/Scala; 105a art direction Lizá Ramalho and Artur Rebelo (R2), design by Lizá Ramalho and Artur Rebelo (R2) and Nadine Ouellet, client Teatro Bruto; 105b Museum fur Gestaltung Zurich, Poster Collection. Photo: Franz Xaver Jaggy © ZHdK. © DACS 2011; 106a © DACS 2011; 107 illustration Mirko Ilic, art direction Minh Uong; 108 artist Alex Gopher, director H5 (A. Bardou-Jacquet and L. Houplain), production company Le Village; 109 Photo Scala, Florence/BPK, Bildagentur fuer Kunst, Kultur und Geschichte, Berlin. © DACS 2011; 110 Bibliothèque Forney/ Roger-Viollet/TopFoto; 111a *Diffraction* (Torre Agbar) by Yann Kersalé, architect Jean Nouvel; 112b © Ed Ruscha. Courtesy Gagosian Gallery; 114 design firm Methodologie, Seattle, strategic director Janet DeDonato, creative director Dale Hart, designer KJ Chun, project manager Andreas Holmer, production Derek Sullivan and Harry Wirth, installation Lisa Hein and Bob Seng, writer Bo Gilliland, editor Paula Thurman; 115 Photo: Les Arts Décoratifs, Paris / Laurent Sully Jaulmes. © ADAGP, Paris and DACS, London 2011; 116–117a Raymond Loewy™ is a trademark of Loewy Design LLC. www.RaymondLoewy. com; 118 © The Josef and Anni Albers Foundation/VG Bild-Kunst, Bonn and DACS, London 2011; 119 © Victor Moscoso; 121a Art Direction and Design by Chipp Kidd, Photography by Daniel Hennessey, Illustration by Mark Zingarelli; 122–123a Digital image, The Museum of Modern Art, New York/Scala, Florence; 123b designed by Milton Glaser for Lincoln Center; 124 Museum fur Gestaltung Zurich, Poster Collection. Photo: Franz Xaver Jaggy © ZHdK. © DACS 2011; 125a poster for L'Hippodrome, two-color silkscreen; 126–127a © TfL from the London Transport Museum collection; © 2011. Digital image, The Museum of Modern Art, New York/Scala, Florence; 128a design by Studio Dumbar (Erik de Vlaam) for Pulchri Studio, The Netherlands; 128b Courtesy of Tomato; 129 © ARS, New York and DACS, London 2011; 131 Mirisch-7 Arts/United Artists / The Kobal Collection / Saul Bass; 133 © Robert Crumb; 134 © 2012 DER SPIEGEL; 135 Designed by John Gorham and Howard Brown; 136 Bauhaus-Archiv Berlin. © DACS 2011; 137 Luis Carlos Morales; 138 *Against poverty and precariousness*, poster by Secours Populaire Français asking people to act against poverty; 139 © www.guidodaniele.com; 142a identity and visual communication for Amsterdamse School voor de Kunsten (Amsterdam School of the Arts); 143 © Fanette Mellier, Ministère de la Culture et de la Communication, Centre National des Arts Plastiques; 144b Prospect, 4 Bath Street, London EC1V 9DX, www.prospect.eu, strategic director Richard Eisermann, creative director Anja Klüver, design director Chris Clegg; 145 courtesy of the National Library Board, Singapore and MIS Union, Singapore; 146a © DACS 2011; 146b Museum fur Gestaltung Zurich, Poster Collection. Franz Xaver Jaggy © ZhdK; 148 Courtesy of The

Advertising Archives; 149 Courtesy of Google; 152 Museum fur Gestaltung Zurich, Poster Collection. Franz Xaver Jaggy © ZhdK; 153a Museum fur Gestaltung Zurich, Poster Collection. © DACS 2011; 153b Museum fur Gestaltung Zurich, Poster Collection. Franz Xaver Jaggy © ZhdK; 154–155a Bildnachweis: Bauhaus-Archiv Berlin. © DACS 2011; 156b © Prologue Films; 160 One More Production, Patrick Jean, Matias Boulcard; 161 © Seymour Chwast; 163 Niessen & de Vries; 165 © Lars Müller Publishers; 167 Courtesy of The Advertising Archives; 168–169a design by Jonathan Barnbrook in collaboration with Adbusters, photography Tomoko Yoneda; 168b Copyright © by Guerrilla Girls, Inc. Courtesy www. guerrillagirls.com; 170a Design by Tomato/Rick Smith, Karl Hyde & Darren Emerson trading as Smith Hyde Productions; 171 The Museum of Modern Art/Scala, Florence; 172b akg-images; 173 Museum fur Gestaltung Zurich, Poster Collection. Franz Xaver Jaggy © ZhdK; 175a © Robert Massin; 175b Museum fur Gestaltung Zurich, Poster Collection. Franz Xaver Jaggy © ZhdK; 177 © Robert Crumb; 181a Courtesy: Jenny Holzer / Photo: Lisa Kahane / Art Resource, NY. © ARS, NY and DACS, London 2011; 181b graphic designer Malte Martin, *Théâtre, théâtre*, poster for Athénée, Paris; 186–187a © Henry Chalfant; 186b Museum fur Gestaltung Zurich, Poster Collection. Franz Xaver Jaggy © ZhdK; 187b © Henry Chalfant; 188a © Jonathan Barnbrook; 188b Beach Packaging; 189 Michael Mescall, Cross Associates; 190 photography Véronique Vienne; 191 concept and creation Anette Lenz and Vincent Perrottet, photography Richard Pelletier, client Pierre Kechkéguian, Le Nouveau Relax, Chaumont; 192a © Phil Baines; 192b Holland Festival Programme cover, design Studio Dumbar, photography Lex van Pieterson; 193 Museum fur Gestaltung Zurich, Poster Collection. Franz Xaver Jaggy © ZhdK; 194b cover design Mike Weikert, photography Nancy Froehlich, editor Ellen Lupton, published by Princeton University Press; 195 Grapus, commissioned by Pentagram, London; 197b Minutes Diary designed by Struktur Design; 201a agency Serviceplan Campaign, advertiser's supervisor Anne-Catherine Paulisch, executive creative director Matthias Harbeck, creative directors Helmut Huber and Florian Drahorad, copywriter Nicolas Becker, art directors Christian Sommer and Ivo Hlavac, consultants Michael Freitag and Britta Christoph; 202–203a eboy, 2003; 202b Charis Tsevis (Tsevis Visual Design) in collaboration with Indyvisuals Design Collective; 204a design Ralph Schraivogel, silkscreen printing Serigraphie Uldry, client Sacha Wigdorovitz; 204c Raymond Loewy™ is a trademark of Lowey Design LLC. www.RaymondLoewy.com; 204b © 2007 Volatile Graphics; 205 design and lettering art John Langdon. Additional photography by Jason Ribeiro and Ida Riveros.

Acknowledgments

Much gratitude to Laurence King, whose belief in this project and the 100 Ideas series has been a great boon to design history and design scholarship. Thanks to Jo Lightfoot for her direction in the early stages of the book. And much appreciation to Clare Double and designer Roger Fawcett-Tang, who did double and triple duty making the disparate pieces of this puzzle come together.

We appreciate all the designers who generously agreed to share their work or contacts with us in the gathering of the visual material. Specifically thanks to Pierre Bernard, Etienne Hervy, Jocelyn Cottencin, Pascal Béjean, Ludovic Houplain, Anette Lenz, Vincent Perrottet, Evelyn ter Bekke, Dirk Behage, Rudi Meyer, Antoine+Manuel, Malte Martin, David Poullard, Michel Quarez, Alain Le Quernec, Etienne Robial, Yann Kersalé, Jean-Louis Fréchin, Helena Ichbiah, Piotr Karczewski, Catherine Zask, Fanette Mellier, Sheila Hicks, Marsha Emanuel, Daniel Kunzi, Stephan Bundi, Alex Trochut, Niklaus Troxler, Karel Martens, Marty Pedersen, Lizá Ramalho, Artur Rebelo, Base Design Brussels, Victoria Allen, Chip Kidd, Christoph Niemann, Laurie Rosenwald, Maira Kalman, Rick Meyerowitz, Woody Pirtle, Stefan Bucher, Richard Eisermann, Studio Dumbar, Luis Morales, Thonik, Niessen & de Vries, Ralph Schraivogel, Daniel Eatock, Indyvisuals Design, K.J. Chun, Martin Woodtli, Cyan, Pinar Demirdag, Adam Machacek, Sebastien Bohner, Leonardo Sonnoli, Tomato Ltd., 2xGoldstein, Pyramyd, Why Not Associates, Seymour Chwast, Milton Glaser, Estate of Paul Rand, Louise Fili, Charles Spencer Anderson, Jonathan Barnbrook, Matteo Bologna, Bruce Mau, Stefan Sagmeister, David Lance Goines, James Victore, Marian Bantjes, Deborah Adler, Piet Schreuders, Noma Bar, David Tartakover, Shepard Fairey, Jennifer Wang, Willi Kunz, Elaine Lustig Cohen, Rian Hughes, Jeffrey Tribe, Henrich Drescher, Ellen Lupton, Rudy VanderLans, Tod Lippy, Scott Stowell, Paula Scher, Victor Moscoso, R. Crumb, Jean-Pierre Kunkel, Paul Bacon, Massin, Chris Ware, Alex Steinweiss, Art Paul, Michael Gross, George Lois, eBoy, Mirko Ilic, and John Langdon.

And to all the designers who exemplify these 100 ideas our thanks for your myriad contributions.

Steven Heller and Véronique Vienne.

Published in 2012
by Laurence King Publishing Ltd
361–373 City Road
London EC1V 1LR
Tel +44 20 7841 6900
Fax +44 20 7841 6910
Email: enquiries@laurenceking.com
www.laurenceking.com

A catalogue record for this book is available from the British Library.

ISBN-13: 978 1 85669 794 1

Designed by Struktur Design
Typefaces: Swift and Gotham
Picture research by Amanda Russell
Printed in China

The image on page 2 shows Piet Zwart, for the Trio printer, 1931 (see p.66).